WEB JOURNALISM

Practice and Promise of a New Medium

JAMES GLEN STOVALL

University of Alabama

Boston ■ New York ■ San Francisco
Mexico City ■ Montreal ■ Toronto ■ London ■ Madrid ■ Munich ■ Paris
Hong Kong ■ Singapore ■ Tokyo ■ Cape Town ■ Sydney

Series Editor: *Molly Taylor*
Series Editorial Assistant: *Michael Kish*
Marketing Manager: *Mandee Eckersley*
Editorial-Production Administrator: *Anna Socrates*
Editorial-Production Service: *Omegatype Typography, Inc.*
Composition and Prepress Buyer: *Linda Cox*
Manufacturing Buyer: *JoAnne Sweeney*
Cover Administrator: *Kristina Mose-Libon*
Electronic Composition: *Omegatype Typography, Inc.*

For related titles and support materials, visit our online catalog at www.ablongman.com.

Between the time web site information is gathered and then published, it is not unusual for some sites to have closed. Also, the transcription of URLs can result in unintended typographical errors. The publisher would appreciate notification where these errors occur so that they may be corrected in subsequent editions.

Library of Congress Cataloging-in-Publication Data

Stovall, James Glen.
    Web journalism : practice and promise of a new medium / James Glen Stovall.
        p.   cm.
    Includes bibliographical references and index.
    ISBN 0-205-35398-3
    1. Electronic journals.   2. Journalism.   I. Title.

 PN4833.S76 2004
    070.4—dc21

                                                                2003048084

Printed in the United States of America

10 9 8 7 6 5 4 3 2 1   08 07 06 05 04 03

This book is dedicated to the student staff members of Dateline Alabama, the news web site of the College of Communication and Information Sciences at the University of Alabama, who allowed me to believe that I was teaching them about web journalism when it was really the other way around.

CONTENTS

CHAPTER NINE

Audio and Video: Sound and Little Fury   153

CHAPTER TEN

Design on the Web   167

CHAPTER ELEVEN

Engaging the Audience   189

CHAPTER TWELVE

Media Law Online (by Amelia Parker)   201

PREFACE

One morning during the spring of 2002, when I was writing this book, I did the following things in my study at home:

- Checked Dateline Alabama, the news web site for which I am the faculty adviser at the College of Communication and Information Sciences at the University of Alabama
- Checked my email through a web site account that picks up mail from several servers
- Sent out various emails
- Talked on the phone
- Got news from several favorite web sites
- Made notes (handwritten) for this book, and in the process checked several relevant web sites
- Read the newspaper
- Downloaded (legally) some audio files from a commercial dealer with whom I have an account, and burned a CD
- Called a university number and checked the messages on my office phone
- Listened to music on the radio
- Thought about the opening of baseball season and remembered that I needed to renew my audio account (for a fee) with Major League Baseball, so that I could listen to radio broadcasts of the games throughout the summer
- Listened to music on an Internet radio station

All of this behavior is both typical and idiosyncratic media behavior. Each of us has a way of reading through a newspaper or flipping through television channels that is our own. We do these things in combination with other activities in our lives, but the combinations are ours alone.

To write about the Internet and the World Wide Web in the early twenty-first century may be a dangerous act. Fifteen years ago, the Web did not exist. Five years ago, it was far different from what it had become in the middle of 2002.

Some currently argue that the Web has approached a plateau and that the innovation that has occurred along with its explosive growth will give way to development of existing ideas and concepts. The dot-com crash of 2001–2002 has put the brakes on many new ideas, and while we continue to see the number of sites and the amount of usage grow, what we are actually seeing and doing on the Web will be what we see and do for a long time to come.

Maybe.

However, in one area of the Web—web journalism—we are just beginning to explore the possibilities that this medium offers. To this point, most journalists have simply transferred their content, practices, and look to the Web, without giving much thought to the medium itself.

Many in the traditional media have resisted doing even that. Newspaper publishers and television station managers refused to establish web sites until they were compelled to do so by the fact that "everyone else had done it." They have viewed the Web as ephemeral, scary, or profitless—or all three. They have continued to invest in stronger signal towers or new printing presses without thinking much about the idea that a new generation of consumers will prefer to get their news without the aid of trees and delivery trucks.

Media traditionalists have recited several mantras to convince themselves that they can finish their careers without having to deal with the Web or its implications:

"I like to hold a newspaper in my hands. I like the feel of it. You can't get that with a computer."

"You can't take the computer to the bathroom with you."

"No one ever made any money on the Web."

Today, of course, a notebook computer is easier to hold than a newspaper (and in some cases it's lighter). It can certainly be carried into the bathroom, and with a wireless Internet connection, you can read your local newspaper or the *New York Times Book Review* there, at the breakfast table, or in the stadium between innings at a baseball game.

And, today, billions of dollars in business is being transacted over the Web. The people making these transactions are not doing it as a hobby. Somebody, somewhere, is making money.

The Web is a scary thing to many journalists. It offers the prospect that not only will journalism practices change, but also that the basic journalist–audience equation may shift. What we know about the Web at this point seems to portend that readers and viewers will be more active in journalistic decision making and presentation.

This book has been written to explore the changes that are taking place in the journalist world because of the Web. My hope is that together we—students, teachers, and professionals—will better understand them. My goal is to get us to think about what we are doing and how the medium is changing our practices and attitudes.

Unlike some of my colleagues and friends in the academy and the profession, I do not view our Web future with trepidation. I believe it offers journalists extraordinary new opportunities to tell their stories and communicate with their audiences. In these first years of the medium, imagination and creativity—coupled with a thorough grounding of the basic practices and culture of journalism—will be at a premium. Those who exercise these qualities will have a profound effect on their profession. If this book sparks an idea here or there, it will be a success.

All efforts like the writing of this book are the products of many people, and this one is no different. My colleagues, particularly Ed Mullins, Matt Bunker, Bailey Thomson, and Kim Bissell, were invaluable to me as I bounced ideas, one after another, off them.

Amelia Parker, a Dateline Alabama veteran and the author of the chapter of legal issues (Chapter 12), deserves special thanks not only for the chapter but for other help she gave to me in putting this book together.

Web journalists around the country were generous with their time and ideas, particularly the people at MSNBC.com in Redmond, Washington, where I spent two days researching this book. I am especially grateful to Tom Brew, the executive editor, Angela Clark, Meredith Burkitt, Jonathan Dube, and many others who let me look in on their professional lives.

I would also like to thank the following reviewers for their helpful comments: Mindy McAdams, University of Florida, and Ron Roat, University of Southern Indiana.

My wife Sally and son Jefferson have now suffered through yet another book manuscript, and as usual, their support and encouragement literally made this book possible.

This book is dedicated to the students who have worked with me for three years on Dateline Alabama, the news web site of the College of Communication and Information Sciences at the University of Alabama. Their support, ideas, and enthusiasm inspired this effort.

J.G.S.

CHAPTER 1

LOGGING ON TO THE WEB

MAJOR THEMES

■ The World Wide Web is a news medium in the sense that all web sites need to post new information to keep visitors coming back.

■ As a news medium, the Web is neither print nor broadcast; it contains characteristics of both, but it is quite different from either when considered on its own.

■ The Web is destined to change journalism, particularly in its news-gathering and presentation functions.

■ The most profound change the Web offers to journalism is its quality of interactivity and the possibility of changing the relationship between the journalist and the audience.

■ Slate.com sprang forth onto the World Wide Web in 1996 as Microsoft's hip, cheeky contribution to web journalism. Six years later the web magazine (webzine, e-zine) was still hip and cheeky, although a little chastened by its brief and unsuccessful life as a subscription publication in a world of free content. Rather than just writing about the bankruptcy of Enron and the subsequent fallout, Slate developed the Enron Blame Game in February 2002, shortly after Enron's bankruptcy had been announced. The "game" consisted of a graphic that looked like a game board with pictures and icons. A reader could click on any part of the board and find out whom that person was blaming for the bankruptcy or what was being blamed for it. Despite its journalism-with-attitude demeanor, the graphic contained a lot of information and made the point that no one really knew very much about why Enron had failed. (http://slate.msn.com/?id=2061470)

■ Glenn Reynolds, an energetic University of Tennessee law professor, has established a weblog (a web site that allows him to post his opinions and to accept and post entries from others—see Chapter 2) called Instapundit (www.instapundit.com). He updates this site with his opinions and information throughout the day. The writing is short, lively, and provocative. His entries and the ones from others that he posts contain lots of links that take readers to other sites. Reynolds (as of April 2003, about this docuverse Xanadu, the precursor of the World Wide Web that we know today. Although Nelson is given great credit for his vision, he remains openly dissatisfied with the Web and is still pushing for a radical reformation that includes his original ideas.

The second thread was technological, and there were two "problems" that needed to be solved here. One was communicating over long distances, a problem that had existed from the time that individuals realized people lived beyond a day's walk. The other was a much more current problem. In the post–World War II nuclear age, the U.S. Department of Defense was fearful that a single, well-placed nuclear blast would eliminate the ability of the United States to communicate and defend itself. In the 1960s, the department's Advanced Research Project Agency (ARPA) began developing an information distribution system that would not be knocked out with one blow.

The product of ARPA's work was a series of connected computers and computer networks called the Internet, which was first instituted in 1969. Slowly and somewhat fitfully through the 1970s and 1980s, protocols for transferring information—email, online research tools, and information and even discussions groups—were formed.

In 1991, Tim Berners-Lee, a physicist working for a European research consortium in Switzerland, developed a hypertext system to allow people to share what they had through the Internet. It required a software program to be installed on an individual computer, and the information to be shared had to be formatted with a set of tags (hypertext markup language, or HTML). The browser that would allow all this to happen was called WorldWideWeb. More sophisticated browsers were later developed by others, but the name and the system that Berners-Lee donated to the world (he has never made any money off his work) stuck.

The work of Berners-Lee and others took the Internet—previously confined to computer geeks and computer bulletin board users—and placed it into the hands of the general public.

And the public ran away with it.

Getting Connected

By the beginning of the twenty-first century, there were millions of web sites and web pages (collections of text and images) that represented individual people, organizations, companies, governments, and ideas. A survey by the U.S. Department of Commerce in September 2001 found that more than half the population was using the Internet, and the number of users was growing by about 2 million people per month. If this growth were to continue, by 2004 more than 75 percent of the nation would be using the Internet (U.S. Department of Commerce, 2002).

The Commerce Department report also said that 90 percent of children from ages 5 to 17 used computers, and 75 percent of 14- to 17-year-olds were on the Internet at some point in their lives. In addition, 45 percent of the entire population used email (up from 35 percent in the previous year), and 36 percent used the Internet to search for product and service information, such as finding airline schedules and buying books online (U.S. Department of Commerce, 2002).

In its short life (about ten years at the time this is written), however, the Web has changed. It is certainly bigger, with more sites and more information. It is also technically easier to browse, or surf, and to find information. New design tools have made web sites easier to create and have allowed users increased ease of navigation. People who design and produce web sites have also become more sophisticated in presenting information and more adept at determining why people visited a web site. The biggest change, however, has been in our attitude toward the Web.

Initially, the Web was a curiosity and a good place to hang out. Many portals, and many web sites themselves, used to tout what they called the "cool site of the day." These were the sites that web producers thought users would enjoy because of their graphics, animation, or clever organization. It did not matter that the subject of the site (e.g., Mama Jewel's Restaurant or the Bureau of Indian Affairs) did not interest the visitor. Rather, the visitor should go to the site just to check out the cool goings-on.

Today, though, the Web is a place where people *do* things. They don't just hang out. One of the chief Web activities is getting information. People want airline schedules, recipes, Sunday school lessons, wedding registrations, the bestseller list, the latest prices on new computers—a wide variety of information that has one thing in common: it must be current. That is why, above all else, the Web is a news medium.

People who surf the Web know this instinctively. They race around the Web, landing here and there, always in search of the latest information about whatever topic is of interest to them at that moment. Much of this activity is driven by current news events, as we saw at the beginning of this chapter. News drives the Web. The coming of spring, for instance, brings with it March Madness—the NCAA basketball tournament—and sports fans are after the latest information. That's why web sites such as SportsLine.com had an increase of 36 percent in its traffic (1.4 million visitors) during the first week of March 2002, when March Madness had barely begun. ESPN.com had an 11 percent increase (3.4 million visitors) and SportingNews.com had a 21 percent increase (440,000 visitors) during that same period (Lasica, 2002).

People want news, and they want it immediately. Even when the information is not "breaking news," they expect the web sites they visit to be different whenever they show up. People rarely return to a web site if they keep seeing the same information. Web site producers quickly realize this, even though they may have begun their site with the idea that they could put it up and just leave it there. Web sites are not billboards: in order to maintain and increase their traffic, they must be changed often. The monster, as many webbies have found, must be fed.

This is, of course, what news organizations do, and this is why the Web is a news medium.

WHAT'S DIFFERENT ABOUT THE WEB?

The essence of the World Wide Web is news, but the Web is not a newspaper on a computer screen. Nor is it a broadcast station that you can pick up through a browser. It is different from traditional media in some significant and profound ways.

■ ■ ■ ■ ■ ▬▬▬▬▬▬▬▬▬▬▬▬▬▬▬▬▬▬▬▬▬▬▬▬▬▬▬▬▬▬

SIDEBAR

SEPTEMBER 11, 2001

Shortly before 9 a.m. on Tuesday, September 11, 2001, a hijacked airliner loaded with passengers flew into the North Tower of the World Trade Center. A few minutes later, another airliner coming from the opposite direction slammed into the South Tower. Within an hour and a half, both buildings—two of the tallest in the word—had collapsed. Meanwhile, another airliner was flown into the west side of the Pentagon, headquarters of the U.S. Department of Defense, in Washington, D.C. A fourth airliner, which passengers struggled to retake from its hijackers, crashed in a rural area of Pennsylvania. Those extraordinary events provoked the following:

- From the time the second tower was hit (9:05 a.m.), the CNN web site got 9 million hits an hour; that number increased to 19 million an hour by the next day. At that time, CNN had been getting about 14 million hits a day.
- MSNBC reported that in the first twenty-four hours of the disaster, 12.5 million people logged onto its site; the previous record had been 6.5 million on November 8, 2001, the day after the disputed presidential election.
- Television was the chief source of information for people on September 11, but 64 percent of those who used the Internet said they got some of their information about the events from the Web and that they got details that were not available from other sources.
- The web portal Yahoo had forty times its usual amount of traffic during the first hour after the attack on the Trade Center.
- To handle the increase in traffic, many web sites, including those of the *New York Times* and CNN, stripped off advertising and graphics in order to increase loading speed for visitors.
- People trying to check on friends in New York and Washington found phone lines clogged and resorted to email and instant messaging.
- Yahoo and other sites posted lists of victims and missing persons.
- Amazon.com, one of the major booksellers on the Web, set up a donation center for disaster relief for the Red Cross. By Saturday night, four days after the attack, the site had raised $5.7 million.

Capacity

A newspaper reporter might be confined to writing five or six hundred words for a story. A photographer might spend all day covering an event and expect to have only one picture in print. A graphics journalist might get a one- or two-column space. At a broadcast station, a reporter would have only forty seconds to tell a story, and a five-minute statement from a news source would have to be reduced to a seven-second sound bite. All of these journalists experience the two great frustrations of professional journalism: the lack of time and space.

The Web greatly mitigates, if not eliminates entirely, these limitations. A reporter can take as many words or as much time as is necessary to tell the story. A photographer can post ten pictures of an event, not just one. A graphics journalist might be limited by screen width (around ten inches or so), but even this limitation represents a vast expansion of the space he or she is normally allotted.

On the Web, news reporters can include with their reports the full text of speeches they cover; biographical information on their sources; maps, charts, and pictures that help expand the reader's understanding of the subject. They can include audio of the sources and video of the scenes where the story took place.

To be sure, there are limitations. Servers, the computers on which information for web sites is stored, do have a finite capacity, but generally it takes a long time before those limits are reached. More practically, the limitations of the Web have to do with the size of the screen that visitors are using, the time it takes to load the information onto the visitor's screen, and the time and effort the reporter wants to spend (and the news organization is willing to support) in gathering the information.

The Web offers more possibilities for presenting more information in more ways than either print or broadcasting.

Flexibility

The Web can handle a wide variety of forms for the information it presents: words, pictures, audio, video, and graphics. In this regard, it is far more flexible than print or broadcast.

This book explores some of the ways that these forms are being used by web journalists, and in some places it speculates on how these forms might develop. The relative newness of the Web as a medium, however, means that many of these forms have not been fully explored and there is a great deal of room for imagination and creativity on the part of people who enter this field. For instance, the *New York Times,* like many other news organizations with substantial Web sites, regularly posts picture galleries of photos that the paper's far-flung set of photographers have taken. At many of these galleries, not only can visitors see the pictures and read the cutline text, they can hear an audio of the photographer talking about his or her work.

The audio picture gallery is a new form of presenting information that the Web has spawned. There are many other forms waiting to be created and developed by imaginative journalists.

Those who enter the field of web journalism are joining a profession in which traditional walls are being eliminated. The journalist who says, "I am a word person" or "I am a photographer" or "I am a graphic artist" runs the risk of severely limiting his or her capacity to take advantage of the many forms the Web offers. No doubt, there will be specialists—people whose main job is to write or to shoot video or research and produce charts and graphs. But entry-level web journalists will be asked to do it all, and veterans will be required to think about their information and decide how it can best be presented to viewers.

Immediacy

The Web can deliver information immediately, often as events are unfolding. Broadcasting, particularly television, can do the same thing and with great impact, as many of us experienced on September 11, 2001. But the Web's qualities offer an immediacy that broadcasting cannot match in four important ways.

The first is variety. Most major breaking news events are multifaceted. That is, they involve a variety of people, places, and activities. The terrorist attacks of September 11 are a dramatic case in point: many things were happening to many people in a variety of locations. At the same time the towers in New York were collapsing, a plane was crashing into the Pentagon, and the government was shutting down air traffic across the country. Locally, school systems and government offices were deciding whether to remain open. A mother wondering if she would have to pick up her child at school that day probably could not have found that information on television. But a good local news organization could have put that information on its web site so that it could be accessed immediately. Many sites did just that.

In a less dramatic vein, let's say you want to know the score of a sporting event. How likely are you to find that out immediately when you turn on the television or radio? Even if you are looking at ESPN's scores rolling across the bottom of the screen, you are probably not going to see the score you are interested in immediately. You can find that information far more quickly on ESPN's web site (as well as many other sports-oriented sites).

The second quality of the Web's immediacy is expansion. As noted earlier, the Web has a huge capacity to hold and display information. For instance, in any major disaster story the names of victims are important and of interest to many people. Yet those names rarely make it onto a televised news broadcast. Limited by a finite amount of time, television cannot be expected to fill the information needs of viewers about a major breaking news story. Television generally only shows us and tells us one thing at a time. (Split screens give television the capacity to show more than one picture at a time, but they are rarely used.) It may or may not be what we are interested in or what we want to know.

The Web can often satisfy our need for information more immediately. It can provide a variety of information that viewers can select. One may want the names of victims, another may want background about the disaster, another may want the latest developments, and so on. A good news web site can provide all of these things so that readers can choose.

Depth, the third part of the immediacy characteristic of the Web, is closely akin to capacity, but what we are really talking about here is quality. Information can be posted immediately on a web site, but to get it ready, it must undergo at least minimal editing. The broadcasts of a breaking news event, though often done by people who are thoroughly professional, have no buffer between their creation and their distribution. Because the Web is essentially a word medium (see Chapter 5, on writing for the Web), web journalists have some opportunity to edit their work or to let others look at it before it is disseminated.

Finally, the Web can offer immediacy with context, something broadcasters find difficult to provide with their breaking news stories. The limitations of television to provide context are evident in the live coverage of many events. Take golf matches, for instance. The camera and announcers may concentrate on a single player or a single shot while a graphic overlays part of the screen showing the leader board. Still, those two things may not tell the whole story of the match because other important actions may be occurring on different parts of the course (or even off the course). Watching a golf match on television is undoubtedly dramatic for those interested in the sport, but television has difficulty giving a complete picture until the match is finished. The Web has the power to summarize and update, while adding information in various parts of the coverage. (See Figure 1.2, posted a few moments after the NCAA announced sanctions against the Alabama football program in February 2002.)

Permanence

Describing the Web as a permanent medium may seem silly to someone who has worked for hours on a document only to erase it with a single keystroke. Or to someone who tries to find a news story on a newspaper's web site that is more than a few days old. In these instances, the Web can seem almost as ethereal as broadcasting.

Yet the Web is the most permanent of media in the sense that it does not deteriorate. Nothing *need* be lost. Properly archived and maintained, data on the Web—because of its electronic form—can exist far beyond any tangible medium we now have. This permanence is an often overlooked quality of the Web, but it is one that

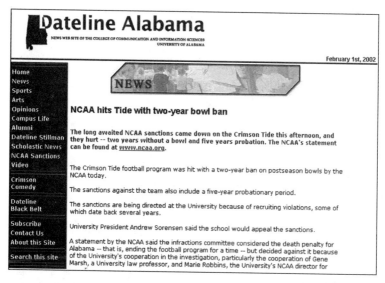

FIGURE 1.2 Instant Coverage. The Web allows local media to give immediate coverage to stories of local interest. The University of Alabama's news web site posted this story a few minutes after the NCAA announced its sanctions of the Alabama football program in February 2002.

gives the medium great power. Paper deteriorates, and videotape and audiotape degrades. Information on the Web, however, stays put unless someone makes it go away.

It has taken us some time to recognize the permanency of the Web and to put that permanency to good use. Web sites have been abandoned, addresses have changed, and data have been overwritten without being properly saved. Much that has been created during the first decade of the Web has been lost, but those losses are not due to a failure of the medium. Rather, they are failures of the operators.

This permanency leads to two other qualities about the Web that render it so powerful: duplication and retrievability. Because the Web is such an open medium and because the technology that creates a web site is shared, any part of a web site (or the whole web site itself) can be duplicated and stored in a different location from where it originated.

Duplication renders information on the Web safe because it can be stored in various places; retrievability renders it powerful, particularly in the area of web journalism. A simple example of this characteristic is the murder that is thoroughly covered by the local press. Six months later, someone is arrested and accused. Six months after that the trial begins. A reporter covering the trial may be new to the news organization, but he or she can easily retrieve what has been written before to become informed about the background of the story. Stories about the trial will probably have at least a paragraph or two of background material, but they can also contain links to earlier stories that will allow readers to gain insight into the case. Journalism is sometimes criticized because of its episodic coverage and lack of context. Retrieving previous stories for the reader is just one way that a single article can be shown to be part of a continuing story over days, months, and years.

Interactivity

All of the qualities of the Web listed above (capacity, immediacy, flexibility, and permanence) have the potential of changing journalism as it is practiced on the Web, but those qualities pale against the potential the Web has for interactivity. This quality portends a new relationship between journalist and reader/viewer/consumer, and that new relationship could mean a new form of journalism.

All news media are interactive to some extent, of course. Television viewers and radio listeners must turn on their sets and select channels. Remote controls allow users to switch between channels at will. Beyond that, however, these media offer no opportunities to interact. They provide no choices and no feedback loops while programs are being broadcast.

Newspapers and magazines are more interactive in the sense that readers can choose what parts to read and what parts to ignore. Headlines, refers (text that directs readers to another part of the paper), layouts, and sectioning help readers make these choices. But print media offer no channel through which readers can respond to what they are seeing and to interact with the journalists who have produced the publication— except in an entirely separate medium and context (such as mail or the telephone).

Web journalism offers the same choices that print media offer, only more of them. Whereas the choices in newspapers are pages and headlines, the choices on the

Web can be built into the articles and web pages themselves, using hyperlinks. These allow readers to veer off within a story to information that is most interesting or relevant to them. An array of choices gives readers more control over what they see and read, and it heightens the nonlinearity of the Web itself.

Where the Web is really different, however, is the immediate feedback channel that it offers to users and journalists alike. News web sites have only begun to explore the techniques for channeling this feedback, using techniques such as instant polls, email, forums, bulletin boards, discussion groups, and online chats with reporters, editors, and sources themselves. These channels can be immediate and active, and as web journalism develops, they will become an increasingly important part of the journalist's milieu.

This new relationship will have profound effects on the way journalists gather information and make decisions. Readers are likely to become sources of information and lead journalists to new inquiries and stories. They could provide valuable perspective to journalists who are new to a story or not part of the community they cover (two of the major criticism of journalists today), offering points of view that journalists would not normally hear in talking with "official" sources about their stories (see Chapter 4). The public journalism movement (often called civic journalism), which seeks to involve the community in journalistic decision making, could be taken to a new level with the Web.

The other side of interactivity is that while the audience can reach toward the news organization, the news organization can find out more about the audience. An organization may ask or require that users register to see its site. (The *New York Times* does this and gains valuable data on who is looking at its site.) But the technology of the Web allows those who run web sites to be less intrusive in finding out information about their visitors. Data can be gathered on where hits are coming from—both from individual computers and the URLs immediately before the hit. The web site can also track a user's progress through the site even to the point of seeing how long the user spends looking at a particular page. Developing email lists, bulletin boards, and forums is yet another way of gathering information about users.

With these and other methods, it is very easy for an organization to see what the most popular parts (and least popular parts) of a web site are, and to make editorial and advertising rate decisions accordingly. Few news organizations have gone that far yet, but they inevitably will do so. Such data will allow news organizations to develop content to better serve general and specialized audiences.

These characteristics—capacity, immediacy, flexibility, permanence, and interactivity—set the Web apart from traditional media. They will be the continuing themes that will be developed in the subsequent chapters of this book.

DISADVANTAGES OF THE WEB

The previous section set out in some detail the characteristics of the Web that seem to suggest the Web has advantages as a news medium over print and broadcast. In general, this is so, but the Web still has major disadvantages that those interested in developing web journalism must acknowledge.

The first of these disadvantages is that the Web is expensive for users. Even if an individual does not have to pay the costs personally, an organization must buy a computer and establish an Internet connection, and neither of these things is free.

Second, the Web is stationary and awkward. The old saw, "I can't take it into the bathroom with me," still holds true for most people, despite the availability of portable computers and wireless connections. Newspapers, magazines, and books are much more convenient to use than the Web, and they undoubtedly will remain so, at least for a while.

Finally, from the user's point of view, the Web can be confusing and frustrating. The multiplicity of voices that the Web has spawned makes selection difficult, and finding precisely the information you want can be mind-numbing. Many web sites are not well organized or well designed. They do not give users what they promise, and they cannot sustain the demands of keeping content fresh or current.

On the part of the web producer, the major disadvantage of the Web is that it is simply not print or broadcast; that is, it is not an established medium, and relatively few people have the "web habit." While that is changing, news web site producers must contend with the fact that the business models that ensure profitability have still not been developed and tested. This disadvantage is currently exacerbated by the expectation of users that they do not (and should not) pay directly for the content they receive from a site. It is unlikely that free content will continue to be the norm. While web sites are relatively inexpensive to establish and post, good content is costly, and eventually the users will have to pay. (For a more complete discussion of this issue, see Chapter 11.)

WHITHER WEB JOURNALISM?

Despite its current lack of profitability, the Web has too many advantages and is too well established as a part of people's lives to fall into disuse. The Web will be in our future, and as such it is likely to alter fundamentally the way journalism is practiced.

The development of web journalism will allow, if not force, journalists to examine some basic questions about how we gather, process, and distribute information, and what our relationship with the audience is. The journalist process itself is unlikely to shift dramatically as we enter this new medium. The culture of journalism is that we tell ourselves about ourselves; we try to do so with accuracy and grace and with the least harm, but we know that sometimes harm or discomfort will be the result.

How we do what we do is the question that is fascinating many web journalists in this era. The Web offers many possibilities and permutations on those possibilities, and anyone with energy, imagination, and a sense of adventure will enjoy the web environment for the next decade. New forms of storytelling and information presentation will be developed. Some will be discarded, and some will remain and mature. Watching and participating in this process will be fun.

The last question—the relationship of journalists with their audience—will probably be the most vexing and ultimately the most important one of all. How do we give the audience what it needs when there will be increased pressures to give the audience only what it wants? What kind of a dialogue should we develop with the audience, and when and how should the audience participate in the journalistic process? What standards of accountability will both journalists and the audience accept? Finally, how will web journalism achieve the ultimate goal of the journalist—to tell ourselves about ourselves in order to build a healthier community of people?

The journey of web journalism is just beginning, and the purpose of this book is to deal with many of these questions.

COOL IDEAS

Don't Read and Drive; Listen Instead

No time to read the newspaper in the morning before you drive to work? The web site of the *San Francisco Chronicle* (www.sfgate.com) has the answer: a CD containing selected portions of the newspaper that you can listen to on your commute. Readers can specify what sections of the newspaper they want to hear and tell the web site about how long their commute lasts. Then they leave a blank CD in their computer before they go to bed.

While the readers sleep, special software from MobileSoft burns the CD. Alternatively, it will make an MP3 file or a sync to a PDA (personal digital assistant).

The next morning, readers of the newspaper can become listeners to the paper and feel fully informed by the time they pull into their parking spaces at work.

DISCUSSION AND ACTIVITIES

1. The author speaks glowingly of the characteristics of the Web that distinguish it from other media. These are capacity, immediacy, permanence, flexibility, and interactivity. Is there a downside to these qualities for journalism?

2. What is the future for newspaper journalism? Television journalism?

3. What web sites do you visit most often? Why? Try to list some categories for your personal use, and then list web sites under them.

4. Imagine yourself as a web journalist. What would you like to be doing in five years? Ten years?

SELECTED BIBLIOGRAPHY

Beck, Margery. "Warren Buffet Sees Problems for Newspaper Industry." Associated Press, April 30, 2001.

Bush, Vannevar. "As We May Think." *Atlantic Monthly,* July 1945, pp. 101–108. www.theatlantic monthly.com/unbound/flashbks/computer/bushf.htm.

EPN World Reporter. "Scrapheap Beckons for Trad Journalists?" August 5, 2002. www.epnworld-reporter.com/news/fullstory.php/aid/374.

Farkas, David K., and Jean B. Farkas. *Principles of Web Design,* Allyn & Bacon, Boston, 2002.

Gates, Dominic. "Newspapers in the Digital Age." *Online Journalism Review,* May 5, 2002. www.ojr.org/future/p1020298748.php.

Langfield, Amy. "Democratizing Journalism." *Online Journalism Review,* April 3, 2002. www.ojr.org/technology/1017872659.php.

Lasica, J. D. "Net Gain: Journalism's Challenges in an Interactive Age." *American Journalism Review,* November 1996. www.ajr.org/Article.asp?id=2217. (This remarkable series of articles was written in the early days of the Web and foresaw, with striking clarity, the importance of the interactive characteristic of the Web to journalism.)

Lasica, J. D. "Internet Journalism and the Starr Investigation." January 20, 2000. www.well.com/user/jd/starr.html.

Lasica, J. D. "Swift and Deep." *Online Journalism Review,* March 19, 2002. www.ojr.org/orj/lasica/1016607119.php.

Rogers, Michael. "Can the Internet Save News?" *Newsweek,* March 2002. www.msnbc.com/news/719816asp?cpl=1.

Rosenberg, Scott. "The Media Titans Still Don't Get It." Salon.com. August 13, 2002. www.salon.com/tech/feature/2002/08/13/media_titans/print.html.

Shapiro, Andrew. "The Drudge Factor." Mediachannel.org. (undated). www.mediachannel.org/original/shapiro-druge.shtml.

U.S. Department of Commerce, National Telecommunication and Information Administration. "A Nation Online: How Americans Are Expanding Their Use of the Internet." February 2002. www.ntia.doc.gov/ntiahome/dn/index.html.

WEB SITES

Online Journalism Review (www.ojr.org)

This site is a must-visit-regularly spot for those interested in journalism on the Web. Larry Pryor, executive editor of Online Journalism Review, writes of the site that he oversees: "As a journalism review based online, we are committed to covering the full range of journalistic issues in all media, but with a particular emphasis on the Internet. Since our March 1, 1998, launch, we have devoted most of our resources to evaluating the emerging field of online journalism, providing readers commentary, monthly features and Web resource databases. Our purpose is to be useful to journalists and anyone interested in where journalism is going in cyberspace."

Poynter Institute (www.poynter.org)

"The Poynter Institute is a school for journalists, future journalists, and teachers of journalism," in the words of its web site. "Our students come here in a search for excellence. Our teachers provide focused instruction and personal support in that quest." The web site is full of interesting articles on all phases of journalism, particularly online journalism.

W3 Consortium (www.w3.org)

The World Wide Web Consortium (W3C) describes itself as a site that "develops interoperable technologies (specifications, guidelines, software, and tools) to lead the Web to its full potential. W3C is a forum for information, commerce, communication, and collective understanding."

Jakob Neilson (www.useit.com)

Neilson is a guru of web writing and usability. His ideas are sometimes controversial, but he holds strong opinions that cannot be ignored. He describes the site simply as "usable information technology."

CHAPTER 2

NEWS WEB SITES

MAJOR THEMES

- Traditional news organizations—newspapers, television stations, radio stations, news magazines—dominate the field of news web sites, often acting as reflectors or spinoffs of the traditional news product.

- Although most news web sites have not been profitable in the first decade of the Internet, many signs—especially the demographic indicators—point to their eventual profitability and even dominance of journalism.

- News web sites need to take advantage of the aspects of the Web to distinguish themselves from the traditional news products of the newspaper, news magazine, or television station.

- Currently, the organization and copy flow of a news web site resembles that of a traditional news organization, but there are likely to be shifts in both organization and operation in the future.

- Many difficult issues, including profitability and quality control, face news web sites, and people entering journalism at this point will be called upon to resolve these issues.

News web sites of the early twenty-first century represent a curious hybrid. They contain the content of media that are from seventy-five (television and radio) to four hundred (newspapers) years old, presented with a technology that is still in its first generation. Where did news web sites come from? What are they now? What are they likely to be in both the near and distant future? None of these questions is easily answered, and maybe none is ultimately that important as the Web develops and changes. But the news web site—whatever it was and is and will be—is the major form of the practice of web journalism and will be for the foreseeable future. Thus, this chapter looks at what news web sites are, where they have come from, who operates them, how they work, and why all of the major issues of journalism are beginning to revolve around them.

News web sites will change substantially, if not radically, during the first decade of this century. No news web site is coming close to using the Web to its full potential yet. The Web's capacity, immediacy, flexibility, permanence, and interactivity have not been fully explored or exploited by any news organization. Newspapers, news magazines, radio stations, and television stations, whose history and investments have been in other products, have been timid in approaching the Web. However, the strength of their acceptance by the public as credible sources of news and their financial commitment to the production of news makes them the first and foremost players in this new field of web journalism.

DEFINED AND CURRENT

A news web site is a site that is devoted to delivering timely news and information to its audience. Those who produce the site observe the traditional customs and practices of journalism (many of which are discussed throughout this book) in gathering, writing, and presenting the news. A news web site is a means for a news organization to display and distribute its content. That content is directed at an audience that is defined either by interest or geography.

A news organization's web site can follow one of the following four methods of populating the site with content.

Shovelware

The term *shovelware,* often used in a denigrating way by people interested in web development, refers to the practice of simply shifting the content produced by the organization for another medium (newspaper, radio, or television) to the web site with little or no change. What you see in the newspaper or hear on the television is what goes on the web site.

Most news organizations use shovelware for a variety of reasons. First and foremost, it is cheap and easy. The news stories and pictures are already there, having been produced for the traditional medium, and they can be easily transferred to the web site. Many newspapers have software that allows them to do this almost seamlessly from their editing systems. Consequently, it takes little time and effort (and little extra money) to get content onto the web.

Another reason for shovelware is that it works. News stories written in an inverted-pyramid form (see Chapter 5) are appropriate for the web. They give the most important or interesting information first and then present information in descending order of importance. Ideally, they are written concisely and precisely, all qualities that good writing for the Web demands. News organizations that shovel their print content onto their web site come away with a well-populated site at little or no extra cost. They have extended their brand to the Web, they have reached people who might not be subscribers, and they have created new advertising opportunities. The information comes in a form readers are used to seeing—the news story.

So, what's wrong with shovelware? Why do webites denigrate it? There is really nothing wrong with shovelware as a first step to web site production. It does have all of the advantages listed above—low cost, easy to get to the web site, familiarity. The reason people interested in web site development speak despairingly of it is that many news organizations never go beyond this first step.

Shovelware does not recognize the Web as a separate medium and does not take full advantage of qualities offered by the Web (see Chapter 1) that are not found in the traditional media. One example will suffice. Most news stories that are shoveled onto a web site do not contain any links to other information that might be helpful to the reader. Links, which require setting up a URL address within or at the end of a story, are not part of the traditional news process. Many newspaper editors, worried about meeting their print deadlines, do not want their reporters or copy editors spending time creating links that will have no use in the print product. Thus, shovelware misses one of the basic advantages of the Web by not linking readers to past stories about an issue or independent information from another source.

Shovelware does not allow the news organization to use the immediacy of the Web to present information quickly to the reader. Many shovelware programs used by news media hold stories until they are uploaded to the live web site at certain times of the day (usually, only one time during the day). Consequently, because print or broadcast deadlines are being followed, readers of the web site are being deprived of information that the news organization has.

Another reason that shovelware is not highly regarded is that if it is all that a web site offers, there is little reason for a reader—particularly one who is a subscriber—to visit the web site. There is nothing new there, just the same things that he or she might more conveniently read in print. Shovelware simply gives the news organization a presence on the Web. It does not do much for the consumers of news.

Moderate Updating

Some news organizations have discovered the immediacy function of the Web. They have also discovered that a growing number of their audience turn to the Web when breaking news occurs or when that kind of information is anticipated.

For instance, a local college basketball hero is eligible to enter the National Basketball Association draft at the end of the season even though he has another year of eligibility left in his college career. Once the last game has been played, he calls a press conference for 1 p.m. the next day to announce his decision. The next newscast from the local television station is at 5 p.m., and the local newspaper will not be out until the next morning. The local television station has decided not to cover the press conference live (too expensive) and not to break into programming to announce the decision (too costly in other ways).

But thousands of people who are interested want to know the decision as soon as it is announced. The logical alternative is the news web site, which can be updated as soon as the information is known.

This process, however, is not as easy for some news organizations as it sounds. News organizations that are using rigid content management system software (see sidebar) may not have the ability or the technical expertise to move stories quickly onto a web site. Some news organizations have web sites managed by outside companies, and it may take some special arrangement with that company to break the normal cycle of when stories and pictures are posted.

■ ■ ■ ■ ■ ▬▬▬▬▬▬▬▬▬▬▬▬▬▬▬▬▬▬▬▬▬▬▬▬▬▬▬▬▬

SIDEBAR

CONTENT MANAGEMENT SYSTEMS

Good-bye, HTML!

Not so fast. It will probably be a while before the Web abandons the hypertext markup language (HTML), which has been used to build most web pages. But there are ways to get onto the Web without much knowledge of HTML.

Web editors such as Adobe GoLive and Dreamweaver have been great leaps forward for the individual web designer, but faced with building and managing an entire news web site, even these programs need a boost.

Enter content management systems (CMS). These systems are specially written software programs that go beyond web editors by allowing journalists to upload their content onto a news web site without knowledge of the first HTML tag. They are designed to fit into the process of copy flow for a news organization. As soon as an article has been read by an editor, it can be uploaded into the system with little or no additional work.

In a CMS, most of the formatting decisions are made as the system is established. A reporter or editor does not have to decide about size or placement of items on the web page. Some systems will provide some options for editors, but the options are limited. Thus, a good CMS provides a fast, efficient way for stories, headlines, graphics, pictures, and cutlines to be loaded onto a site. Logos, navigation bars, and other standard items on a page reside within the system and are automatically called onto a page.

A content management system is a good way for a news organization to get its copy onto a web site, but it does not offer much flexibility if the organization wants to develop nonprint or nonbroadcast elements on the site. Its efficiency can become a crutch for editors that prevents them from exploring possibilities on a web site. And the formatting function can prevent a site from having much visual variety.

Content management systems are entering their second generation, as editors are demanding more efficiency and flexibility. These editors are discovering they need systems that allow imagination and creativity in exploring the use of the Web as a news medium.

Still, some news organizations are recognizing that those arrangements must be made, and the programs they have to manage their sites must be flexible enough to allow for immediate posting. They must also have someone in the newsroom who is adept at this process. They can take advantage of the multimedia aspects of their organization by cross promotion. That is, they can say in their traditional products (newspaper or newscast) that the audience should visit the web site to find out the latest developments on a story. And they can use the web site to direct the audience back to the traditional product (and, in the case of the newspaper, give them subscription information).

The events of September 11, 2001, moved most shovelware web sites into the moderate-updating category, at least for the day. The news was so powerful and so important that news organizations could not ignore any means of presenting it to the public. Many web sites moved back into the category of shovelware after that day, but at least for once they saw the necessity of using the Web to give readers immediate, up-to-date information.

Aggressive Updating

The owners of a news organization at some point may catch a vision of the possibilities of the Web—especially its quality of immediacy—and move toward an aggressively updated site. This type of site employs staff members who post new items on a site throughout the day, and the software the organization uses allows for this to happen easily and quickly.

This kind of updating begins with the shovelware that the organization has produced for its other product (print or broadcast). The web site staff look at these stories and see which ones might involve breaking news. For instance, a newspaper might run a preview story in the morning edition about a meeting of the city council scheduled for that day. The council, the story says, is set to vote on a proposed increase in property taxes. The web site staff will make arrangements with the reporter who is covering the council meeting to find out how the council voted soon after it happens, and will update the story accordingly. (This process of rewriting an existing story, or rewriting the top paragraphs of a story with new information, sometimes takes on the old wire service term of a "writethru.")

The web site staff may also look for ways to enhance content that does not need to be updated. For instance, a newspaper may have room to run just one picture along with a story. The web site can accommodate many more than that, and the staff may want to set up a photo gallery if the photographer has other good shots that were not used. Likewise, a television reporter may have audio or video related to a story that could not be included in the regular newscast but may be suitable for the web site.

News organizations that subscribe to the Associated Press or some other news service may build in a "feed" for those services to the site. As stories are produced and sent by the wire service, they automatically appear on the site. A new story can show up every few minutes, and on the splash page of the site, headline links to these stories will be constantly changed.

Having the site change every few minutes or even every few hours is one of the hallmarks of aggressive updating. Those who work with the Web believe that a site should continually change and present new information. Some content management systems allow editors to mark more than one story or picture that should be placed at the top of the opening page or section page. These items then "rotate"; that is, they change positions on the page as the page is refreshed. This rotation gives the site the appearance of having new information all the time.

Aggressive updating is done for a variety of purposes. One is that news organizations recognize they are in the news business, not in the business of printing newspapers or broadcasting newscasts. They understand the nature of news, and the hunger that audiences have for it.

Another purpose for aggressive updating is to build the audience for the site. This audience would consist of loyal readers and viewers of the traditional product, but it would also include people who are accustomed to using the Web for their work and leisure. Having these people showing up at a web site enhances the news organization's place in the community and offers additional advertising opportunities.

Original Content

A few news organizations have gone a step beyond aggressive updating to more extensively developing original content for their sites. These organizations have developed staffs who are devoted to using the web site for original reporting. They work with software packages, often involving a variety of software programs that allow maximum flexibility in developing pages and forms of presentation.

Web sites with the original-content philosophy use stories, pictures, graphics, and other information that have been put together for the traditional medium. They also work with the news staffs on important stories, so that the Web presentation of those stories can use the advantages of the Web as a medium.

Because they are produced by news organizations, these original content web sites also incorporate the aggressive-updating philosophy. Their first job is to try to stay on top of events, and the staffs feel they can prove their worth most readily when breaking news occurs—particularly in their local areas—and they can provide information that no other organization is providing.

But much of the normal day-to-day activity of the staff is devoted to developing and managing content for the site. A big-city web site might gather crime statistics for neighborhoods around the city to form an interactive map (as the *Chicago Tribune* web site did in the early days of news web sites) that readers could click on and find crime information for a single neighborhood. The web site staff might set up an interactive chat session with a reporter who had a covered a big story, a columnist, or a local celebrity. The staff could help a photojournalist produce an audio photo gallery for a story the photographer has been shooting.

Original-content sites (such as the *Topeka Capital Journal;* see Figure 2.1) are likely to have their own advertising staffs in addition to editorial staffs. Advertising managers and salespersons are not only involved in selling ads for the site, they also track site hits and try to keep up with the demographics of site users. To the extent that the leadership of the news organization demands it, these Web ad staffs work with the advertising staffs for the traditional media to enhance the sales for both.

Original content sites walk an identity tightrope. Because they have sprung from another medium, they are obligated and often mandated to pay attention to the health and welfare of the newspaper or television station. They must maintain good relationships with the traditional staffs because they depend on them for much of their content. Still, as professional journalists, they usually have something of a competitive spirit and want to show off the advantages of their medium. They also want to be first in presenting information, which they often are because of the immediacy of the Web. Maintaining healthy and productive connections with the traditional medium requires strong and thoughtful leadership throughout the news organization.

OWNED AND OPERATED

Who owns a news web site? As we alluded to in the previous section, most news web sites are owned by traditional news media companies—newspapers, television

FIGURE 2.1
CJonline.com. Thought to be one of the best and most innovative web sites in the nation, CJonline.com, the site of the *Topeka Capital Journal,* has won many awards from the Online News Association and other organizations. It attracts great attention from those who wish to enliven their own sites.

stations, a few radio stations and news magazines. Most news organizations have web sites that are actively maintained and updated periodically.

The major news web sites—the ones that draw the largest audiences—are the *New York Times* (nytimes.com), MSNBC (msnbc.com), CNN (cnn.com), the *Washington Post* (washingtonpost.com), the *Chicago Tribune* (chicagotribune.com), the *Los Angeles Times* (latimes.com), ABC News (abcnews.com), CBS News (cbsnews.com), and Fox News (foxnews.com). The *Wall Street Journal* (online.wsj.com/public/us) has a large web site that was an early leader in gaining paid subscriptions to most of its content.

A somewhat different approach can be found at NBC News. That organization has joined with computer giant Microsoft to produce an excellent and extensive news site, MSNBC (msnbc.com); this site also includes items from the *Washington Post* and *Newsweek*. CNN (cnn.com), one of the leading sites in drawing visitors, has done something of the same thing by pairing with *Time* and *Sports Illustrated* magazines for some of its content.

All of these web sites use the name of the news organization and are active in extending the brand of the company. Each has enjoyed a measure of success in being innovative and in developing repeat visitors.

Another approach to news web sites has been taken by Newhouse Newspapers. In the late 1990s, Newhouse decided that its corporate philosophy would be to build sites that did not use the brand name of its newspapers but rather would attempt to build a new brand for the site itself. Thus, we have Cleveland Live (www.clevelandlive.com) Alabama Live (al.com), and New Jersey Online (nj.com). These sites use the content of the Newhouse newspapers in that state in order to build a statewide site, but the sites themselves add little to this content. They also do not promote or emphasize the individual newspapers that provide the content.

Critics of this approach abound, and their criticisms include the following.

- The individual newspapers have no web site (and are thus abnormal among their peer news organizations) and generally do not feel invested in the statewide or regional site.
- The newspapers are deprived of an opportunity to develop local online audiences and to provide local information online that would not fit into their newspapers.
- Consumers who try to access local news through one of these statewide sites often find them confusing and disorganized. That's not surprising, because the people who operate these sites are getting content from multiple sources that has been produced under varying circumstances. Editors of these sites find it difficult to resolve all of this content into a single organization scheme.

DEVELOPING A WEB SITE (OR NOT)

During the first decade of the World Wide Web, no one knew exactly what the Web would become or how people would view it. Inside the news organization, the Web was limited to those who had computers with connections to it, and the connections themselves were often slow or even inoperable. Many people had a hard time conceptualizing how it could be that people could sit at their homes and read a copy of the *New York Times,* view paintings in the Louve in Paris, or shop for a dress at Land's End. Businesses could see no useful purpose for the Web, thinking that it could provide very little in the way of real goods and services. Communicating, the central function of the Web, could be done by many other means.

The news media's early approach to the Web was checkered with visionary action, misguided concepts, and curt dismissal. Some organizations such as the *Chicago Tribune* took to the Web early. The *Tribune* built a site, hired a staff, and set to work creating original and innovative content. Many in the company were disappointed with the audience's response, particularly advertisers, who seemed unconvinced that advertising on the site would be a good investment. The *Tribune* web site was overhauled, reorganized, and eventually reduced a number of times. It never achieved the status within the company and the profitability many had hoped for.

The *News York Times* committed itself to a web site in the mid-1990s. From the time the site was launched in January 1996, it has been considered a leader in web site development. The *Times,* like the *Tribune,* had a staff that could produce original content, but the newspaper itself was foremost in the thinking of the company. The *Times* sought to extend its brand to the Web audience, so the web site at first looked very much like the distinctive appearance of the newspaper itself. It even carried headlines in a font that emulated the type font of the paper's headlines. The web site was rarely allowed to get ahead of the paper in covering the news, even though the Web was more immediate than the printing press. Fierce battles within the organization about the purpose and role of the site occurred, and stories are told that at one point, information could not be posted on the web site until it had appeared in the newspaper. Still, the site has developed steadily, adding features and building audiences, so that in mid-2002 (as this book is being written) it was attracting more than 10 million viewers a month and is looked to as the top newspaper web site in the country.

Even as a clearer view of the Web and its use has emerged, finding the will in many news organizations to build and maintain a web site has not been easy. Editors and publishers have been committed to their medium as much as to the news business itself, and this commitment has colored how they view the web site and how they treat it as part of the organization. Web sites sometimes take on the role of Harry Potter in the Dursley family—a nuisance, to be tolerated when necessary, ignored when possible, and abused at any opportunity. The web site can be the place where incompetent employees are exiled. It can be viewed as competition for the print or broadcast product and thus denied resources for development. Most devastating of all, the web site has been wrapped with the aura that it is not profitable and can never be profitable (an issue we will deal with later in this chapter and through this book).

Yet some in the news business are opening their eyes to the possibility—or even inevitability—of the Web. Arthur Sulzberger, the publisher of the *New York Times,* has spoken frankly about the Neanderthal attitudes that many in his business have had toward the Web and has concluded, "Newspapers cannot be defined by the second word—paper. They've got to be defined by the first—news. If we're going to define ourselves by our history, then we deserve to go out of business."

GROWING THE WEB SITE

Some news organizations never suffered from the Web myopia described in the previous section. Or, if they did, they are over it, and their managers see the possibilities of the Web for expanding their product and their reach. News organizations that recognize they are the chief information-gathering components of the community, that they print or broadcast only a fraction of the information they gather, and that this additional information could have value, see the Web as a logical outlet.

This recognition has led to extension sites and full-blown spinoffs that have their own corporate identities, news staffs, and sales forces, sometimes not even using the name of the parent company from which they sprang.

A good example of an extension site is the New York Times Learning Network. A link to the network is often located prominently on the splash page of the *New York Times* site, but once you get into the network, you find something entirely different from the newspaper itself. The network contains a number of education-related news articles, but there is also likely to be a teacher's lesson plan related to the article. The network provides information that teachers can use about holidays and significant events in history. The network takes articles in the *New York Times* about science or technology and expands them into lessons for school children. It offers slideshows, question-and-answer sessions, audios, videos, and even games and crossword puzzles that will help teachers explore a topic. There is a daily news quiz, and chat sessions are often scheduled with reporters who have covered significant events. The site also has special sections for teachers, students, and parents, and these sections cover a wide variety of topics. Over time, the web site has developed a deep set of archived material that is easily accessible.

Some news organizations have recognized what is important about their city or region and have tried to capitalize with spinoff sites. For instance, in moderate- to large-sized cities, entertainment news—theater, movies, music, arts—often gets short shrift in the newspaper. All of these activities could produce lucrative advertising for the news organization, and some organizations have developed sites that emphasize these activities. Other news organizations have found that focusing on the travel and tourism industry can attract a wide audience and advertisers who want tourism rather than local trade. Weather, tides, and fishing information are just some of the types of content these sites offer. What they are trying to do is become the chief source of information for people who may be coming to the area. As such, the news organization can then go to local businesses that cater to the tourist trade (motels, restaurants, etc.) and offer them a targeted, nonlocal audience.

Other news organizations realize that sports, particularly college sports, is a major area of interest to many of their local citizens as well as to citizens beyond their circulation or broadcast areas. They have established sports web sites keyed to college teams, and fans of the team—local and nonlocal—understand that they can get the most and latest news about these teams from these sites. A good example of this kind of spinoff is GoVols.com and GoLadyVols.com, two sites operated by the *Knoxville* (TN) *News-Sentinel* that post news, information, and views about the University of Tennessee sports programs (see Figure 2.2). These sites not only draw readers but also attract customers for t-shirts, sports paraphernalia, and souvenirs that no fan can do without.

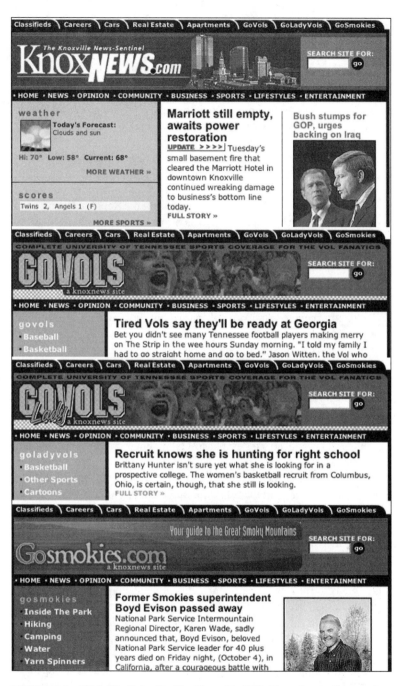

FIGURE 2.2 **Web Site Spinoffs.** The *Knoxville* (TN) *News-Sentinel* is one of a number of newspapers that developed a spinoff web site, allowing it to cover parts of its community with more emphasis. In this case, the *News-Sentinel* is taking advantage of the many people interested in sports at the University of Tennessee and in the nearby Great Smoky Mountain National Park. (To view the site, go to www.knoxnews.com.)

INDEPENDENTLY OWNED

Some news web sites do not come from established news organizations but spring from the minds and efforts of individuals or small groups. They are produced for various reasons and with a variety of approaches, but always under the assumption that on the Web, at least initially, a Matt Drudge can look as big as the *New York Times*.

Matt Drudge, of course, is one of the leading examples of this phenomenon of individual journalism. Independently owned and operated sites are hailed by those who see the Web as providing a forum to people who would otherwise not have a voice. In this way, the Web harkens back to the early days of the Republic, when a single printer could start a newspaper and espouse his or her faction's point of view. Indeed, producing and posting such a web site is vastly less expensive and far easier than printing and distributing any sort of publication. A web site can be produced in less than half a day and can cost less than $100 in out-of-pocket expenses.

Some web sites in this category are built to cover subjects and stories that are being ignored by the traditional media. Some of these topics would not be considered news at all by normally accepted standards of journalism. For instance, Brooklynite Ira Stoll has produced a site (smartertimes.com) devoted to criticizing the *New York Times* and pointing out its errors, shortcomings, and perceived bias. He does so because, in his words, "New York's dominant daily has grown complacent, slow and inaccurate. Even an ordinary, semi-intelligent guy in Brooklyn who reads the newspaper early each morning can regularly notice errors of fact and logic." The *Times* will not comment on the site or acknowledge its existence. That web site exemplifies a feeling among some that what the media are least likely to cover are the media themselves.

Many individually produced sites emphasize commentary rather than news and information but should be considered here because of the people involved. Journalist Andrew Sullivan (andrewsullivan.com), for instance, is a conservative writer who is openly gay and has written for a number of major publications (such as the *New York Times Magazine*). His web site is a daily, sometimes hourly barrage, of comment, reaction, and exchange between him and his readers, which can be highly entertaining and sometimes informative.

Individual sites rarely produce enough income to sustain the producer on a full-time basis. In fact, they rarely produce income at all. But they do offer an opportunity for individuals to break the hold that traditional media organizations have had on communicating with wide audiences and on the definition of journalism itself. These sites can build small but significant followings, can engender lively discussions, and can give voice to points of view that would not normally appear in traditional media.

Swimming in more traditional channels, a few news-oriented Web-only publications are beginning to appear. These sites emulate the sites of local newspapers or broadcast entities. These have news and advertising staffs that post new information on a daily basis and are directed at serving a geographic region, such as a city or county. Examples of such sites are the Oswego Daily News (oswegodailynews.com) and the Fulton Daily News (fultondailynews.com). Sites such as these emphasize local news, or hyperlocal news as webites sometimes refer to it. They are born of a dissatisfaction with a local metropolitan daily newspaper that does not—and cannot—cover the news of local communities in any depth. They are sustained initially by local businesses that find advertising in larger newspapers too expensive and too inefficient in that the ads reach an audience the advertiser does not need. These sites build a local audience by writing unpaid obituaries, covering the activities of local civic clubs and kids' soccer leagues, and posting pictures of newborn babies. These are items that larger newspapers and broadcast stations would ignore, but they are important to the lives of individuals.

Web-only publications are more likely to resemble traditional magazines than newspapers, however. Part of the reason for this is that news—information on breaking stories—is difficult and expensive to gather, and meeting daily deadlines can be a wearing process. A magazine is produced with longer deadlines, and the readership does not expect it to keep up with breaking news stories. One of the most successful of the early webzines was Salon (salon.com), which was begun in 1995 as an intelligent but middle-brow publication that commented on politics, news, people, and life in general. Salon was part of a series of original-content publication sites and online communities. David Talbot, the founder, and his staff sought to explore how the Web could be used to deliver information and comment that people would want. They also attracted advertisers and eventually sectioned off part of the site as "premium," for which subscribers are charged a fee.

Salon was followed in 1996 by Slate (slate.com), a publication sponsored chiefly by Microsoft. The company managed to attract the high-profile Michael Kinsley, then a host of CNN's *Crossfire,* to move from Washington, D.C., to Seattle to become its editor, and the site quickly won praise for its provocative commentary. Slate drew a large audience, but that audience dried up when Slate began charging a subscription price for most of its content. That plan was soon dropped, and the site has since tried to generate revenue through advertising and sponsorships.

Both Salon and Slate post new content every day and are a timely part of their readership's lives and thinking. They even occasionally break news stories themselves, although that is not their mission. The experience of each has taught the Internet world lessons in producing content and in surviving rocky economic times.

A more comprehensive and ambitious web site was created by noted radio host Tom Joyner in 2001, when he began BlackAmericaWeb. Joyner had developed top-ranked radio programs in two major markets, Dallas and Chicago, and he used this celebrity to put together a site that is "an interactive, easy-to-use Internet community and comprehensive source of information for and about African-Americans." The site is a set of partnerships that include BlackEnterprise.com, BlackPressUSA.com, Soul ofAmerica.com, BlackHealthNetwork.com, NandoMedia.com, Thomasoncapital.com, and StreamingFaith.tv, among many others. The site posts information provided by all of the partners and leads its splash page with news reports of events likely to interest black Americans.

Some news web sites are devoted to a subject rather than a group of people. WebMD (webmd.com) tries to satisfy the needs of consumers for medical and health-related news. By concentrating all of its efforts and expertise in this one area, the site can produce news that, according to its own site description, is "more reliable. In a medium often accused of providing outdated and inaccurate information, WebMD stands out as a credible, authoritative source of health news." The site goes far beyond just providing massive amounts of news and information that include sections on hundreds of diseases and conditions. The site attempts to build communities of people interested in a particular health-related topic. It sponsors live chats with experts and celebrities and sends out dozens of topic-specific newsletters. It allows a user to build a medical profile and to edit that profile as conditions change. The profile is used to provide the user with specific information about topics of interest. The site also helps consumers find doctors, treatments, and eligibility for programs and support. A part of the site even offers a management program to help physicians operate more efficiently. The site (as of the summer of 2002) attracts more than 15 million visitors a month, and its Medscape information portal, which is aimed at physicians and health care professionals, has more than a half-million doctors registered.

NEWS SITES THAT DIDN'T MEAN TO BE

Major League Baseball, or officially, The Office of the Commissioner of Baseball, located in New York City, is not a news organization. It is the association of major league baseball organizations around the country that has been existence in some form since the 1870s. The organization oversees scheduling of games, television contracts for the All-Star game and the World Series, player drafts and trades, implementation of rules, and many other matters having to do with the operation of the game. The commissioner, in name at least, is responsible for the general welfare of the national pastime, from the Major Leagues to Little League. The web site for the commissioner's office did not mean to be a news web site, but that's what it is.

Every day, especially during the baseball season, thousands of people land on the site (mlb.com) to get updated scores, to watch pitch-by-pitch Flash presentations of games, to listen to live radio broadcasts, to see video highlights, to read about trades, team controversies, ballparks, rookies, veterans, and anything baseball. In 2001, the site (through the commissioner's office) forced all twenty-six teams to channel their individual game radio broadcasts through the site and then charged consumers a $10 annual subscription fee to listen to the games. About 120,000 people paid the fee. (Do the math.)

That's not the only way the site gets revenue. It has a variety of subscription packages that range from the Press Pass (where you can read game notes before the game and get caught up on the latest statistics and team reporters just as if you were a reporter covering the game), to searchable video, to baseball history, to various aspects of fantasy baseball. And, of course there is a single subscription package ($9.95 each month) that gets you everything. In addition, the MLB.com Shop will sell you a jacket, cap, or almost any other item of clothing with your favorite team's logo on it, as well as a wide range of other items from baseball's history to the upcoming All-Star game.

The basis of the site, however, is news. Even in the off-season, MLB.com has a daily roundup of stories about trades, injuries, team movements, and rumors. The baseball junkie is never without an information fix if he or she can get to MLB.com.

And if you are an aficionado of crime news and the criminal justice system, what sites are bookmarked on your browser? Chances are, one of them is Court TV (courttv.com), the web site for the cable television channel famous for showing live trials around the country. The Court TV web site devotes much time and effort to promoting the channel's television schedule, but it has expanded into much more. It runs many articles about crimes that have not yet made it to court. Many of these reports are written by staff members, but others are gleaned from wire services to which the station subscribes. In addition, the site contains analyses, expert opinions, court documents, and a variety of material that television programming could not show or would not have the time to discuss. The site offers in-depth coverage of trials that are being broadcast as well as famous trials where television cameras have not been allowed.

The site has many other features, including chat sessions with lawyers, judges, and experts; sections on famous crimes and trials in history; an extensive description of its nightly dramatic fare (such as reruns of the televisions series *NYPD Blue* and *Homicide*). A "Smoking Gun" section exhibits extensive information about odd or unusual items related to crime and punishment (such as a wrestling web site run by a Catholic priest in Pennsylvania; the site advertised for sale hundreds of photos of young, scantily clad boys in "wrestling poses"). And, of course, the site has a section where visitors can purchase videotapes, books, and even a *Homicide* beach towel.

These and other sites like them were conceived for one purpose but have fallen under the spell of news. Information, particularly recently gathered information about topics of interest, is a powerful draw for people and can become a lucrative commodity. Web sites such as Major League Baseball and Court TV are just two of

FIGURE 2.3 VOA News. The Voice of America is the nation's broadcasting arm that broadcasts news and information outside the borders of the United States. VOA broadcasts in more than fifty languages around the world. Converting its content to a web site was a monumental task, not only because it took VOA from a sound to a text medium but also because of the many languages the VOA uses. (For more information, go to www.voa.gov/index.cfm.)

many examples. These sites may have instant credibility because of the organizations they represent; they use that credibility to dispense information and to create audiences and revenue for their organizations. Each of these sites is an example of the way journalism—its standards and conventions—has insinuated itself into non-news situations and organizations.*

WEBLOGS: A NEW FORM OF JOURNALISM?

What if there was a newspaper to which readers contributed news items and essentially decided what was in the newspaper by their contributions? Or a broadcast station for which viewers produced the stories that were seen by the rest of the audience? And the reporters could—in fact, were expected—to sprinkle their reports with a bit of attitude, or at least to let their point of view show?

And no item could be longer than three paragraphs (in the newspaper) or one minute (broadcast)? And everybody who read or watched was interested in the topic that was being reported? And anyone listening or watching could respond by disagreeing with the reporter, correcting information, or just offering another point of view, either directly to the reporter or to the group as a whole? And while some topics would die for lack of new information, interest or responses, other topics might stay alive for days, weeks, or months?

To some this would not be much of a newspaper or news broadcast, and it certainly would not be journalism. After all, journalism should be practiced by trained journalists. Their work should go through the standard editing process, and it should be presented to the audience with little indication as to how the reporter feels about the information. And while members of the audience might want to respond, their responses would be confined to phone calls to reporters and letters to the editor, usually published several days after the original item appeared. Corrections, when absolutely necessary, would be placed obscurely on an inside page of the newspaper or broadcast rarely on a television station. Now, that's journalism.

Or is it? What is described at the beginning of this section is neither a newspaper nor a news broadcast and would probably be completely unmanageable in either of those media. On the Web, however, such "publications" are called *weblogs,* and they are growing in number and audience. The weblog is a powerful manifestation of the interactive qualities of the Web, and many people believe that this interactivity will spark a dramatic change in journalism itself. J. D. Lasica, senior editor of the Online Journalism Review, says that the weblog is a grass-roots phenomenon "that may sow the seeds for new forms of journalism, public discourse, interactivity and online community" (Lasica, April 29, 2002).

A weblog can begin as an entry in a personal journal that is posted on a web site with an invitation for anyone to respond; or it can start as an entry that will lead to a

---

*To demonstrate that the Major League Baseball site is not a propaganda tool of club owners, many of the stories that MLB.com runs end with the sentence, "This story was not subject to the approval of Major League Baseball or any of its clubs."

directed discussion by a specific set of participants. There are many variations. What is necessary for a weblog are the following:

- A web site or section of a site devoted to the weblog
- Someone in charge of posting—an editor, manager, director, or just an individual who does not mind spending time in front of a computer screen
- Software that allows users to submit their entries
- Rules for participating in the discussion (sometimes there simply are no rules)
- And a beginning entry

Unlike bulletin boards, weblogs are not simply places for people to spout off or "flame" another participant and then move on. The point of a weblog is to share information as well as points of view. Consequently, most weblogs have editors or managers who are there to control but not necessarily censor the content. These editors can prevent an item from being posted if it is inappropriate in tone or subject matter, but their main job is to see that the weblog itself continues in operation and to keep discussion moving.

Some weblogs have rules that participants must follow. Metafilter (metafilter.com), one of the most popular general weblogs, requires that participants register and that they wait at least one week before posting anything. "The lag is built in to allow new members to get used to the place and to understand what other members consider good links," Matt Haughey, Metafilter's creator and editor, says (Metafilter.com/about.mefi, downloaded April 17, 2003).

The usual form of a weblog entry is a short piece of writing (fifty to a hundred words) that introduces a topic or refers to a previous entry. Writers often share some information that they have found elsewhere on the Web, and they provide a link to the information. A writer might want to comment on some development and include a link that is an example of what he or she is talking about. The writer is also free to include editorial comments or phrases that reveal a point of view or attitude toward the information. The following is an entry from E-media Tidbits, a weblog on web journalism operated by the Poynter Institute.

A TIMES EPIC IN MULTIMEDIA

Steve Outing on online storytelling

Did you catch the epic New York Times September 11 package over the weekend? In exhaustive coverage, Times reporters combed through cell phone and e-mail records of the World Trade Center victims to document their final minutes of life after the planes hit the twin towers. (It's a powerful read. I sense a Pulitzer in the future for this.) While much of the package is text that's been repurposed on the NYTimes.com website, there is a very well done multimedia presentation featuring Times journalists narrating infographics that explain the effects of the plane impacts on various floors, and the people working there. This is an effective way to consume this story, an alternative to reading thousands of words of text. In my case, I viewed the multimedia first, then was engrossed and went on to read the whole package. I also loved the opportunity to hear the print journalists' voices—something made possible by the Web. (It goes to show the new importance for print journalists to be trained for also doing audio and/or video work.)

[Discuss THIS item | See ALL Tidbits discussions]

Participating in a weblog is called *blogging,* a term derived from combing the last letter of the word "web" with the word "log." Another term to describe an entry is *microcontent,* which refers to the brevity of the writing that has become a standard expectation of bloggers.

Weblogs have proliferated since their beginning in 1997 and 1998, due in part to several sources of free software that are available to those who want to begin a weblog. There are literally thousands of weblogs, ranging from free-form journals where comments about any topic are welcomed from anyone who cares, to tightly controlled discussions with a limited list of contributors. In this latter type of weblog, noncontributors can watch the discussion and can post comments on items in the log, but they cannot initiate their own items. (The *Guardian* newspaper in London once went even further in shutting out contributors. During the summer of 2002, the paper ran a weblog that simply gathered information and links from around the world about the approaching World Cup soccer tournament in the Far East that fall. No one outside the staff contributed or commented.)

Is this journalism? Weblogs have some of the elements of traditional journalism in that they dispense information to an audience, but they lack the traditional editing process that should include some independent assessment of the accuracy of the information being presented. Bloggers argue that contributors to weblogs feel an obligation to their potential audience to present information that they think is correct. Further, they say, a weblog is a self-correcting entity; inaccurate information can be corrected, or at least challenged, as discussion of a topic continues. In this sense, weblogs may be compared to talk radio—a comparison that many bloggers do not appreciate.

To be fair, contributors to weblogs are usually identified (unlike people who call in to talk radio shows), and many seem to take seriously their responsibility for contributing substantial information to the discussion. And, on some topics, weblogs are a source of up-to-date information that no media organization attempts to match. In addition, weblogs have an inherent respect for their audiences and take advantage of their wide-ranging knowledge and expertise. While contributions may not come from trained journalists and may not be vetted through a traditional editing process, weblogs offer the possibility of presenting a much wider range of points of view about information than would be possible in the traditional media.

Consequently, those who are committed to weblogs believe they have seen the future, and they expound this belief with almost religious fervor. Rebecca Blood, who has operated a personal journal weblog called Rebecca's Pocket (rebeccablood.net), has articulated those feelings eloquently in an essay about weblogs:

> Traditional weblogs perform a valuable filtering service and provide tools for more critical evaluation of the information available on the web. Free-style blogs are nothing less than an outbreak of self-expression. Each is evidence of a staggering shift from an age of carefully controlled information provided by sanctioned authorities (and artists), to an unprecedented opportunity for individual expression of a worldwide scale. Each kind of weblog empowers individuals on many levels. (Blood, 2000)

Weblogs are a powerful demonstration of the interactive and personal qualities of the Web. They are likely to change journalism, but how profound that change will be depends neither on journalists nor on bloggers. It will depend on the readers themselves. Will news consumers continue to want their information filtered through the standard journalistic processes? Will they prefer it varnished with the overt point of view of the writer? Or will they find the information and presentation of a weblog more informative, more provocative, and ultimately more useful? If the answer to the last question is "yes"—and many bloggers believe that it will be—then journalism is in for a radical change. Certainly journalists need to take note of weblogs now for their information value and for ideas about the ways in which they may use the Web to help readers become more fully informed.

WHITHER WEB SITES?

A news web site has been the way in which news organizations have presented the news content—pictures, stories, graphics, video, etc.—to audiences over the Web. These sites not only have shown the content, they have also reflected the structure, appearance, and even values of the news organization itself. In short, they have been an extension of the brand of the news organization.

As the Web travels through its second decade and develops in new and sometimes unexpected ways, news web sites have become more difficult to define or even categorize. News web sites range from the "traditional," which use the content, look, and feel of the news organization it represents, to the highly innovative, which seek to evolve the site into a different entity.

And, as we have seen, news web sites are not the exclusive purview of news organizations. Individuals, small groups of interested people, and corporations of every size have gotten into the news business by producing web sites. In fact, these non-news organizations have demonstrated the nature and power of the Web, and the expectations that people have for finding new information. The Web has made them into news organizations, whether they intended to be that or not.

The Web is making the production and distribution of news more democratic. The institutions that once controlled much of this production and distribution—and protected the journalistic foundations on which the news was based—now find themselves in a sea of competition that not only challenges their supremacy but may rewrite the definition of news itself. Some of the issues involved in the future definition of news are discussed in the next chapter.

COOL IDEAS

Throw Away the Keyboard, Toss the Notebook

Tired of typing and want to get back to the way Thomas Jefferson wrote the Declaration of Independence? (He actually wrote it, quill in hand.) The tablet PC that works like a real tablet is here.

Handwriting recognition programs have been around for a while (since the early to mid-1990s), but all they did was convert scribbles to text—and sometimes not very well.

With a note-taking utility called Journal from Microsoft, the tablet PC not only recognizes text and makes it Web-ready, it also preserves the original handwriting. Now the notes you write can be saved as text and searched, or they can be saved as HTML documents and put on your web site.

Handwritten web sites? Maybe penmanship will make a comeback in the school system. (Find out more about all of this by checking the Business 2.0 article at www.business2.com/articles/mag/print/0,1643,42148,FF.html.)

Permanence—Back to 1786

The Augusta (GA) *Chronicle* has been publishing since 1786, and just about everything it has ever produced has been preserved in hard copy or on microfilm. All of this is now available on the newspaper's web site—all 1.2 million pages—and there's an added perk: it's all searchable.

All of the microfilm was scanned by Morris Communications, and the pages were converted to PDF files, easily readable for any user who downloads Adobe Acrobat reader for free. The archives have not only the text but the pictures, graphics, advertisements, and other items on the page as well.

The *Chronicle* charges a fee for outside users to gain access to these archives, located at AugustaArchives.com., but officials at the newspaper say they have had a heavy and positive response from users around the world.

DISCUSSION AND ACTIVITIES

1. The author says that on the Web a Matt Drudge can look as big as the *New York Times*. What does he mean by that? Do you agree?

2. Is a weblog a news web site?

3. Baseball has MLB.com, as well as many other sites devoted to the sport. CourtTV is devoted to crime, courts, and punishment. Is there any subject or issue that needs a good news website devoted entirely to that subject? What would it take to start a news web site on that subject?

4. Find some examples of local news web sites providing minute-by-minute coverage of a breaking local news story. Analyze the coverage. What kind of information did the site present? You might want to call the people at the site and talk to them about what happened, how they got information and processed it, and how often they posted information during the event.

SELECTED BIBLIOGRAPHY

Auletta, Ken. "Synergy City." *American Journalism Review,* May 1998. http://216.167.28.193/Article.asp?id=2446.

Baum, Gary. "Tweaking the Times' Nose." *Online Journalism Review,* March 27, 2002. www.ojr.org/ojr/workplace/1017265278.php.

Blood, Rebecca. "Weblogs: A History and Perspective." *Rebecca's Pocket,* September 7, 2000. www.rebeccablood.net/essays/weblog_history.html.

Colgan, Craig. "Creatures from the Web Lagoon: The Blogs." *National Journal,* August 2, 2002. http://nationaljournal.com/about/njweekly/stories/2002/0803nj_colgan.htm.

Cone, Edward. "Writing in 3-D in my Blog." *Greensboro News and Record,* May 19, 2002. http://www.news-record.com/news/columnists/staff/cone0519.htm.

Kramer, Staci. "The Times They-Are-a-Changing." *Online Journalism Review,* March 13, 2002. www.ojr.org/ojr/kramer/1016056980.php.

Kramer, Staci. "Will Kinsley's Slate Get Wiped." *Online Journalism Review,* August 15, 2002. www.ojr.org/ojr/kramer/1029281360.php.

Lasica, J. D. "After the Meltdown." *Online Journalism Review,* March 25, 2002. www.ojr.org/ojr/future/1017079354.php.

Lasica, J. D. "Independent's Day." *Online Journalism Review,* April 2, 2002. www.ojr.org/ojr/workplace/1017771181.php.

Lasica, J. D. "Weblogs: A New Source of News." *Online Journalism Review,* April 18, 2002. www.ojr.org/ojr/workplace/1017958782.php.

Lasica, J. D. "Blogging as a Form of Journalism." *Online Journalism Review,* April 29, 2002. www.ojr.org/ojr/workplace/1017958873.php.

Lasica, J. D. "Oklahoma: Where Convergence Is Sooner." *Online Journalism Review,* July 26, 2002. www.ojr.org/ojr/lasica/1027636058.php.

Lasica, J. D. "Innovation in the Heartland." *Online Journalism Review,* August 20, 2002. www.ojr.org/lasica/1029874865.php.

Scheirer, Eric. "How Media Companies Should Structure Online." *The Forrester Report,* February 2, 2000. www.forrester.com.

Stevens, Jane. "TBO.com: The Folks with the Arrows in their Backs." *Online Journalism Review,* April 3, 2002. www.ojr.org/ojr/workplace/1017858030.php.

Stone, Martha. "Breaking Stories and Breaking Even." *Online Journalism Review,* February 1, 2002. www.ojr.org/ojr/workplace/1015015509.php.

Tedeschi, Bob. "Downloading Magazine Replicas." *The New York Times,* August 5, 2002. www.nytimes.com/2002/08/05/technology/05ECom.html.

WEB SITES

Two web sites noted at the end of Chapter 1 are indispensable for keeping up with web journalism. They are the site for the Poynter Institute (www.Poynter.org) and the Online Journalism Review (www.ojr.org). Here are a couple of others.

CyberJournalist.net (www.cyberjournalist.net)

This site is run by Jonathan Dube, technology editor for MSNBC. Here's his description of his site: "CyberJournalist.net focuses on how the Internet, media convergence and new technologies are changing journalism. The site offers tips, news and commentary about online journalism, digital storytelling, converged news operations and using the Internet as a reporting tool." CyberJournalist.net is a service of The Media Center at the American Press Institute.

Editor and Publisher (www.editorandpublisher.com)

Editor and Publisher is the major trade magazine for the newspaper industry and deals with a wide variety of issues, from the technology of printing and Web publishing to the ethics of newsgathering.

New Directions for News (www.newdirectionsfornews.com/)

This site and sister sites serve as homes for ideas in digital storytelling. Its site description says, "NDN produces work products on topics vital to news organizations and society in the rapidly evolving media environment." The site is funded primarily through a grant from the McCormick Tribune Foundation. It is based in Minneapolis in association with the University of Minnesota.

■ ■ ■ ■ ■

CHAPTER 3

NEWS
EXPANDING THE DEFINITION

MAJOR THEMES

- Much of the old thinking about news—news values, for instance—will transfer into web journalism, but these values will be mixed with some radical new ideas.
- The ability of the Web to hold vast amounts of information allows it to fill voids that traditional media cannot, or do not choose, to fill.
- The egalitarianism of the Web will profoundly change the nature of news.

Imagine this:

- When you read a story on your favorite news web site about something—a new line of shoes endorsed by Michael Jordan, the latest novel from your favorite science fiction writer, a new variety of rose, a cell phone that has a bell or whistle yours doesn't have—you can click on a button on that page and buy it. In the case of the cell phone, you can click on another to buy a classified ad and sell your old one, or simply put it up for auction.

- You're reading a story about recent Academy Award winners. Beside the story is a box listing the movie theaters in your area that are showing the winning entries, along with showtimes. A button beside each entry allows you to purchase tickets.

- Your favorite Busch Cup NASCAR driving team is entered into a race in Bristol, Tennessee. The race began an hour ago but is not being televised, and you would like to know how your guys are doing. You call up your favorite news web site on your computer to find the current standings—updated within the last ten minutes—and get a report from the infield on the progress of the race.

- You read a local story on your favorite news web site, a story about which you have some personal knowledge, and you believe the reporter got it wrong or left out some important information or point of view. You click a button on that page and email the site with your concern. Within the hour, your comments are posted at the end of the story along with the comments of others who have read the story. Two hours later, another reader has responded to your comments, and that response is posted right below yours.

■ When you go to your favorite news site on the evening after the NASCAR race, the lead story is about the race because when you personalized the site, you told the editors that you always wanted NASCAR stories to be the lead stories. Also on the splash page is a story about a new rose variety (see above), because you have told the web site one of your hobbies is growing roses.

OLD NEWS, GOOD NEWS

Every good journalism student knows news values. These values are the things about an event that make it news in a journalistic sense.

■ *Impact.* An event that affects many people or involves many people is news. The event does not have to be dramatic. For instance, a city council can raise the city sales tax by a voice vote and without debate. That event could affect thousands of people.

■ *Conflict.* An event where there is conflict—physical, verbal, or even psychological—can be considered news. Differing points of view constitute conflict.

■ *Currency.* Events that surround or involve issues under public discussion are said to have currency. Currency can die quickly, however. In the summer of 2001, a story many in the media paid attention to involved the disappearance of an intern in Washington; she had been involved with a U.S. congressman (see the next news value) and for lack of any other viable news that summer, this story was the talk of the town in Washington and elsewhere. After September 11, this issue completely lost its currency.

■ *Prominence.* When prominent people participate in events, that is likely to be news. We know more about the President of the United States than we do about most of our neighbors, because he is the most prominent political figure in the nation.

■ *Unusualness.* Events that are out of the ordinary can be considered news. They do not have to be particularly important or have a lot of impact. They simply need to be unusual enough that we pay attention to them.

■ *Proximity.* This value refers to location, and it can lift an event into the realms of news. A car accident two hundred miles away that kills two people is probably not something you are going to hear about. If one of those people is from your hometown, however, you may well hear about it. And if the accident occurred on a downtown street in your hometown rather than two hundred miles away, a local editor or news director might consider it worth reporting.

■ *Timeliness.* Events are generally thought to be news only if they occurred recently—within the last few hours or the last day or two. This is the value that almost all news events have in common.

■ ■ ■ ■ ■

SIDEBAR

THE PRESIDENT AND THE INTERN

The Saturday meeting of editors at *Newsweek* magazine can be a lively affair, but the third one in January 1998 was particularly memorable. Reporter Michael Isikoff had been tracking rumors that President Bill Clinton had been having an affair with a White House intern. The reporter had solid information confirming the story, but the editors decided to hold off for another week.

Their decision filtered out of the office and into the gossip circle of a few insiders in New York and Washington. That circle included Matt Drudge, producer of a one-person web site in Hollywood, California, called the *Drudge Report*. The site specialized in rumor and innuendo, particularly about the Clintons. Drudge, too, had heard about the possibility of a presidential affair from his contacts among the anti-Clinton right. The delay by the *Newsweek* editors was the pretense he needed to circulate the rumor. He posted an item, not about the presidential affair, but instead saying that *Newsweek* editors had killed it.

Relatively few people saw the posting itself, but now the rumor grew legs. It was picked up by a variety of newsgroups and reposted, giving it a small but general circulation. The next morning, on a nationally broadcast news talk show, an anti-Clinton guest mentioned the rumor that was in circulation. It was later mentioned again on another TV talk show, and the buzz had begun.

Over the next forty-eight hours, the world came to know the name Monica Lewinsky.

Most journalists do not think much about news values when they are deciding what to report, because the journalistic process has become so institutionalized. Journalists routinely know what is news; they know what they think about an event or idea for a story, and they usually know what their editors or news directors will think about it. In other words, as any editor will tell you, news is what he or she says it is.

After an event, idea, or subject has been deemed newsworthy, journalists use certain criteria to decide how important it is. These criteria are fairly simple to understand:

■ Is death or injury part of an event? On a daily basis, death is the most serious fact that journalists have to report. Any story about a disaster will prominently feature the number of people killed or injured in that disaster.

■ How widespread is the event or its effects (the news value of impact)? The more people who are involved or who are affected by an event, the more important it is.

■ Has property been destroyed? If so, how much? Where? To whom does it belong? Destruction of property is a powerful news force because of its unusualness and because it makes compelling pictures.

■ How much money is involved? An event that involves a lot of money is thought to be important because of the high value that our society—and human beings in general—place on money.

■ Who are the people associated with an event (famous and not-so-famous), and will people be interested in their actions? Judging the interests of the audience is one of the most important actions a journalist takes. Much of what appears in a newspaper or on a news broadcast is defended by the words, "We thought people would be interested in that."

These news values and criteria of importance are mixed together in every news organization that is independent of some outside force (such as government). They are the ideas and concepts that produce the day's news. They are not foolproof, and they are not always used well by journalists. Stories that are important are sometimes missed. (Heat, for instance, is a much deadlier natural disaster than floods, hurricanes, or tornados, but it is rarely reported as such.) In general, however, journalism gets it right and covers the stories that need to be covered.

The good news is that this will probably not change much in the world of web journalism. Many of the same editorial decisions that are made at newspapers and broadcast stations will be made in the news meetings of news web site staffs, at least for the foreseeable future.

Nor will the old forms of storytelling and presentation be abandoned (see Chapters 4 and 5). The inverted-pyramid story structure, a staple of presenting news in print, has proved remarkably resilient for many years and has characteristics that make it an ideal form for the Web. Feature stories and styles, photography techniques and video styles, and the conventions of graphic presentation have been carried over into the Web with good effect. They are useful modes of giving information to the reader and viewer, and they are likely to continue to be in use.

Given that, what will change with web journalism, particularly in the way we approach news? The answer is that a great deal is likely to change. While the changes will not be sudden and traumatic, they will occur because the medium allows it, and the audience will demand it.

NEWS, AND MORE OF IT

The first big change that the Web has brought to journalism is the ability to handle far more information than any traditional medium. Web journalists are learning to think "laterally" about their stories. Instead of just gathering enough information to write a single, inverted-pyramid story, a web journalist must consider various types of information that could be included as parts of a story package.

For example, a famous author may come to a local college campus to give a speech. The print reporter will attend the speech and write a story about the event. A photographer may also show up to shoot a single picture of the author giving the speech.

The web journalist needs to think beyond these simple actions. That reporter could produce any of the following items:

■ An inverted-pyramid news story
■ The text of the speech

■ ■ ■ ■ ■

SIDEBAR

THE STARR REPORT

Nine months and millions of investigative dollars after Matt Drudge posted his item about *Newsweek* (see sidebar, "The President and the Intern"), special prosecutor Kenneth Starr was ready to release a report on President Clinton's affair and other legal problems. His report was to go to the Judiciary Committee of the Republican-controlled U.S. House of Representatives. The committee had already voted to make the report public almost as soon it was received. There was little suspense about it: Clinton had confessed to the nation three weeks before and had been repeatedly asking for forgiveness since then. According to well-placed sources, however, what Starr had written contained salacious details of the President's sexual encounters.

The Starr Report, as it became known, would likely be the basis of an impeachment move that Republicans were planning against the President. Word was that Starr and his investigators had talked with everyone they could, and the report was massive and specific. Speculation about when the report would be made public had swirled for several days.

Finally, on Friday, September 11, 1998, the 450-page report was placed on the web sites of the House of Representatives, the Judiciary Committee, and several news organizations. After that:

- The House and committee web sites—which normally had about 10 millions hits (Internet calls to a web site) for both sites each month—got 10.2 million hits from Friday through Sunday.
- The web site of the U.S. Government Printing Office, where the hard copy of the report was being printed, got 1.4 million hits that weekend.
- The Library of Congress web site, another location for the report, had 3.9 million hits on Friday alone, compared with 269,000 on the previous Friday.
- CNN, the first news organization to have the report, had 300,000 hits per minute on its web site after it had posted the report. MSNBC broke a record for that day with nearly 2 million visitors. One estimate was that traffic on the Web increased 175 percent from the previous day and that 20 million Americans read parts of the report online by Sunday afternoon.

A survey of daily newspapers later found that 17 percent had published the full report in print, while 70 percent ran substantial excerpts; 64 percent of these papers put the report on their web site, and those that did had 80 percent increases in their web site traffic.

- A digital video clip of the most important or interesting parts of the speech
- Biographical details obtained at the author's web site or at a web site maintained by the publisher
- Links to any online book reviews that have been posted about the author's book

Web journalists should remember that people come to the Web for information, and that information may not always fit into the traditional definitions of news.

The Web characteristic of near-infinite capacity, combined with the relatively low costs of production, has allowed the Web to become a substitute in covering some major news stories that traditional media have abandoned. A good case in point was the 2000 national political conventions. Thinking that the conventions were too settled and scripted for much attention, the major television networks all but ignored them. But even at conventions where the presidential nominees are undisputed, there can be a tremendous amount of energy and activity that is of interest to a large number of people not in attendance. That activity was chronicled by a large number of sites in 2000, and predictions are that in the next quadrennial the presence of news web sites will be even more dominant.

NO MORE DEADLINES

Another aspect of traditional journalistic practice in dealing with news that will be revised (if not discarded altogether) is the concept of deadlines. Television is bound by time. Deadlines are fixed and absolute, as much for the viewer as the journalist. Viewers who miss the broadcast cannot retrieve it. Print publications are bound by publication schedules. Readers have no access to the news until after those schedules have been met. But once the print product is in their hands, they can retrieve it as they wish. The journalists who produced it relinquish their control over it.

The Web is more organic than print or broadcast in that both readers and journalists have constant access to it. A reader can check the *New York Times* web site (or any other news site) several times a day and expect to find something different there. The people who produce a web site do not have to wait for a publication schedule. They can post items on the site almost instantly.

Not only does this destroy the concept of deadlines, it means that information—articles, pictures, graphics, etc.—can go onto the site incrementally, as they are ready. A reporter does not have to prepare everything having to do with a story before parts of the package can be disseminated.

Let's go back to our example of the author visiting campus (previous section). Much of what was suggested as part of the story package could be prepared and posted before the "event," the author's speech, had taken place. Readers could read biographical information and book reviews before the speech was given, possibly helping them decide if they want to attend the speech itself. And let's say that the author was scheduled to spend the next day on campus, talking to classes and giving readings of his work. What we have is a continuing story that could be continually updated on the web site. A reporter could cover the appearances of the author, and people who heard him could post their reactions to what he said.

NONLINEARITY

The Web can be a linear medium, just as broadcast and print are linear. That is, a reader or viewer starts at the beginning and reads or watches until the end of the story.

Television is highly linear, print less so. You have to watch a television program in the sequence in which it is broadcast. With print you have more choices—reading the story, looking at the pictures, studying the graphic—but still there is a strong tendency to go from first to last.

Because the Web can be either linear or nonlinear, web journalists will have to understand both concepts and be skilled enough to present information in both forms. The Web can break up information and allow readers to veer off on a tangent if they choose. In viewing an account of a baseball game, a reader might look at the box score, read the injury report, visit a team's web site, and watch a video highlight before ever getting into the game story.

Web journalists must understand that various types of information should be presented with a story, and that links to that information should be set up to satisfy the reader. The trick will be for a journalist to be clever enough to organize the information so that a reader can go through it using a variety of routes. We have yet to settle definitively on any organizational schemes, but research, practice, and trial and error may give us some indicators as to what organizational plans work best as the Web develops.

AUDIENCE-GENERATED NEWS

The structure of the production of news, as noted earlier in this chapter, leaves the definition of news almost completely in the hands of journalists. The news audience has to accept that definition. The Web has the potential of altering that imbalance. News, at least some of the time, may be what the reader says it is.

The interactivity function of the Web will foster participation by readers in newsmaking decisions more than ever before. This already happens on many web sites in a variety of ways.

■ *Email.* Many news web sites include an email address for the reporter, so that readers can get in touch quickly if they have questions, suggestions, or news tips. One college site, Dateline Alabama at the University of Alabama, includes the email address of the copy editor in case a reader detects a spelling or grammar error in the story. Another use of email that many sites contain is a button that allows a user to email the story to someone else; thus the visitor becomes an editor and distributor, deciding what content is good enough for someone else to view.

■ *Online polls.* This device allows news sites to post a question and ask readers to submit an answer. The results are then posted and even commented upon by the site producers. The results have no scientific validity and cannot be generalized to any population—even to users of that web site—but they are a way of generating interest in the site and engaging visitors.

■ *Bulletin boards, forums, and discussion groups.* Many web sites provide areas where readers can post their information, ideas, and opinions about various topics. They can actually engage in online discussions with others who are interested in the topic. The subjects of these topics can be anything from the latest Supreme Court decision to book reviews to sports predictions. They can be short-term or range over many months. Many visitors will look at the bulletin boards and watch the discussions take place without ever participating in them, but they inevitably become part of the information mix of the site.

■ *Online chats with reporters or newsmakers.* The technology of chat rooms has reached a high degree of sophistication, and a number of web sites sponsor regular chats with reporters or people in the news. Participants have the opportunity to ask questions and engage in discussions that illuminate news events.

These are just a few of the low-technology and standardized ways in which web sites are interacting with their audiences. The technology of the Web is rapidly developing, as are the imaginations of those who use it. Consequently, many interactivity schemes are on the horizon.

For example, one proposal from the web denizens at Hypergene.com suggests setting up a web page for a story that looks like a page from Amazon.com, the famous Web bookseller (see Figure 3.1). Readers would gain points for their participation in a story package. Reading a story would be worth a certain number of points; emailing the story to a friend would be worth more points; asking a question, engaging in a discussion group, posting a news tip—all would gain the reader points, which could be redeemable for merchandise or some other reward.

This concept is just one of many ideas about how to get readers involved in a site and how to make a site valuable to its audience. All of these methods of interactivity are valuable both to the visitors and to the web site itself. They enhance the viewers' relationship with the site, and they allow viewers to raise questions and offer news tips to the journalists on the site. In the near future, the reputation of a news web site— both its credibility and its ability to draw visitors—may rest largely on what kind of interactivity it offers its readers how it responds to what the readers have to say.

PERSONALIZED NEWS

In journalism, editors select news and information, package it, and present it to their audience. The process is at the heart of journalistic practice. It is considered essential to the concept of news. Editors give; audiences receive. Personalized news, while maintaining that process in some respects, moves the decision making toward the individual user.

Personalized news is a concept that allows the individuals in the audience to decide what they want to see on the site. The reader of a newspaper can make the same kind of decision if he decides to toss aside the front sections of the paper and read only the sports section. The technology of the Web allows the reader to make choices so that as the site loads, it will show the things the reader wants to see, not necessarily the items the editor thinks are important.

Many news web sites have tried personalization and are becoming increasingly sophisticated about it. (Some, such as CNN.com, as this is written, have tried it and abandoned it.) A variety of approaches and methods to personalization exist. Probably the most common is to personalize on the basis of the content that the individual

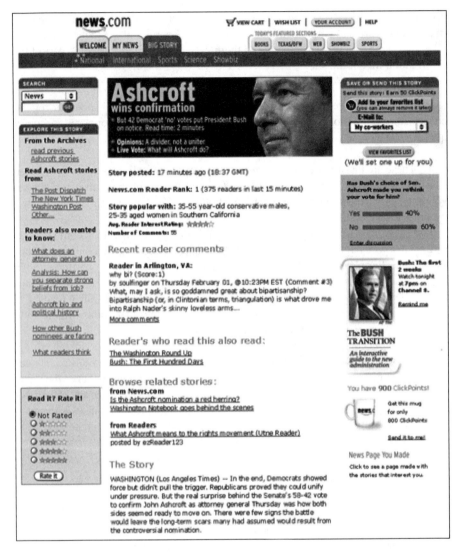

FIGURE 3.1   Amazoning the News. These two concept pages, one of a professional basketball game and the other a political story, were developed by Hypergene and based on the way Amazon.com, the bookseller, presents information to the reader. These two examples show how information about a topic can be presented in a nonlinear fashion. A full explanation of these concepts can be found at the Hypergene web site, www.hypergene.net/ideas/amazon_1.html.

would like to see. And this personalized content can be based on a relatively small amount of information.

MSNBC.com, for instance, asks visitors to enter their postal Zip code. With these five numbers, the site can know the geographic area of the visitor and can automatically produce the weather for that area whenever the individual logs on. Because

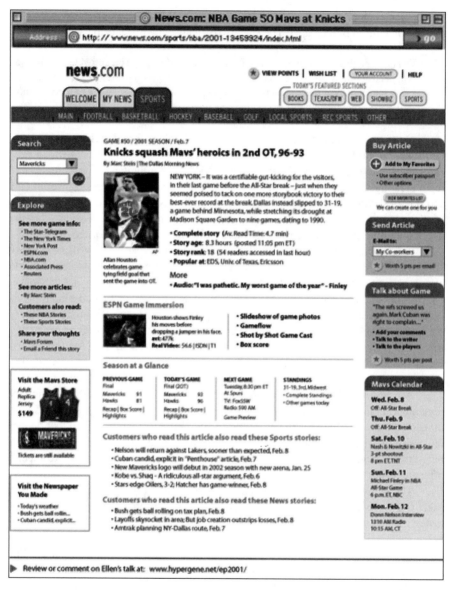

FIGURE 3.1 **Continued**

of its network of NBC stations, MSNBC can grab the headlines and links off the local channel's web site and put them on the splash page that the individual sees. MSNBC places all of this information below the images and text that it creates for its main page so that the local information becomes an individualized supplement.

The web site of the *Washington Post* (washingtonpost.com) takes something of the same approach by asking individuals to register (at no cost). The *Post* asks readers to give their country, gender, email address, Zip code, and whether or not they subscribe to the print edition of the paper. The site also explains why it wants that information:

> Our primary goal in collecting personally identifiable information is to provide you, the user, with a customized experience on our network of sites. This includes personalization services, interactive communications, online shopping and many other types of services, most of which are completely free to you. (washingtonpost.com, downloaded April 16, 2003)

Once registered, the user can select categories of preferred content—movie reviews, sports, gardening, etc. For those who live in the Washington, D.C., area, the *Post* can generate a great deal of information about local communities, such as real estate reports, ratings and test scores of local schools, lists of administrators of governments and school systems, crime reports and traffic conditions, just to name a few. As users continue to engage with the site, the site editors can gain more information about the user's preferences and can continually increase the personalization of the content.

A somewhat different approach to personalization is taken by the *New York Times,* which has chosen to emphasize services rather than content. Readers of the *New York Times* (nytimes.com) have to register before they can go beyond the splash page of the site. The site offers a variety of email newsletters that it can send to readers on subjects such as baseball, political campaigns, dining, travel, and health; there are also special offers from advertisers. Readers can change their preferences at any time. The *Times* offers specialized news alerts that it will email to individuals when breaking news about a particular subject occurs. It also has a premium account that offers items such as archive searching and crossword puzzles to users for a fee.

Amazon.com, the giant Web bookseller, has set the pace in personalization by remembering the transactions (and even the browsing) of individuals. A person who makes a purchase from Amazon gives the site certain information. When that person returns to the site, he or she will see recommendations for other books and products based on previous transactions. Amazon, too, uses email newsletters to make special offers and alert users when items are available that may be of interest.

The technology of the Web makes personalization possible, but many editors ask, "Is it really a good idea?" Personalized news does mean a shift toward user control of the site that may, in fact, prove unsatisfactory for the reader. What is also uncertain at this point is whether or not profits will follow personalization. Many believe that in the long run, personalization will be profitable, but how long will it take? Will news web sites ever be able to recover the investment that they have made in the technology and labor it takes to bring a high level of personalization to the site?

J. D. Lasica, a senior editor of Online Journalism Review, who has written extensively on many issues concerning news on the Web, believes that personalization is too strong an idea to die anytime soon.

> True personalization, in short, augurs a revolutionary shift in the balance of power between news provider and news consumer. Traditional assumptions about who gathers the news and who consumes it go out the window. Journalists now entering the field may be collecting, processing and disseminating the news in complete novel ways. How we think about news itself may be transformed, from a solid if predictably plodding prod-

uct, scripted by a professional priesthood for a mass audience, to a more free-flowing fount of information that serves the individual needs of the consumers.

Personalization is not just a cool feature of new media; it is intrinsic to new media. Unlike radio, television, or print, the Internet is the only medium that is inherently personalizable. Users can be reached simultaneously with one-of-a-kind messages. The old formula of editors and news directors having sole say in determining what is important has become an anachronism in cyberspace. The user, after all, is in the best position to know what he or she finds most interesting, valuable, useful—and newsworthy.

AND FINALLY . . .

Will the Web kill journalism? Will news as we know it cease to exist? Probably not. Journalism with all of its faults is of great value to society in that it knits our communities and our nations together with a common commodity—news. However news is produced in the future, ultimately it will require journalists to produce and legitimize it. These are people who are steeped in the language and who are discerning and objective observers of the world around them. No matter how open or participatory or personalized our definition of news gets, not everyone can be a journalist.

COOL IDEAS

If Readers Could Choose

What if readers, not editors, could choose the stories that are most interesting to them—and make those decisions for other people, not just themselves (exactly like editors)?

A number of web sites give you some insight into what readers would choose by listing stories that readers view the most, email to friends, or rate as most useful.

MSNBC.com puts a list of top-rated stories by readers on the front page of its site. While many of the items on this list line up with what the editors have chosen as the top stories, some do not. For instance, health-related stories are regulars on the Reader's Choice list. Stories with bizarre twists are often there, too.

The *New York Times* web site contains a list of its "most emailed stories" in the last twenty-four hours (www.nytimes.com/gst/pop_top.html), as does ABCNews.com (http://sendtofriend.abcnews.go.com/sendtofriend/mostsent). Yahoo lists its "most-viewed stories" (http://story.news.yahoo.com/news?tmpl=index2&cid=1046&/) and its "most viewed photos" (http://story.news.yahoo.com/news?tmpl=index2&cid=1047). CNN.com updates its "ten most popular stories" list every twenty minutes (www.cnn.com/userpicks/).

Such lists might let editors rethink their own selection processes.

DISCUSSION AND ACTIVITIES

1. Will the definition of news change because of the Web? What does the author say? What do you think?

2. Compare the coverage of an event using three web sites and three newspapers (not those of the web sites). Start with the amount of coverage and the forms of presentation (news stories, pictures, graphics, etc.) What are the differences and similarities in approach?

SELECTED BIBLIOGRAPHY

Bamrud, Joachim. "The News on 3G." TheFeature.com, August 14, 2002. www.thefeature.com/index.jsp.

Barringer, Felicity. "Web-Leery Olympics Limit News." *The New York Times,* September 25, 2000. www.nytimes.com/2000/09/25/technology/25WEB.html.

Goldstein, Jon. "Web Journalists Hope to Fill News Void." SunSpot (BaltimoreSun.com), July 30, 2000. http://cnew.tribune.com/news/tribune/story/0,1235,tribune-elections2002-7128.00-htm.

Kampinsky, Ellen, Shayne Bowman, and Chris Willis. "Amazoning the News." Paper presented at the IFRA Newsroom Convergence Conference, Barcelona, Spain, May 10, 2001. www.hypergene.net/ideas/amazon_1.html.

Landler, Mark, "A Medal for Aussie Cell Phones." *The New York Times,* September 25, 2000.

Lasica, J. D., "The Promise of the Daily Me." Online Journalism Review, April 4, 2002. www.ojr.org/ojr/1017778824.php.

Marinucci, Carla. "New Media Casts a Wider Net at Conventions, *San Francisco Chronicle,* July 29, 2000. www.sfgate.com/cgi-bin/article.cgi?file=/chronicle/archive/2002/07/29/MN25158.DTL

Outing, Steve. "Immersed in the News." Poynter.org., June 6, 2002. www.poynter.org/centerpiece/immerse/immerseive.htm.

Tedeschi, Bob. "Sports Sites Revamp Strategy." *The New York Times,* September 4, 2000.

Wendland, Mike. "Forget Deadlines, Think Online." Poynter.org., January 20, 2000. www.poynter.org/centerpiece/012000-index.htm.

WEB SITES

The Poynter Institute (www.poynter.org), Online Journalism Review (www.ojr.org), and Cyberjournalist (www.cyberjournalist.net)—referred to at the ends of Chapters 1 and 2—are particularly relevant for keeping up with how news is evolving on the Web. In addition, you may want to visit the following on a regular basis.

Online News Association (www.journalists.org)

The Online News Association is an association of more than six hundred professionals whose principal livelihood, according to the association's description, "involves gathering or producing news for digital presentation. The membership includes news writers, producers, designers, editors, photographers and others who produce news for the Internet or other digital delivery systems, as well as academic members and others interested in the development of online journalism." The association's annual awards are some of the most prestigious in the business. The site carries much information relevant to the online journalist.

The Future of News, Online Journalism Review, 2002 (www.ojr.org)

This series of articles offers a valuable variety of subjects and viewpoints about the changes that the Web will make in news and news coverage.

J. D. Lasica's Online Journalism site (www.well.com/user/jd/webjournalism.html)

Lasica is one of the leading thinkers and writers about online journalism. He is a senior editor of the Online Journalism Review, but he maintains this web site to host writing that he does for the review and other publications (including the *American Journalism Review*) and web sites.

■ ■ ■ ■ ■

CHAPTER 4

REPORTING
GATHERING INFORMATION
FOR THE WEB

MAJOR THEMES

■ The basics of journalism, gathering important, interesting and timely information and presenting it to an audience, will remain the substantive part of journalism on the Web.

■ The Web is likely to alter reporting procedures.

■ The Web is also likely to change the relationship between the reporter and the audience.

■ Reporters will have to understand the concept of lateral thinking in planning their approach to reporting, and they will need to layer information so that the audience can have access to it and understand it.

SOMETHING OLD, SOMETHING NEWS

Once, not too long ago, the life of a reporter could be relatively simple. If you worked for a newspaper, you got your assignments or you worked your beat. You had to find sources who would talk with you. You had to worry about the demands of the inverted-pyramid story structure (see Chapter 5), and make sure that what you wrote was attributed properly. You had word limits—usually less than what you needed to tell the story properly—and deadlines, always deadlines.

If you were a broadcast news reporter, you had to find stories that had visual elements, and you had to worry about carrying various pieces of heavy equipment. You had to hope that your on-camera sources would say things you could edit into five- or ten-second bites. And you had to get all this together by the time the newscast occurred.

If you were a photographer, you had to worry about film, cameras, and getting to the place where the picture could be taken. You had to make sure you got names and information for cutlines. Then there was processing the film and editing the contact sheets and hoping there would be room in the paper for at least one of your photos. And all of this had to be done as you faced an ever-approaching deadline.

Maybe it wasn't so simple after all.

Simple or not, the Web promises to make the life of a reporter much more complicated. Consider these snippets as we migrate toward reporting in a Web environment.

■ *Writing for Aunt Matilda.* Traditionally, print journalists have been told to write for a "typical" member of the audience—someone who is intelligent enough to understand a story but not as well informed as you are. This would be your Aunt Matilda, and you had to keep her in mind when you were composing a story. Make sure your Aunt Matilda can understand this, your editor would say.

Web journalists may still have to worry about Aunt Matilda understanding their stories, but they will have to keep a number of other people in mind as they compose a variety of forms—people from the uninitiated to the highly interested to the experts. Web journalists will have to satisfy a variety of audiences in a variety of ways.

All news is local. At least, all of the news that traditional reporters were involved with was local—local events and local sources. The Web, however, creates the possibility of a nonlocal, indeed a worldwide, audience. People who look at the work of a web journalist will be those who are interested in the subject, not necessarily local residents. The Web also opens up a variety of ways to get in touch with sources who may be outside the local area.

■ *I'm trying to make a deadline (part 1).* The clock always weighs on the traditional journalist. Presses need to run at certain times so delivery trucks can make their rounds; newscasts occur at definite hours, no matter what. Not so with the web journalist. There are no deadlines. The web journalist can post a story when it's done. That's the good news. However, there is also some not-so-good news.

If there is no deadline, there is no postdeadline. That is, some stories seem to take on a life of their own, and it may be a while before they go away. A reporter can learn new information after the story is posted and will need to update the story. A reader can send in new information, forcing the reporter to check out new leads. Inaccurate information has to be corrected. Points of view omitted from the original story may need to be included later. A story may not be confined by an event itself but rather by the amount of continuing interest that it generates.

■ *I'm trying to make a deadline (part 2).* There is no deadline in web journalism, so for breaking news, the deadline is *now.* This minute. And again in the next ten minutes.

Let's say a car crashes into city hall in the middle of the day. The newspaper reporter, whose deadline is 7 p.m., has a few hours to put the story together. She can talk to sources and witnesses. She can call the hospital to ask about the injured. She can spend some time gathering her thoughts and composing a lead, a second paragraph, and a third paragraph that will convey the full story to the reader.

The web journalist has to go up immediately with whatever information is available, and then he will have to update that information continually through the afternoon: What happened? How did it happen? Who was hurt? How badly? What kind of damage was done? People around town will hear about the event and start logging onto the web site immediately to find out about it. The web journalist cannot head to Starbucks to mull over the story for a while. The deadline is now.

Travel Light

Once, all a reporter needed was a notebook and maybe a tape recorder and access to a telephone. Back at the office, a reporter's technical skills needed to extend only to knowing how to fire up a computer and get to the word processing program.

Web journalists will need to carry a laptop and know how to make an Internet connection through either a phone jack or a wireless network. On that laptop will be a variety of applications with which they can download and process still pictures from the digital camera and moving pictures from the video camera. The journalists will have to edit video, scan documents, and make them into Web-ready PDF files. They will also have to be familiar with the basics of HTML tags so their copy will look right on the web site. They will need to be able to get into the back door of the database program that powers their web site so they can upload their copy immediately.

Know How to Use Many Forms

The print journalist works with the inverted pyramid, the broadcast journalist with dramatic unity story structure. Each has its demands and limitations.

The web journalist needs to master these and other writing forms, such as headlines, summaries, slideshow cutlines, frequently asked questions (FAQs), polls and quizzes, weblog entries, and other forms yet to be developed. That should not be a big problem if the reporter is an expert in the English language. Facility and confidence in using the language—always important for the journalist—will gain added significance.

Aunt Matilda's Revenge

The traditional journalist could write for Aunt Matilda (as noted above), but chances are the journalist would never actually hear from Aunt Matilda. Aunt Matilda's understanding of a story or her attitude toward it was never much of an issue. Aunt Matilda was just a concept, not somebody you had to answer to.

The web journalist, however, may well hear from Aunt Matilda soon after the story is posted. As a former English teacher, Aunt Matilda may want to point out a grammar or spelling mistake. She may want to join a forum or discussion group to discuss the story. She may have additional information or a new lead for you to follow up. She may have a different take on how some of the information has been presented or interpreted. Aunt Matilda may not like the way the journalist has handled the story, and she may have the editor's email address.

Sell Your Story

The print journalist has to worry about getting good placement on the page; the broadcast reporter wants enough time on the newscast to tell the story. Both are a matter of pride in a profession that sometimes does not have many rewards.

The web journalist needs page hits. She cannot just post a story and hope people will show up. The journalist may be required to visit and post on bulletin boards devoted to the story's subject and try to direct traffic to the story. The journalist may also have to contribute to a weblog or newsgroup so that the story will be seen by the right people. The editor will have page hit data available immediately to see what people are reading—and what they aren't. Will the web editor use that data to make assignments or personnel decisions?

The web journalist has a brave new world to face. There will be new procedures and new demands. Still, a reporter is a reporter. The basic job itself will remain essentially the same.

REPORTING: WHERE JOURNALISM BEGINS

Reporting is the central act of journalism, no matter what the medium. Writing, editing, design, and presentation are vital to the journalistic process, but the purpose of journalism is to present information to an audience. This does not happen without reporting. Someone must gather the information—and not just any information. It must be information that meets the specific demands of journalism and comes from certain kinds of sources. It must be news.

News can be defined as timely information that is of interest and importance to a broad audience. What is interesting and important? People in the twenty-first century have a variety of interests and expectations that constitute the fabric of their lives. They have families, both immediate and extended; they have professions and means of making a living; they have hobbies and ways of spending leisure time; they have interest in and connections to groups of people through civic, religious, and social activities. Journalism supports these interests by providing information so that people can share it, can use it to make decisions about their lives, can be entertained by it, and can use it to help them define their world.

Information about any aspect of human activity is not necessarily news, however. Two characteristics must be present in this information to bring it into the realm of news. One is that the information must be of interest to more than a small circle of people. That is, the fact that as a student you had trouble signing up for classes would certainly be important to your life. It would not be news, however, unless what happened to you was an experience that others had shared. The fact that many other people also had difficulty registering would constitute news. One of the first things that journalists learn is how to distinguish between information that is of interest to individuals or small groups and information that has a broader audience.

The second characteristic of information necessary to make it news is timeliness. Information, in this sense, is like produce in a grocery story: it is perishable. News, as the word implies, is made up of information that has some recency. To be news, an event must have occurred in the recent past, or a topic must be one that is currently on the minds of more than a few people. Last week's weather is of little interest to most people—even though occasionally that weather may have a continuing impact. Today's weather, however, is of great interest and importance. The information about these two events—last week's weather and today's weather—is essentially the same, but one is current and the other is not.

It is difficult to be more definite than the paragraphs above about what news is or isn't. Journalists are asked on a daily basis why they did not put information about certain events or topics in their publication or on their newscasts. A standard answer is, "We didn't consider that news." What they are revealing is that news is a judgment call: what is news is not always obvious.

Still, reporters learn by training and by trial and error what their news organization considers news. This understanding often comes from knowledge of what the news organization has done in the past. Events and topics that have never been covered in the past are unlikely to be covered in the future. Journalists have traditionally made these "news decisions" in isolation; that is, the audience or the general public has not been involved. The culture of web journalism is more participatory and interactive with the audience, and this isolated decision-making process is likely to change, as we shall see later in this book. (See Chapter 11.)

WHAT MAKES A GOOD REPORTER?

Reporters must come to journalism with personal characteristics and inclinations that will allow them to be successful. They must then develop a set of professional characteristics that will help them do their jobs and survive in a demanding and competitive environment. Those personal and professional characteristics are outlined below, as well as the demands of the journalistic culture itself.

Personal Characteristics

All types of people become reporters, so reporters are hard to characterize. Yet there are some personal traits that many reporters share and that seem to be necessary for success. One is curiosity: a good reporter wants to know things and experiences some satisfaction in finding them out. This is a trait that a reporter will develop if he or she doesn't have it to begin with. The best reporters have what is called a "nose for news." They can see or sense that something will make a good story. They recognize when an item of information is a bit unusual or when things don't quite add up the way one might expect.

Another characteristic is at least a bit of boldness. A good reporter must be confident and assertive, even in the face of having to stand out in a crowd or of making someone angry. A reporter occasionally has to ask the awkward, embarrassing, or even rude question. A reporter has to go where he or she may not be wanted.

Tenacity helps a person be a good reporter. Even if he or she is rebuffed, a good reporter continues to pursue the information that is necessary for a story. The reporter may have to look for the same information in different places or may have to devise different means of getting that information. A reporter is always looking to expand his or her sources so information can be complete and confirmed.

A reporter should have a retentive memory. He or she should remember where information is or from whom it can be obtained. The good reporter is able to connect disparate facts.

A reporter should develop the ability to listen. Much of a reporter's professional life is spent interviewing people. The reporter who is in love with his own voice is probably not going to be a good reporter. Tom Clancy, author of *The Hunt for Red October* (which was made into a blockbuster movie), said this about the value of good interviewing:

> Every person you meet—and everything you do in life—is an opportunity to learn something. That's important to all of us, but most of all to a writer because as a writer you can use anything. . . . I never even got aboard a nuclear sub until *Red October* was in final editing. On the other hand, I have talked with a lot of people who are or were in this line of work. (Clark, 1994, p. 146)

Reporters must be persuasive. They have no subpoena power over their sources. People do not have to talk with them or give them information. Reporters sometimes have to convince their sources that it is worth their time and effort to help the reporter.

Attentiveness to details is another part of the good reporter's personal arsenal. In gathering information, a reporter has to make sure that every detail is understood, that every legitimate source has been contacted, and every logical interpretation of information has been considered. Reporters know that interviewing is not just another form of casual conversation. The reporter is after certain information, and he or she must be sure that information is obtained. It has to be right, and it has to be verified.

Finally, the willingness to work hard is undeniably a characteristic that every successful reporter must have. Reporting is difficult, exhausting, and often frustrating. Obtaining quality information can be arduous and even occasionally hazardous. People who get turned away from a story too easily do not become good reporters.

Professional Abilities

No skill in journalism—or in the media in general—is valued more highly than the ability to write. Journalists must know and respect the language. They must understand the various forms of writing for the mass media and the reasons why those forms exist. They must also understand and be attentive to the rules and conventions of writing, especially style rules. All journalists and journalists-in-training pay attention to their writing. Most are on a constant quest for improvement. In Chapter 5 we will examine writing—and particularly writing for the Web—in some depth.

Reporters must also be able to gather information, assess its quality, and consider it creatively. Assessing information—and the source of that information—is the next crucial step in the process of the reporter being able to do his or her job.

Much is said and written these days about "critical thinking." Journalism, and particularly reporting, is a practical application of that concept. Reporters have to put together information in such a way that they create a context and thereby an understanding of the information. This is a subtle process that takes better than average intellectual skills. Not all reporters are geniuses, certainly, but the better reporters have honed their critical thinking skills and apply those skills to their jobs every day.

Another important professional characteristic is integrity. That might sound like a personal characteristic—and it is—but in a professional realm it takes on a somewhat different meaning. A reporter has to look at information honestly; a reporter needs to examine the assumptions or prejudices he or she brings to the analysis of that information.

The journalistic personality should contain a healthy dose of skepticism. Journalists should not be gullible; they should question what they hear, what they read, and especially what they see. They do not want to be taken in by those who give them false information. At the same time, they should not be cynical, disbelieving everything that is said to them. Instead, they should always be willing to question their source and check what they have against other information they might receive.

Ultimately, reporters survive in the tough, competitive journalistic culture because they have a sense of "greater good." Reporters generally believe they are in journalism for reasons other than making money or making a living or even for satisfying their personal desires. They generally hold to the belief that good information is good for society—that sharing that information helps society function.

SOURCES AND PROCEDURES

Sources of information are the *sine qua non* ("without this, nothing") for journalists. A reporter must know where information is and how to get it. Much of a reporter's time, particularly at the beginning of a career, is spent developing sources of information and methods of research.

Reporters work with three types of sources: personal (people); observational (events, places, etc., that a reporter can see); and stored (information in books, reports, libraries, etc., in print or electronic forms). Developing each type of source requires a different skill.

Most of the information that a reporter uses comes from personal sources—that is, people to whom the reporter talks. People have more current information than can usually be found in stored sources, and reporters can rarely be on the scene when news events actually occur. Consequently, the main job of the reporter is to find the people who have information or whose point of view is relevant to the reporter's story.

This is true even in the age of the Web, with all its immediacy. Information on the Web did not get there automatically or by any force of nature. At some point, a human had to process that information in some way. Reporters learn quickly that people are the most important and vital parts of any story they pursue, not just because of the information they have but also because they inject vitality into a story. Talking with people—getting them to part with information—is a skill that any reporter needs to develop and practice.

The Web (and the Internet) can help a reporter in developing personal sources in several ways. One is in simply finding people. A number of good telephone directory sites are located on the Web, and the operators of these sites make great efforts to see that the information is as up to date as possible. In addition, companies and organizations that have web sites often list employees and sometimes even list telephone numbers. Finding appropriate sources of information is not nearly as difficult a task as it was in the pre–World Wide Web days.

Email is another part of modern technology that can help a reporter develop personal sources of information. Many people, even high-ranking business officials, answer their own email these days. (In the future, this may not be the case.) Email often represents the only way a reporter can get in touch with someone who is busy or well protected by secretaries and assistants. Some reporters even conduct interviews by email or personal messaging systems rather than by telephone. Most reporters believe that face-to-face interviews are the most valuable kind of interviews, followed by telephone interviews, because they give the reporters clues about nonverbal reactions a source may have to a question. Sometimes, however, an email or personal message interview is the only way to the information a reporter needs quickly, and in those instances they should be used. One advantage to an email interview is that it provides a written record of the exchange and should prevent any misquoting on direct quotations.

The second kind of informational source, observation, means that a reporter should be on the scene of a news event. Here, modern technology seems to be of little use. Reporters must use their eyes and ears, and they must be able to interpret the information they are seeing. They must understand why they are at a scene and what they can get from being there. They must have the skill to place themselves in a position to get the information they need to cover the event properly. They must be alert for unexpected occurrences or people. Some resources on the Web may help them prepare for being on the scene, but once they are there, they need to rely on their physical resources.

The third kind of source—stored sources—is where the Web has made an enormous difference in the lives of reporters. The effects of the Web on reporting will continue to be far-reaching as web journalism develops.

STORED SOURCES

Casey Stengel, manager of the New York Yankees baseball team in the 1940s and 1950s, would often give long, involved, and stupefying confusing answers to reporters' questions. Then he would punctuate his circumlocutions by saying, "You can look it up!"—a challenge to those who might not believe what he had just said, if they understood it at all.

What Stengel told reporters is what we know today: a vast amount of information is available to be "looked up." This stored information includes books, reports, articles, press releases, and documents. And now there is the Web, with its amazing array of information.

Stored sources of information are vital to the journalist. The age of the Web has made retrieval of stored information a standard part of the reporting process. But delving into the vast array of information that is available on the Web can be a daunting task. Where do you start? That depends on the topic and what information a reporter needs to know about it, of course. Many experienced Web surfers use web sites that offer "search engines" to find web sites and web pages that contain information about a topic. Search engines have become increasingly sophisticated and efficient in finding information and in grouping that information into clusters that will be useful to the searcher. Essentially, there are two kinds of search engines: human and crawler.

The human-powered engine takes submissions and organizes them into directories. These directories begin with general topics (e.g., science) and then get more specific (astronomy), then offer even more specific categories (astronomers, auroras, eclipses, etc.) The person searching for information clicks down through a path of these directories and subdirectors until he or she finds the information that is sought.

Search engines that use "crawler" techniques depend on software that accesses web pages and looks for key words in the title of the page or in the text that the page contains. This software "crawls" and "spiders," two terms that refer to the way the software looks at a site and then at the pages in the site. However, a search engine crawler may find thousands of web pages with the word "eclipse" in it, and only a fraction of them will have anything to do with astronomy. How does it separate the electronic wheat from the chaff if what you are looking for has to do with astronomy?

Most search engines use a combination of human and crawler search techniques. In addition, search engine operators write into the software some method of analysis that allows the engine to determine if the web site or web page is relevant to the topic that is being searched. Consequently, the word "eclipse" might have to appear close to a word such as "sun" or "moon" to be included in a listing of astronomical eclipses. How search engines work in this regard is often a closely guarded trade secret that goes beyond the scope of this book. What the web journalist is interested in is the results of the search. Does the search engine have speed, and does it return good results? Because search engines work in different ways, they will produce different lists on the same topic. Consequently, many web journalists get into the habit of using more than one search engine to find as much information as possible about a topic.

A web journalist can work more efficiently, however, if he or she has a more specific idea about where information is located, so that search engines may not be necessary. As we alluded to earlier, there are some standard sources of information that journalists return to again and again because of the nature of what they cover and the kind of information that becomes news.

One such source is governments—local, state, and federal. One of the major jobs of any governmental agency is gathering information. (The other is providing services.) Consequently, one of the best ways to get information on crime (homicide rates, victims, juvenile delinquency, etc.) is from the U.S. Department of Justice and one of its departments, the Federal Bureau of Investigation. The U.S. Department of Agriculture provides information on what crops are raised, where they grow, and the latest techniques on cultivation. Information about education, from prekindergarten to postgraduate work, can be obtained from the U.S. Department of Education. And the Census Bureau, part of the U.S. Department of Commerce, has information on many aspects of the population and life in the United States. These are just a few examples of where information can be obtained. State governments have comparable agencies that provide state-level information, and local governments gather much information pertaining to their political districts.

Outside the realms of government, journalists can get information from trade associations and independent associates that are interested in particular topics. Almost every profession and industry has a major trade association—sometimes several such associations—that keep up-to-date information on employment, productivity, and other trends in the field. The American Medical Association for doctors and the American Bar Association for lawyers are two major examples, but there are many others. The American Cancer Society, Major League Baseball, the Red Cross, the Boy Scouts, and the College Board (for higher education) are examples of agencies or companies that collect information related to particular topics. Just about anything you can think of—any topic of interest to more than a few people—has some organization that gathers information about the topic.

Companies, organizations, and individuals maintain web sites designed specifically to disseminate information about themselves. One useful aspect of many of these web sites is that they list people in the organization who can be called by a reporter trying to gather information for a story.

In addition, the Web has fostered its own specialized source of information about almost any topic: newsgroups. Newsgroups are bulletin boards related to a single topic, where messages can be posted, discussions can take place, and questions can be asked and answered. Got a question? Find the right newsgroup, and you are likely to find a number of experts who can give you the answer. (Newsgroup topics range from car repair to fantasy baseball to cancer survivors.)

Journalists may also seek stored information in online or electronic information services. Such services provide subscribers with fingertip access to a wide range of information, such as newspapers, magazines, television transcripts, governmental reports, legal opinions, encyclopedias, library card catalogs, and many other sources.

Stored information, whether it comes from a library or from the Internet, presents the reporter with three basic problems. The first problem is management: how do you find what you need? Sometimes, just "looking it up" is not nearly as simple as it sounds, and when you are faced with the enormous amount of information that is available through the Internet, the problem is compounded. Most reporters develop strategies for exploring information sources, mainly through experience. The more a reporter uses a library or an Internet search engine, the more he or she will understand what information is available and where it is likely to reside.

A second problem is managing the information. So much information is now available on almost any topic that a reporter must have a keen sense of what is necessary for the journalistic goal and what is not. Again, experience is the reporter's best friend in keeping all of the information he or she has under control. It also helps to have an organized filing system so that time is not wasted gathering the same information more than once.

The third problem is reliability. Is the information that a reporter gets correct? How do you know? Assessing the reliability of information has always been a problem for reporters, but it, too, has been compounded by the expansion of information that is available. Reporters should consider carefully the source of the information in assessing its reliability. They should also try to find the same information from another source, if possible, and if there is some doubt about the original source. They should remember that just because something is in a book in the library—or posted on a web page on the Internet—does not make it accurate.

SPEED AND NO DEADLINES

The Web brings special pressures and opportunities to the reporting process. Journalists who join news web sites—especially those who have experience in newspapers or television—find that while the basic ways of gathering information are the same for any medium, the Web makes special demands and calls forth different skills. These demands and skills are tied to the special characteristics of the Web—immediacy, capacity, interactivity, flexibility, and permanence—that were discussed in Chapter 1.

The Web moves at broadcast-level speeds (see Figure 4.1), and so do web journalists. News on the Web has become an immediate expectation of the audience, just as real-time live events of importance are expected to appear on television. But the demands of the Web for immediate information are much different than those of broadcasting. Much of broadcasting's live coverage is based on live camera shots of the scene of an event, with an announcer or reporter providing commentary; this might be interspersed with interviews with principals in a story or experts on the story's topic. Because much of this coverage is live, it does not go through an editing process.

Words, not pictures, remain the coin of the realm for the web journalist. A web reporter not only must gather information but must put that information into some written form so it can be posted on a web site. Wire service reporters have been operating under this pressure of immediacy for decades, but reporters for other print media

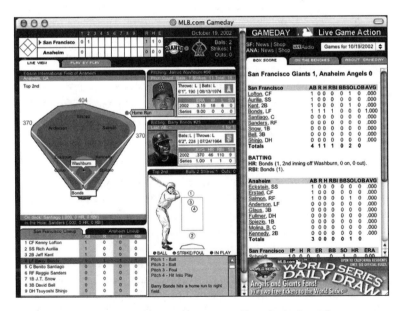

FIGURE 4.1   World Series Coverage—Immediacy in Action. The person feeding the Major League Baseball web site during a baseball game has to record every pitch and every play; the information is posted almost immediately on the web site. (Pictured here is what the site looked like when Barry Bonds hit a home run during the 2002 World Series.)

generally had at least some time between gathering the information and seeing it through to publication. The Web eliminates that time and makes wire service reporters out of everyone.

This acceleration of the reporting process has a profound effect on journalists—many of whom come from the traditional print media—and how they work. Many events, even though they are breaking news, are expected to happen. For instance, in the summer of 2002, negotiators for Major League Baseball's owners and players stayed up all night trying to come to an agreement before a strike deadline. Reporters covering the event knew that at some point shortly before the deadline there would be an announcement that an agreement had or had not been reached. Thus, they could plan for such an event by writing the body of the story about the possibility of a strike and the ongoing negotiations before the announcement was made. When the announcement was made (a settlement was reached and there was no strike), the reporters could then write the top of their stories to go up immediately on their web sites.

For events that can be anticipated, planning is a key element of the web reporting process. Thinking about what might happen and putting packages of information together before an event occurs is part of the standard procedure of the good web journalist.

But what about those events that cannot be planned, that happen with no notice—a major downtown fire, a surprise announcement from the White House, or two airplanes slamming into the World Trade Center?

The keys to covering such events well are knowledge of sources and facility with the language. A good web journalist needs to know where information is located—whom to call, where to go, and what stored resources are available. The reporter needs to think creatively about the people and places that would have information about a breaking news story. One of the first places to look is the news organization's archives, where related stories, maps, and other information might be stored. Such was the case in newsrooms all over the world on September 11, 2001, when journalists desperately sought names and phone numbers of friends (and friends of friends) who lived in New York and might be witnesses to events there. They also combed atlas archives to find the exact locations of the Trade Center towers, the Pentagon, and Somerset County, PA, the crash site of the fourth plane.

With unplanned breaking news, confidence in using the language is a must for web journalists. If information is to be posted immediately, time for editing is necessarily minimal. A journalist must be able quickly to form the information into words and phrases that make an event understandable to a mass audience.

Even when an event is not breaking news or of huge impact to the audience, speed is of the essence in web journalism. As we alluded to earlier in this chapter, deadlines have a completely different character in web journalism than in the traditional media. Deadlines may exist because of the editing procedures and schedules of the news organization itself, but once the editing has been completed, a story or story package can go onto the site immediately. Reporters are no longer pressured by a printing and distribution schedule or by a set of broadcast times. If they need more time to confirm a story and find out additional information, they can have it, particularly if they are in a noncompetitive environment.

VERSATILITY AND TEAMWORK

Because the Web is a flexible medium—that is, it can handle various forms of information—web journalists must also have the flexibility to work with the different means of gathering and presenting the news. They must not only be able to put information into a variety of written forms (see Chapter 5), they must know the kinds of information that need to be gathered to satisfy these forms. For instance, a cutline for a picture will require different information than information for an "explainer" box for a graphic.

Journalists will also need to know how to handle digital cameras (still and video), sound recorders, scanners, and other devices the web site may use for processing information. They will also have to be trained on the software that drives this machinery. The use of this equipment and software may be little more than elementary, but journalists will need to develop a basic understanding of what these things can contribute to the reporting process.

The smaller the news organization, the more likely the management will expect web journalists to acquire a variety of reporting skills. At larger news organizations, however, journalists may have to learn a different skill—teamwork. Chances are that a set of reporters with a variety of skills will be needed on many stories to satisfy the voracious demands of the Web and its audiences. Reporters will need to learn that they are part of a team of reporters who are there to contribute the mix of information that the web site wants to provide. They will need to be supportive and complementary in their efforts to present a unified package to an audience.

Such story packages will likely be built around a central narrative that the reporter gathers together and writes. As such, the reporter is likely to be the leader in the team's coverage of an event or issue and may even be given the task of organizing the team and assigning tasks to individuals of the team. Knowledge and understanding of the subject or event are certainly necessities for the reporter, but the reporter's leadership skills will be just as important—as will the reporter's understanding of the various forms of information presentation that the team might use.

BEYOND TRADITIONAL SOURCES

Sources of information are vital to journalism, as we discussed earlier in this chapter. Part of the culture of journalism is the desire to give readers and viewers the best information available. That means not only the latest information but also information from the most expert and reliable sources. The importance of sources is demonstrated by the fact that they are displayed prominently in journalistic writing through various forms of attribution.

To get good information, journalists have traditionally gone to official or expert sources. These people may be government officials, law enforcement officers, university professors, business executives, or social and civic leaders who have not only information but also influence. They are people with titles, and by including those titles in their writing, journalists make the ad-hoc argument that what is presented in the story is the best information available.

What this means is that knowledgeable people without titles—and without influence—are often ignored as legitimate sources of information. Consider the following.

- For a story about treatment of cancer patients, a journalist would interview doctors, researchers, and officials of cancer treatment centers. Patients themselves might also be mentioned, but their views would not constitute a major part of the story because they lack perspective or broad knowledge about the implications of the treatment.

- A story about drinking and driving would include the information and views of law enforcement officials, legal experts, and people who had studied this problem. It might even include information from someone who had been a victim of a drunken driving accident. Yet your roommate—who has been arrested for drunk driving—would not be considered a legitimate source of information for this story, even though he or she certainly has knowledge about the problem and a point of view that none of the traditional sources has.

- A school board makes zoning decisions for local elementary schools, and a journalist will interview board members, school system officials, and possibly even parents who are affected by it. What about the children who will have to change schools? What about the residents who do not have children but whose property values may be affected by the change? What about the citizens, without titles or official standing in this change, who see the board acting unfairly toward one group of citizens with this change?

Because of the interactivity of the Web, journalists must think more expansively about sources. People whose information and point of view are not normally included in traditional news reporting will be able to react to these stories and connect more easily with the editors and journalists who produce them.

Some news web sites actively seek responses to the news stories they present, and some even go so far as to include those reactions automatically at the end of each story—making the story, in effect, the beginning of a discussion forum about the topic. This expansion of courses and points of view will have a profound effect on web journalism as it continues to mature.

At some news organizations, reporters go beyond poststory responses and actively solicit information and opinions from the public before a story is written. These reporters use their web sites to find additional sources that they might not be able to track otherwise.

LATERAL THINKING: THE MIND
OF THE WEB JOURNALIST

Think about the basic questions that a journalist has to answer:

- *Who.* Who are the important people related to the story? Is everyone included so that the story can be accurately and adequately told? Would background information about the characters in a story help the audience to understand it?

■ *What.* What is the major action or event of the story? What are the actions or events of lesser importance? What are the events or information that can provide more context to the "what" of a story?

■ *When.* When did the event occur? What is the sequence of the events and how can that be clearly related to the audience? Is the event one of a series of events or the result of a string of occurrences?

■ *Where.* Where did the event occur? Is there anything about the place that contributes to the story?

■ *Why and How.* Are there underlying reasons why an event occurred that the audience will need to know in order to understand the event? Are procedures or processes important to the story?

Journalists for traditional media usually cannot come close to answering all of these questions because of space and time limitations. Consequently, they learn to limit their thinking to what will fit into a five-hundred-word article or a thirty-second broadcast story. But what if they could answer all of these questions, even for fairly routine stories?

Consider the following example. A famous football coach from a university outside your area comes to town to speak to the local Quarterback Club. The newspaper reporter will look up some background information on the coach, see how the team did recently, and make sure he or she knows about any controversies surrounding the coach. The reporter may have to write a short preview story about the speech. The reporter will attend the speech and take careful notes for the inverted-pyramid story that needs to be written. The reporter may also carry a tape recorder and a camera, or the newspaper may send a photographer to cover the speech. The reporter may try to talk with the coach after the speech, to ask questions about what the coach has said. The reporter will also talk with the president or someone else in the Quarterback Club to get a reaction to the coach's appearance.

The television reporter will gather enough equipment to shoot a clip of the speech and to conduct a short interview before or after the talk. The reporter will have done enough background research to know if there are any controversies or issues that should be asked about. The reporter will have to put together enough clips and reporting to fill a minute to a minute-and-a-half of airtime at most.

In both cases, once the story is printed or aired, it will be finished. It has a beginning and an end. It is, if you will, vertical.

For the web journalist, the thinking needs to be lateral. The journalist needs to ask, "How can the story expand?" (See Figure 4.2.)

The web journalist does many of the things the print and television journalists do because the main story form the journalist uses—an inverted-pyramid or dramatic-unity video structure—may be the same as the traditional journalist uses. But the web journalist will need to think beyond these traditional forms.

Before the first story is written (the preview to the speech), the web journalist will find any web sites that have information about the coach. Those will be included as links in the preview story. The journalist will also find image sources—sites devoted to the coach that may have usable pictures. (Most major football coaches have

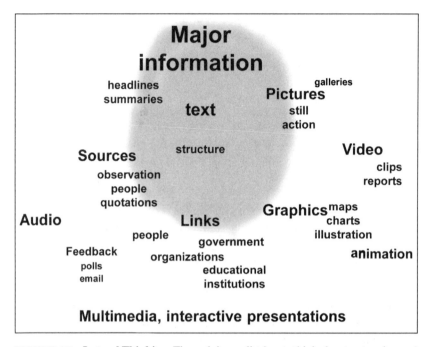

FIGURE 4.2   Lateral Thinking. The web journalist has to think about a story beyond the linear narrative. This usually involves considering the many forms of information presentation that are available for use on the web site. The journalist must decide if any of these forms are appropriate for the information that is being gathered and is needed to tell the story fully.

their own web sites; they will contain photo galleries that are established for just such uses.)

In covering the speech, the journalist will take a still digital camera, video camera, and audio recorder, or a combination of such equipment. A story will be written about the speech—either for posting or for webcasting. In addition, the reporter may have to do one or more of the following:

■ Create a slide show made up of pictures both of the coach appearing locally and of images from other web sites or other sources. Each of these pictures will require some explanation—usually twenty-five to seventy-five words. The journalist may have to record this commentary and integrate the audio with the slide show.

■ Take the video of the coach's speech and edit it down to a forty-five-second clip with an introduction to post next to the story.

■ If the coach used prepared remarks for his speech, the journalist will need to obtain a copy of those to post along with the story.

■ If the coach has written a book about his philosophy of life (as too many have), the journalist will want to establish a link to the book's web site or possibly one of the major booksellers that handles the coach's book; the journalist will also want to find reviews of that book and put links to those reviews on the page that has information about the book.

■ The journalist can put together a roundup of the coach's career, including where he played football, the schools where he has coached, the championships he has won, and the records he has compiled; this information can be linked to the sites for the athletic departments where the coach has been.

■ The journalist can then establish a forum page so that readers who want to respond to what the coach has said—particularly if it is something controversial—can have their say; these responses in turn will generate other responses, and the forum could continue for several days.

The web journalist can do all of this and more. The journalist is no longer limited by too little space in print and too little air time in broadcast. An imaginative and highly skilled web journalist can take advantage of the medium to present a wide variety of information in many ways, to the delight (or maybe consternation) of the readers.

Of course, there are also problems. The first is the age-old problem that every journalist has always had: what information is available about the topic at hand. The assumption of the example above about the coach coming to town to give a speech is that there is plenty of information available. That would probably be the case here, but not always. Specific, timely information may not be easy to come by. Recent pictures may not be posted anywhere on the Web. The coach may not have a prepared text, and he may restrict the recording of his remarks.

Another problem is conceptualizing all of the items of information that might be useful to tell the story. Sometimes reporters do not always have the time, imagination, or knowledge to expand their stories in the ways we have described above. Lateral thinking is a skill that reporters should develop, and one of the ways of doing this is through experience. Any good reporter continues to return to sources that have been productive; that is, you will tend to go back to people who have given you information for previous stories. In the same way, web journalists seeking to expand their stories will develop a good list of sources, web sites, and techniques that they can use to expand their stories.

One quick start toward expansion is collaboration. Bringing someone else in to brainstorm a story is an excellent way to gain ideas and information. Chances are a fellow reporter, editor, or even an interested friend will know something about a story that you do not know or will have an idea that you have not thought of.

A third and more important problem that the web journalist has with lateral thinking is figuring out what he or she needs to tell the story adequately. The Web allows the journalist to do many things. That does not mean that these things should be done. Presenting information in the best, most understandable form is a difficult intellectual task. Reporters have to understand the information and the forms that are available to them. Jonathan Dube, publisher of CyberJournalist.net and technology editor of MSNBC.com, says that a journalist should think about what he or she is trying to accomplish in presenting information and gives this breakdown of form and function (Dube, Cyberjournalist):

- Use print to explain
- Use multimedia to show
- Use interactives to demonstrate and engage

Still another problem for the web journalist is organizing a multiplicity of information and forms. If there is a variety of information, how do you make sure the reader sees it and is not confused by it? In the next section we will discuss layering of information. Web site design—something the reporter may be involved with—may help with this problem. A good web design will anticipate this problem and offer some preset solutions to it, but even the best planning will not anticipate all the decisions that the journalist must make about presenting information.

A fifth problem—and a very practical one—is the personal resources of the journalist. How much time or energy does he or she have to expand the story? This is no small consideration. Even when the medium is as accommodating to the imagination as the Web is, the clock and the body place limits on what a journalist can do. The web journalist has to learn to manage time and energy, just as all other journalist do.

The sixth question is also a practical one: is it worth it? What are the stories that demand lateral thinking and expansion? News organizations develop a set of priorities that take into account what editors feel is important and interesting to their readers. They use these priorities to make decisions about where to spend their resources, to decide what is important for their readers to know and what stories have "legs"— that is, what stories will be of sufficient interest that the readers themselves will want to engage and interact.

Lateral thinking, then, is more than finding links to related information about a story. It involves a pattern of thought that must become second nature to the web journalist. It also involves the techniques of reporting that are necessary for the web journalist to take full advantage of the medium.

LAYERING INFORMATION

All media layer information in some way. That is, rather than trying to give consumers the information about a topic all at once, they provide it in small doses, at least initially. Newspapers have section heads, headlines, and subheads. They also produce pictures, graphics, and other devices to present information; they run sidebars to main stories. Television news broadcasts show teasers and give introductions before they actually get to the story. Books and magazines have tables of contents and chapter and article headings. Layering is giving readers and viewers some indication of the content of a story without making them get into the story itself.

Layering serves two useful purposes: it helps the medium organize itself, and it helps the reader in deciding how deeply to go into a story. For those reasons, it is important to any medium that the conventions of layering be followed.

With the Web, layering takes on additional significance, particularly in helping to organize the information that can be presented about a story. More than any other medium, the Web can present information in quantity and in a wide variety of forms. Appropriate layers allow readers not only to get into a story but also to wander around inside the story package to draw from the story as much as they would like.

Layering is based on a textual and visual logic that allows the reader to see and understand where the information is headed. The textual logic can follow any of a variety of paths or sequences—most important to least important information, most interesting to less interesting, essence of the story to peripheral information. Visually, the logic is large (and relatively unpopulated with text) to smaller (and more populated with text or other items). (See Figure 4.3).

In a newspaper, layers of the story go from headline (large, unpopulated) to subhead to body copy (small, very populated). On the Web, the layering of information can certainly follow the standard newspaper sequence, but it does not have to. The usually beginning is a headline, just as it is in the newspaper and often written in the same manner (cryptic and abbreviated).

Many news web sites use what is becoming a standard form following the headline—a summary. A summary differs from a lead paragraph (see Chapter 5) in that it seeks to present information about the entire story rather than focusing on just the most important information. Summaries can even be used to "sell" a story to a reader—that is, to indicate that the story has some interesting information. Compare these two:

LEAD PARAGRAPH
Agriculture extension officials said today the local squirrel population has grown so fast during the last five years that they may be running out of food and places to live before long.

SUMMARY
Chances are, more squirrels are running around in your back yard than five years ago. Find out why and why agriculture extension officials are concerned.

Not all web sites follow the headline–summary–story sequence of layering, however. Some provide links in the summary to other parts of the story package as well as the main story itself. Others put links to pictures or sidebars at the beginning of the story itself.

One popular method of layering is to embed links to other parts of the story within the main story itself. Visually, these links are usually the standard HTML form—underlined blue text—but a web site can choose to present its links differently. The visual logic of layering should be the same throughout the web site, however, because readers will come to depend on that consistency to navigate through the site.

Print reporters are rarely concerned with headlines, subheads, or layout. They gather the information, write the story, and turn it in to their editor. Someone else writes headlines and subheads and lays out the page.

Web journalists, however, need to understand the concepts of lateral thinking and layering of information as part of the reporting process. As they gather information,

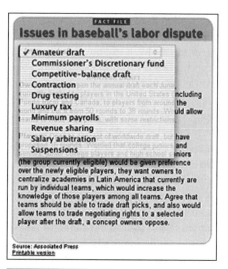

FIGURE 4.3   Layering Information.
This series of screen shots shows how
MSNBC.com presented the issues in the
negotiations between Major League
baseball players and owners during
the 2002 talks that prevented a players'
strike. Ten issues were identified, and
the pull-down menu allowed users to
select what issue they wanted to know
about. A short explanation was provided
for each issue.

they need to think about where that information fits into a story package. They will be
called upon to produce more information in a variety of forms, and they will have increasing control over how that information is presented to readers. They must think
beyond the single-shot story to a broader vista of information to give to their audience. (See Figure 4.4).

WHAT IT TAKES

As web journalism develops, reporters will be called upon to be more skilled in their
reporting and writing techniques and more versatile in their thinking. Coverage of
breaking events will be immediate and continuous, because the audience will expect
to know what the reporter knows when the reporter knows it. Coverage of nonbreak-
ing news will be more thoughtful and complete, because audiences will expect a rich
and varied experience when they visit a news web site.

FIGURE 4.4   Print versus Web Reporting. On the left of this illustration is an inverted-pyramid news story that might appear in the newspaper. On the right is a mock-up of a web page devoted to this story. The web page introduces the reader to a number of forms to tell the story. This introductory page tells the barest facts of the story and then allows the reader to choose what part of the information he or she wants to explore.

The basic requirement for all journalists—facility with the language—will not change, however. It will, in fact, become even more valuable. Reporters will have to use a multiplicity of forms, and they must be confident in using the forms and the language to work with them quickly and efficiently. The next chapter concentrates on how the web journalist can gain those language skills.

COOL IDEAS

More than a Trailer, More than a Preview

Frontline, the Public Broadcasting System (PBS) in-depth news show, aired a documentary on the Al Qaeda terrorist network in November 2002, fourteen months after the September 11 attacks. The show was *Frontline*'s usual job of thorough reporting, but savvy Internet users got something more: Beginning more than two months earlier, they got a running account of how the documentary was produced.

When producers Martin Smith and Marcela Gaviria and cameraman Scott Anger set out for the Persian Gulf, Pakistan, and Afghanistan in August, they sent back reports of where they were, what they were doing, and whom they were talking to. Those dispatches were posted on the PBS web site, and readers could follow their progress, learn of their frustrations, and see with them how the story was taking shape.

Those reports gave the documentary a dimension that it could never have had with traditional broadcasting, and it told readers much about the practice of broadcast journalist.

(To read the dispatches, go to **www.pbs.org/wgbh/pages/frontline/roots/dispatches.**)

DISCUSSION AND ACTIVITIES

1. This chapter says that speed will be a major factor in many stories that web journalists produce. Do you agree? Why?

2. What are the incentives for a person to become a news reporter? What effect will the Web have on those incentives?

3. Practice lateral thinking. Each student should select a different local story from the campus newspaper. What are the elements that could be developed for that story by a well-staffed news web site? Each student should develop his or her own list and then share it with the class. (Listen closely to what other students have to say about their story packages. Could their ideas be applied to your story?)

4. Why should the news web site reporter need to worry about layering?

SELECTED BIBLIOGRAPHY

Clark, Thomas (Ed.). *The Writer's Digest Guide to Good Writing.* Cincinnati, OH: Writer's Digest Books, 1994.

Dube, Jonathan. "Online Storytelling Forms." CyberJournalist.net (no date). www.cyberjournalist.net/storyforms.htm.

Grabowicz, Paul. "Research People on the Internet." *Online Journalism Review,* August 1, 2002 (two-part series). www.ojr.org/ojr/technology/1027538596.php.

Killmer, Kimberly A., and Nicole B. Koppel. "So Much Information, So Little Time: Evaluating Web Resources with Search Engines." *Technological Horizons in Education (T.H.E.) Journal,* August 2002, pp. 21–29. www.thejournal.com/magazine/vault/A4101.cfm.

Overing, Michael S., and Edward C. Wilde. "Research, but Carefully." *Online Journalism Review,* August 8, 2002. www.ojr.org/ojr/law/1028842909.php.

Stovall, James Glen. *Writing for the Mass Media* (5th ed.). Boston: Allyn & Bacon, 2002. www.abacon.com/stovall.

Sullivan, Danny. "How Search Engines Work." SearchEngineWatch.com, June 26, 2001. http://searchenginewatch.com/webmasters/work.html.

WEB SITES

Poynter.org (www.poynter.org), especially Jonathan Dube and Sreenath Sreenivasan, who write "Web Tips from the Pros." This is a continuing item posted on this site that gives excellent tips, particularly on where to find information on the Web.

Cyberjournalist.net (www.cyberjournalist.net/weblogblog.htm)
This site contains an interesting compilation of weblogs devoted to journalism.

MSNBC.com Ombudsman (http://stacks.msnbc.com/news/ombudsman_front.asp)
MSNBC has employed the first online news ombudsman (at this writing it is Dan Fisher), who writes about the leading sites' news coverage.

EPN World Reporter (www.epnworld-reporter.com)
"EPN World Reporter," according to its "About Us" description, "is the online magazine for journalists, editors, and photographers. Covering news and events, from multimedia news reporting, to security training for frontline reporting, to the latest journalism controversy, EPN World Reporter keeps the media abreast of all the latest developments that have an impact on the profession." You are likely to find something useful and interesting there every time you visit.

Consumer WebWatch (www.consumerwebwatch.org)
This site focuses on online credibility. The site says, "Through research, the promotion of guidelines for best practices and other analytical means, we seek to improve the credibility of online information." It is a division of Consumers Union, Consumer Reports' parent company.

■ ■ ■ ■ ■

CHAPTER 5

WRITING
EVERY WORD COUNTS

MAIN THEMES

- Writing is central to the process of journalism, no matter what the medium.
- The characteristics of all good writing, no matter where it appears, include a unifying theme, accuracy, clarity, precision, and efficiency.
- The Web is a word medium and depends on good writing.
- Efficient use of the language makes the most effective writing for the Web.

"In the beginning was the Word" (John 1:1). Without preamble or introduction (like a good journalist), the Fourth Evangelist begins the Gospel of John by declaring the divinity of Jesus. The writer wants the strongest metaphor available. He bypasses wind, fire, mountains, and rivers. He selects the Word.

Words have power beyond measure. They convey ideas and information that can change lives.

It doesn't matter whether words are chiseled on a stone tablet or show up as electronic blips on a computer screen. It doesn't matter that they may be surrounded by pictures or graphics or the hottest Flash presentations. It's the words that really matter.

As playwright Tom Stoppard has said, "Words are sacred. They deserve respect. If you get the right ones, in the right order, you can nudge the world a little."

WRITING FOR THE MEDIA

Those who write for the media take on many responsibilities. Their goal is to present information and ideas to an audience. The purpose of their writing is usually information, and that means they must write with modesty. That is, they must put themselves in the background and mold their writing style to fit the demands of the medium they are using. No matter what the medium, all media writing should attempt to exhibit four characteristics: accuracy, clarity, efficiency, and precision.

Accuracy is the chief requirement of a writer for the mass media. This is not just a journalist's requirement: all writers are expected to present information accurately and to take some pains in doing so. Many of the procedures for writing for the mass media are set up to ensure accuracy.

Clarity means that you should present your information in a context so that it can be easily understood by a mass audience. It should be clear and coherent. Your writing should answer all of the questions that could be expected by the audience (not all of the questions that could be asked, but all those that it takes to understand the information).

Efficiency is one of the most prized writing characteristics. Efficiency means using the fewest words to present your information accurately and clearly. Efficiency is difficult to achieve because most of us write inefficiently, especially on first draft. Most of us do not do a good job editing our writing. The world is filled with inefficient writing, and we often fall victim to it.

Precision means that, as a writer, you take special care with the language. You know good grammar and practice it. You use words for precisely what they mean. You develop a love for the language.

All of these characteristics are audience-driven. That is, they are valued in journalistic writing because they serve the audience, giving news consumers information they want in the way that they have come to expect.

Writing for the Web requires that the writer master the conventions and forms of news writing. Web journalism at this stage of its development is a descendent of print, and the most common form for print journalism is the news story. This chapter will review the techniques and structures of journalistic writing before discussing the forms of writing that are emerging with the Web.

STRUCTURES FROM PRINT

Journalism has developed a number of standard writing structures for both print and broadcasting that use the characteristics discussed in the previous section. These structures were built to serve various purposes, and they have proved remarkably resilient.

Three of these structures, the inverted pyramid, the headline, and the cutline, have proved especially important as the Web develops into a full-fledged news medium.

Inverted Pyramid

The inverted pyramid (see Figure 5.1) is the standard news story structure that is used throughout print journalism. This structure concentrates the most interesting and important information at the top of the story so that readers can get the information they need or want and then go on to another story if they choose. This characteristic makes it an ideal structure for use on the Web.

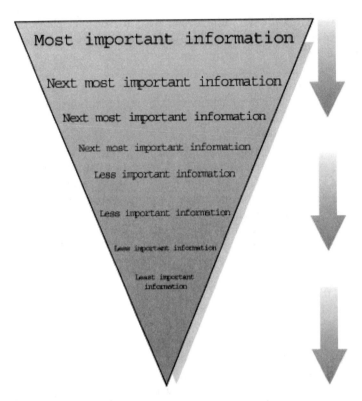

FIGURE 5.1   The Inverted Pyramid. The most common writing structure for news stories in print is the inverted pyramid, which requires that the most important information come first and that information be presented in descending order of importance. This structure works very well for the Web because it gets information to the reader quickly.

The lead (pronounced LEED), or first paragraph, is the focal point of the inverted-pyramid story. A standard lead gives the reader the most important information about an event or issue and answers the who, what, when, and where questions about the story. In most news stories a lead paragraph is one sentence and has a maximum of thirty to thirty-five words. The lead is not a summary of the story. (Summaries will be discussed later in this chapter.) Rather, the writer has to choose the most important or the latest information available to put into a lead.

The second paragraph of the inverted-pyramid structure is almost as important as the lead. The second paragraph develops information that is found in the lead. A good second paragraph will put the readers into a story and will give them incentive to read on.

Somewhere in the top three or four paragraphs should be what some call the "nut" graph. This paragraph contains contextual information about the story and tells the reader why the story is important and why the reader should be reading it.

The inverted pyramid also organizes the information in such a way that the reader can be efficient. Not every reader will read all of every story on a web site. The inverted pyramid allows readers to get enough of a story to know whether they want to continue reading or go to another story.

Another reason the inverted pyramid is ideal for the Web is that it is a nonchronological structure. That is, it presents the most important or most interesting information first, no matter where it might have happened in the story's sequence of events.

The inverted-pyramid structure demands that the writer make judgments about the importance of the information that he or she has gathered—judgments based on the news values discussed in the previous chapter.

Headline

Another standard journalistic writing form that has been adapted by the Web is the headline. (See also the discussion of headlines in Chapter 6.) Most of us are familiar with headlines as they appear in newspapers, magazines, and newsletters. They are cryptic summaries of information that indicate the content of a longer piece of prose. The form that a headline usually takes is that of a complete sentence with a subject and a verb:

President threatens veto of new tax bill

Sometimes a verb or part of a verb form is understood but not stated explicitly:

Midville man charged with larceny

Smith on team's final roster

(In each of these headlines, the verb "is" is missing.)

Notice a couple of things about these examples and the ones you see in the illustrations. First, the headlines are written with present-tense verbs. Second, articles (*a, an, the*) are missing. The third characteristic is specificity; even though just a few words are used, the headline contains specific meaningful information.

Though brief, headlines are not easy to write. They first require that the writer understand thoroughly the article that the headline is for, which requires reading the article carefully, of course. Headlines should not mimic the beginning or lead paragraph of the article, so if the writer wants to use the idea in the lead for the headline, he or she needs to find different words to express it. Many journalists consider the headline to be a sales pitch for a story. The headline should be interesting enough to engage a reader and help him or her decide to read a story. For that, the headline needs specific information and concrete wording. Vague or abstract words do not help build interest.

Most web sites develop a style and set of requirements for headlines. The *New York Times* news site (nytimes.com) requires its headline writers to meet the same standards that print headlines meet; other newspaper sites may not be as restrictive and demanding.

Cutlines

Just as they do in print, pictures need words to help readers understand them. Cutlines are the explanatory and descriptive copy that accompanies pictures. They range widely in style and length, from the one-line identifier called the "skel line" to the full "story" line. Cutlines are necessary for practically all pictures because of the functions they serve: identification, description, explanation, and elaboration.

A well-written cutline answers all of a reader's questions about a picture. What is the action in the picture? What is its relationship to the story it accompanies? Who are the people in it? Where are the events taking place, and when? What does the picture mean? The cutline should answer these and other questions in such a manner that material found in any accompanying story is not repeated verbatim but is reinforced, amplified, or highlighted.

The following are some general guidelines for writing cutlines.

- Use the present tense to describe what is in the picture.
- Always double-check identifications in a cutline. This rule cannot be stressed too much. Many newspapers have gotten themselves into deep trouble by misidentifying people in a cutline, so cutline writers should take great care.
- Be as specific as possible in cutlines. Add to the reader's knowledge, and go beyond what the reader can see in the picture. A cutline is useless if it simply tells the reader what can be seen already.
- Try to avoid cutline clichés. "Looking on," "is pictured" and other such expressions are trite and usually avoidable.

Cutlines have long been a neglected part of a newspaper's editorial process, but on the Web they will take on increasing importance because of the ability of the Web to display more pictures. Many web sites have a picture gallery as a standard part of the site, and whoever is assigned to writing cutlines for the gallery needs to be adept at informing readers about the individual pictures and tying them together with a coherent chunks of prose.

WEB WRITING STRUCTURES

While the Web has used a number of print writing structures, it has also given rise to some writing forms of its own. These forms have been developed because of two interrelated Web characteristics: hypertext and layering.

Although the name is relatively new, hypertext is a concept that was active many years before the Internet. It is a system that allows a user to find a specific bit of information within a large amount of data. Libraries, faced with this problem, developed card catalogs (now pretty much a thing of the past). A person could walk into a library, go to its card catalog, and find the location of a book, magazine, recording, or whatever else the library contained. That person did not start at the beginning of the catalog and thumb through each card. Rather, the user knew that cards would be alphabetized by author, title, and subject, and he or she would go to the point in the catalog where the desired item would most likely be.

On the Web, hypertext allows users to jump from the beginning of the presentation of information to where he or she wants to be. It does this through linking, a function of hypertext markup language (HTML), which is how most web pages are built. Linking lets the user click on a word or an image, and the computer will show a different piece of information. Hypertext gives rise to the reality of nonlinearity (a concept discussed in Chapter 3). A user does not have to start at the beginning and go to the end. Instead, the user can choose what information he or she will see next.

But an important—and often overlooked—point should be noted. Hypertext itself does not give the users choices. Rather, it gives the journalist the ability to set up choices for the user. Consequently, it is incumbent upon the journalist to consider what choices the reader might want and to narrow those choices so that the reader will find them manageable.

The management of information and the choices given to the reader lead to the second major consideration of web writers (and editors): layering (discussed in Chapters 4 and 6). Layering means that information is given to the reader in small doses to begin with and then in larger doses as the reader goes more deeply into a story.

The concept of hypertext and the practice of layering mean that writers will have to use new forms of writing and new organizational schemes to present their information to the reader. Writers will need to organize their information into small portions, or "chunks." These writing chunks may use only a single word or sentence or paragraph, but they must be written so that they are both independent and part of a larger entity. They will have to be packed with information and yet skillfully efficient. More than ever, they will demand that the writer be a master at using the language.

SUMMARIES

The most important new form of writing used to present information on the Web is the summary. A summary is a one-, two-, or three-sentence paragraph that tells what an article or story package is about (see Figure 5.2). Summaries are not new, of course. They have been around in various forms for some time. (In academic writing, they are called abstracts.)

The chief job of the summary is to relate in more detail than a headline what an article is about. The information in a summary cannot be detailed, but it should be specific enough to be informative and interesting. Above all, it should be accurate. A summary that says one thing and an article that says something different is

Engineering students design devices to help handicapped children

Deidre Stalnaker, staff reporter

November 15th, 2002

Mechanical engineering seniors used analysis methods developed during previous engineering courses to design machines to help children with spina bifida get in and out of their wheelchairs and bathtubs. These students gave demonstrations of the devices during a trade show on Wednesday. ...FULL STORY...

M & M's: Melvin to manage Mariners

 The Seattle Mariners will name Arizona Diamondbacks bench coach Bob Melvin as the club's next skipper on Friday at an 11 a.m. PT press conference. Melvin, 41, was the youngest of four finalists for the job and the only one without managerial experience. More >

Tide stages late rally to win Independence Bowl, 14-13

Alabama combined a couple of big plays with a little end-of-game luck to defeat the Iowa State Cyclones 14-13 in the Independence Bowl in Shreveport, La., on Thursday. Does this mean the football program is cured?

Rick Randell, sports editor

Murray's South to a Very Old Place, still provocative after 30 years

Race issues are still very alive in the south, and the book "South to a Very Old Place," written by Albert Murray, the 2001 winner of the Clarence Cason Award for Nonfiction Writing, addresses his experience with these issues. The book is provocative and sometimes confrontational, but once you start, it's hard to put it down.

Pike Stringfellow, book review editor

FIGURE 5.2   Summaries. The summary has become a standard writing form on the Web. A news web site must decide what its summaries should do (summarize, add information, or sell a story) and how much of the writer's personality should be injected into the writing.

a devastating blow to the professionalism of a web site. Writing a good summary means that the writer has read and understands the article. Here are some examples:

HEADLINE
Retirement fund worries continue to plague local workers

SUMMARY
Word that the Fairwether Tire Company Employees Retirement Fund has taken another hit from bad investments has workers in other industries in town wondering about their future. Employees at Beaver Supply, Wally's Wonderworks, and Haskell Industries have asked for meetings with company officials to discuss the status of their retirement plans.

HEADLINE
State wins first game of the season, 14–12

SUMMARY
It took State's quarterback Ronnie Ridell just eight minutes in the first quarter to post two touchdowns against Minnesota Tech in the season opener on Saturday. It took State's defense the next three quarters to maintain that lead and hold off a determined Tech rushing game to secure the victory.

HEADLINE
String of thefts costs University big bucks

SUMMARY
In the past five months, many pieces of electronic equipment have been taken from five campus buildings. The crimes have cost the university over $25,843 to date, and there is no guarantee that this is the end.

Some news organizations attempt to use the lead paragraph of the article as the summary. This practice is easier than writing something new, but it misses a golden opportunity to take advantage of the layering characteristic of the Web and is ultimately unsatisfying for the reader. Lead paragraphs are written to go with the full article, not to stand by themselves on the front page of a web site. In addition, a reader may feel that his or her time has been wasted if the lead paragraph turns out to be the same as the summary. There will be no new information there.

Not only can the summary tell what the article is about, it can also attempt to sell the visitor on reading an article. While giving the reader some information, it attempts to raise a question about the article that the reader will want to have answered. Consider these headlines and summaries:

HEADLINE
University board votes to raise tuition for third straight year

SUMMARY
The bad news is the Board of Trustees raised tuition. The good news is the increase wasn't as much as some had predicted. No matter what, it's going to cost everyone more to attend the University next year.

HEADLINE
Dead Red, latest downtown bar, opens its doors

SUMMARY
Many inside city hall resisted giving a license to an establishment that billed itself as the "baddest bar in town." Why is it so bad? Why did the city give in?

HEADLINE
Basketball team wins third straight, beating Tech 56–52

SUMMARY
The coach called it an "ugly win." There were too many penalties and too many turnovers. Our guys tripped over their own feet. Still, there was one bright spot.

These summaries deliberately, and sometimes blatantly, withhold but point to information contained in the story. They are written to spur readers to follow the links into a story and read what's there. They try to get the readers to find out more information.

What may be noticeable about all of the examples above is that they differ in tone and content from the straightforward newswriting prose that we discussed earlier. Summaries can use literary techniques (repetition, alliteration, puns, proverbial sayings, etc.) to catch the attention of the reader and inform as well as entertain. A summary can even step far enough away from the impersonality of newswriting to show some attitude about the subject of the article and the information it contains. If the editors of a news web site allow it, a summary can be a mini-editorial on the topic.

However, the main purpose of the summary in this realm is to inform. Accuracy, efficiency in using the language, and clarity are the essential characteristics of a good summary.

Still, summaries offer a marvelous chance for a reporter, copyeditor, or editor to be creative and to have some fun with the language and with the information that he or she is presenting.

A different kind of summary can be used to introduce a link to another part of a story package or to a different web site altogether. Writers and editors have not paid much attention to these kinds of summaries, but as the Web develops they will become more important. A link summary gives some information about what the reader will get if he or she clicks on the link. (Often, of course, links are simply self-explanatory labels, and readers do not need that extra information.)

Many link summaries are simply perfunctory:

For more information, click **here.**

Go to the organization's **web site.**

Neither of these summaries is very useful in helping the reader decide to follow the link. The web site would better serve its readers if it gave them some information about what they would find if they followed the link. For instance:

News and information about a variety of journalism issues can be found at the Poynter Institute **web site.**

A description of many of the **hiking trails** of the Great Smoky Mountains National Park is offered by DatelineSmokyMountains.com.

Note that in neither of these examples do you find the "go to" or "click here" clichés that accompany many links. Instead, you see real information—not much, but enough to let you know what is at these sites.

OTHER WEB FORMS: LABELS AND SUBHEADS

Just as summaries have been around for a while, so too have labels and subheads. Still, they constitute an important part of web writing, and they take some skill to produce.

Labels

Labels are the one- or two-word monikers that summarize a large body of content and indicate the overall organization of the web site. Because of their brevity, they do not contain much specific information. Rather, they are general guidelines that tell the reader where he or she is or is going in the site.

Labels must be accurate and as specific as possible. Writers have to understand the widely accepted meanings and implications of words, not just their strict dictionary definitions. They should understand that in some contexts, words that may seem the same carry different connotations. One example of such a pair of words is "story" and "article." Within the confines of some parts of journalism, a "story" is likely to refer to something in a newspaper while an "article" is a magazine piece. In the U.S. Navy, a "ship" refers to a surface vehicle, whereas a "boat" refers to a submarine.

Applying the correct labels to web site content and categories is an important task and sometimes more difficult than it first appears.

Subheads

A subhead is a line of type within the body copy of an article that informs the reader what is coming up next within the copy. Subheads also break up the copy, introducing white space and making articles easier to read.

Subheads are best used at natural breaks in the article rather than being arbitrarily inserted every few paragraphs. They should help the reader through the article rather than interrupting the flow of the prose.

Like all forms of concision, subheads can be difficult to write. They require that the editor read the copy closely enough to capture the essence or the most important idea of the paragraphs to which the subhead refers. Then the editor must state that idea in just a few words—usually no more than three or four.

WRITING FOR VISUAL EFFECT

One of the great demands that the Web makes on writing is efficiency. To write efficiently, to use the fewest words to present the most information, is not the type of writing that most students have been taught in English grammar and literature classes. To write less and say more is a difficult skill to develop.

Writing efficiently is time-consuming because it involves editing and rewriting. Most of us use too many words when we put together our first drafts, and those drafts need to be edited and rewritten.

The words themselves, however, are not enough. A writer has yet another consideration. That is how the words look.

In print this was rarely a consideration for the writer. Designers and editors took care of how the publication looked. On the Web, writers are much closer to the production and distribution of their work. Within the style limits of the web site, they can exercise more control over the appearance of their words, phrases, and paragraphs than ever before (see Figure 5.3).

Why should they? To help the reader. As we have mentioned throughout this book, among the major characteristics of the Web are immediacy and speed. Readers want information quickly, and some evidence suggests that, rather than doing much reading, they tend to scan. Web writing guru Jakob Neilson agrees with that notion, writing:

> Because it is so painful to read text on computer screens and because the online experience seems to foster some amount of impatience, users tend not to read streams of text in full. Instead, users scan text and pick out keywords, sentences, and paragraphs of interest while skipping over those parts of the text they care less about.
>
> Skimming instead of reading is a fact of the web and has been confirmed by countless usability studies. Web writers have to acknowledge this fact and write for scannability. (Neilson, 1997)

Writing for scannability means using visual cues to help readers see the text and figure out what is important to them. Writers can do this by using the following techniques.

Paragraph Spacing

One of the standard design techniques of the Web is a line of white space between paragraphs. This technique helps divide text into manageable chunks for the reader. The downside of this technique is that it increases the necessity for scrolling on the part of the reader. Most web site editors believe that paragraph spacing is worth doing, however, not only for the sake of the reader but also because it produces a clean-looking page.

Short Paragraphs

As we mentioned earlier, writing short paragraphs is probably not something you learned to do in literature class, but using short paragraphs (when it is appropriate) is essential

Paragraph spacing

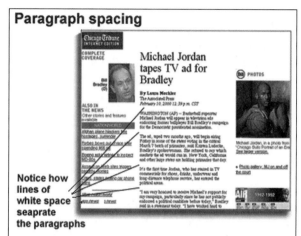

Notice how lines of white space seaprate the paragraphs

FIGURE 5.3   Visual Styles. Writing for the Web requires thinking about how copy will look, not just what it says. A number of techniques have been developed to help readers scan their way through the copy and find the information they want. Writers need to think about what key words may be made into links, where numbered and bulleted lists can be inserted, and when indentations of copy may be appropriate.

Horizontal lines, colored text

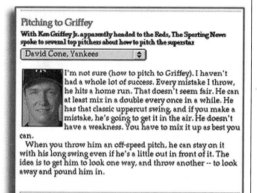

This portion of an MSNBC page uses horizontal lines to set off this text from the rest of the article. Colored text is used to highlight words.

Bulleted text, boldfaced words

The designer of this page helps the reader through it by breaking up the text and highlighting certain words with boldface type.

on the Web. Short paragraphs visibly entice the reader to read. If they have a line of white space above and below them, they can be especially easy for the reader to digest.

Short paragraphs make for easier reading, but they demand disciplined thinking on the part of the writer. Information must be broken into bits that the writer can put together in small portions but also in a manner that is logical and effective.

With this type of writing, transitions are particularly important. The writing must tie the information together tightly, so readers can easily follow it. A new paragraph should be introduced in a way that follows from the previous paragraph; new paragraphs should not surprise or confuse the reader.

Keywords

Keywords are words within text that are most likely to tell the reader what the text is about. They are usually nouns or verbs specific enough to indicate the information being presented. Designers highlight keywords by using boldface or colored type.

> The **Mercedes Widget Company** manufactures a complete line of **widgets** that will meet every widget need.

A reader could glance at this sentence and, without reading it, understand that it is about widgets.

On many web sites, keywords represent links that visitors can use to jump to additional information about that subject. Used in a limited way, keyword links can indicate to the visitor that the site has depth; overused, they can give the reader too many options and become distracting or confusing. Too many boldfaced keywords will leave the reader wondering what is really important about the text. With only one or two, there is much less confusion. For instance, look at the first paragraph of Lincoln's Gettysburg Address:

> Four score and seven years ago, our **fathers** brought forth on this **continent** a new **nation**, conceived in **liberty** and dedicated to the **proposition** that all men are created **equal.**

What is important here? By boldfacing many of the important words in this sentence, the writer has not aided the reader much. Now look at the same sentence again:

> Four score and seven years ago, our fathers brought forth on this continent a new nation, conceived in **liberty** and dedicated to the proposition that all men are created **equal.**

Here the writer has zeroed in on the two ideas about the sentence that he or she believes to be the most important ones—the ones the writer wants the reader to pay attention to.

Colored Text

Most news web sites use black text on a white background, just as black text appears on white pages in print. Print editors do not have the option of easily coloring text, as web editors do, and some web editors try to take advantage of this ability. On most sites, links appear in blue text, and that introduces something different for the reader and is a clear visual cue to the content of the text. Editors need to exercise caution in venturing beyond that, however. Too many different colors or too much of one color can be difficult for the reader and can distract from the content. The key is to help the reader, not just introduce color to the web page.

Indentations

Material that can be set off from the main text, such as a block quotation, can be indented to provide another visual cue for the readers. The indention must be logical, however. That is, it should be readily apparent to the reader why the material is set off and that it actually fits together.

Lists

One of the easiest things to see in text is a list. Readers seem drawn to lists, even when they are not particularly interested in the content of the list itself. Writers for the Web should consider three types of lists for their writing: the numbered list, the unnumbered list, and the bulleted list.

As the name implies, the numbered list is one in which numbers label each of the items on the list. The numbers imply that there is an order to the list, but if the order is indicated in other ways (such as alphabetizing), numbers should not be used.

The unnumbered list does not use numbers and may have no particular order implied by the items in the list. Sometimes an unnumbered list will have the first letters or words in boldface type to help readers discern one item from another.

The bulleted list is one step beyond indention. Bulleted lists are indented and use black dots in front of individual items on the list. A bulleted list may or may not have a particular order to the items in the list.

All of the structures mentioned above will help writers conform to some of the demands of writing for the Web. These forms also help writers deal with large blocks of prose that can be daunting, particularly if they appear in small type on a screen. They aid readers in scanning information and in deciding what information is relevant to their needs. They should be used only when appropriate, however, because the form should support content, not control it.

NEW FORMS OF WRITING

Web journalists, as we have seen, will have to go beyond the standard forms of writing for print media. The ability to write concisely and quickly will continue to be a criterion of success. However, writers will also have to master other forms of writing to be able to survive in the web environment. The following are some of the forms that are being developed.

■ ■ ■ ■ ■

Email and Personal Messaging

The Web has fostered one of the most important submedia of mass communication: email. Its importance is increasing as people discover its speed and efficiency and as technical advances continue to open up more possibilities for its use. Email, once viewed as a personal convenience, has become a tool of mass communication.

As such, professional writers are finding that the informal, grammarless style with which they began using email needs to be set aside for a more formal, disciplined approach to the writing. As with any writing, emails should be clear in their context and their structure. Writers of email messages should consider the reader: What does the reader need to know about the message to respond appropriately to it? Cryptic, nongrammatical messages without context may be fine for communicating between friends or even in chatroom settings, but they simply won't do in a professional environment.

Email newsletters are an increasingly popular form of keeping those with a common interest informed. Many news web sites have established email headline services that tell readers about new and interesting features on the site. Usually, these take the form of headlines and intros or summaries, along with links that allow receivers to go directly to articles and pages being referred to. Other email newsletters, such as A Word A Day (www.wordsmith.org), present a single new item each day and are short enough to be read easily and quickly.

Personal messaging is another popular form of communication, although it is not considered to be a mass medium. Still, personal messaging is useful to the journalist because it represents a way of communicating, particularly with sources of information. Some journalists have begun conducting interviews by personal messaging because it is faster, easier, and cheaper than trying to establish telephone contact.

FAQs

FAQs are pages of "frequently asked questions" that seek to give readers specific information about a topic. The form was originated by utilitarian web sites, those that had users engaging in some specific activity such as buying a product or downloading some software. The questions were based on what authors anticipated would be the most likely questions about the activity or on what questions had been most asked by users.

The form has been adapted by some news web sites as another layer of information to give to the reader about a topic on which there is a news story. An article about an upcoming April 15 tax deadline, for instance, might have an FAQ about the Internal Revenue Service. This is a way of getting information about the IRS to the reader without having to integrate it into the article or other parts of the story package.

WEBLOGS

A weblog is a compendium of short entries on a web site devoted to a particular subject. (See the section on weblogs in Chapter 2.) Often that topic is the originator of the weblog, and as such the log becomes a personal but public journal. Some weblogs have been established to allow experts or people interested in a certain topic to share ideas and information.

Weblogs are relatively easy and cheap to start (software to create and manage a weblog is freely available.). Since they first appeared around 1997, thousands of people have established weblogs, and some are drawing exceptionally large audiences. (Weblogs are discussed more in Chapters 2 and 6.)

The common term for writing for a weblog is "blog" or "blogging" (combining the last letter of "web" with the word "log"), and people who contribute to or read weblogs are called "bloggers."

The entries themselves are short, usually no more than three hundred words or so. The entries describe a topic or issue, or they may pick up on a previous discussion. They often contain commentary or opinion from the person who writes them, and they may include one or more links to web sites where readers can find more information. In a group weblog, anyone in the group can contribute to the log or can comment on the contributions of others. Several discussions can take place at the same time. Following are some examples of weblog entries.

MARC WEISBLOTT: THE WEISBLOGG

ROCKIN' TO THE STONES? YEAH, IN CHAIRS: A marvelous summary from Neal Pollack in the New York Times of what the Rolling Stones "mean" to those of us who were born sometime after Brian Jones drowned. (For the record, the only Stones album I ever bought for more than fifty cents was Exile on Main Street, somewhere around 1987, after being seduced by seeing the reissued double album package front-racked in a record store . . . oh yeah, I shelled out for a cassette of Mick Jagger's first solo album, too.) Also, on behalf of the blogsphere, let me extend a warm welcome to Mr. Pollack, who seems to be in recovery from the precious writing style of the McSweeney's clique from which he hails. Pollack's first few entries are evident here.

Comments?
http://weisblott.com/

GLENN REYNOLDS: INSTAPUNDIT

THE JURIST reports a poll indicating that support for press freedom is diminishing as compared to a year ago.

I wonder if perceived anti-American bias in matters of the war and national security plays a role. Hmm. Looking at the actual poll results, I think the answer would have to be "yes."

posted at 08:57 PM by Glenn Reynolds
http://www.instapundit.com

J. D. LASICA: JD'S BLOG: NEW MEDIA MUSINGS

Remembering Robert Kennedy

Just watched RFK, which aired Sunday night on FX (what can I say, I'm a TiVo kinda guy). We live in a time of cynicism about our leaders, and for the most part, that's justified. RFK was a different kind of leader, and his rhetoric soared like nothing we have heard in the past 40 years. It's hard to imagine but, for all his flaws, it has been two generations since we've seen the likes of a Robert F. Kennedy.

Sometime we'll tell our son that we named him, in part, after RFK.

http://jd.manilasites.com/

DAN GILLMOR: DAN GILLMOR'S E-JOURNAL

Pitches by 802.11 wireless providers:

SkyPilot is putting together a "mesh" system providing very fast wireless connections. The idea is peer-to-peer rooftop antennas connecting to each other, says Duncan Davidson, the CEO and co-founder.

This might be an alternative to DSL or cable. But it's not the answer to true broadband, which is a lot faster and more useful.

I've been corrected. Davidson, who was reading this posting from the stage, says the technology scales far above these piddly speeds. Good news.

Oh, sheesh. The semi-lame Boingo video I saw last week in Orlando is now on the screen. Too many conferences . . .

Sputnik is not Boingo, and not Joltage. But it's another viral wireless platform.

The idea is to put up lots and lots of access points all over the place, getting folks with computers to add their own locations to the network.

David LaDuke, the CEO, is pitching this as an enterprise play. I'm just as interested in seeing it spread as a way of getting more access points out there for regular folks.

LaDuke says it's protocol agnostic. (So is Joltage.) The gateway is supposed to configure itself. It just showed up in my Airport list of wireless networks. I guess it worked.

He's calling this a "smart edge platform." One application is a cache, meaning that content moves out to the edge of the network. (Mike Homer and Ian Clarke, are you aware of this?)

LaDuke just said he hoped it wouldn't offend anyone, but the product is open source. "Anyone" is Craig Mundie from Microsoft, who's in the front row, who wondered if the license is GPL. It is.

There's a proprietary piece—a corporate gateway that will have security and reliability features including, LaDuke says, the ability to detect a war driver. Needed, and welcome.

These mesh networks are increasingly exciting to contemplate.

http://www.siliconvalley.com/mld/siliconvalley/business/columnists/dan_gillmor/ejournal/2938269.htm

As in the examples above, many weblogs are written in a highly personal style and mix information and opinion together freely. Most weblogs that draw large audiences take great care with their use of the language, and they value opinions and discussions over personal attacks and offensive rantings.

Weblogs are growing in use and popularity. They take a step away from the traditional news organizations by allowing an interested group of users to create, contribute to, and participate in what is basically a specialized publication. The weblog is dynamic and organic. Sometimes, contributions never generate any discussion; at other times, discussions can continue for months. Many see them as a new form of journalism that, while it won't replace news web sites, could become a vital part of the mix of news and information available to Web readers.

IT'S STILL ABOUT JOURNALISM

As the Web grows, with more information and wider audiences, clear, concise, and readable writing will become more important. People who can gather together information, synthesize it, and put it into digestible prose will have great value to the growing Web audience.

DISCUSSION AND ACTIVITIES

1. Is the Web so free and open that style rules have no value? The author of this book does not seem to think so. What do you think?

2. Will the weblog phenomenon become an important part of journalism? List the reasons for your answer.

3. Take a long piece of writing from a newspaper (at least twenty column inches) and write a fifty-word summary that simply states what is in the article. Everyone in the class

should do the same article. Compare the summaries and the approaches that each member of the class took. Then discuss among the class members the difficulty of writing such a summary.

4. Take the same article you used in Activity 3 and write a summary that tries to sell the article to the reader. Again, compare the approaches.

5. Take the same article you used in Activity 3 and write an eight-word headline. How difficult was that?

SELECTED BIBLIOGRAPHY

Dougherty, Dale. "Don't Forget to Write." Webreview.com (no date). www.webreview.com.

Gahran, Amy. "Cut the Fluff." Contentious.com, April 6, 1998. www.contentious.com/articles/1-1/cip1-1/cip1-1.html.

Morkes, John, and Jakob Neilson. "Applying Writing Guidelines to Web Pages." Useit.com, January 6, 1998. www.useit.com/papers/webwriting/rewriting.html.

Neilson, Jakob. "Inverted Pyramids in Cyberspace." Useit.com, June 1996. www.useit.com/alertbox/9606.html.

Neilson, Jakob. "Be Succinct! (Writing for the Web)." Useit.com, March 15, 1997. www.useit.com/alertbox/9703b.html.

Neilson, Jakob. "How Users Read on the Web." Useit.com, October 1, 1997. www.useit.com/alertbox/9710a.html.

Neilson, Jakob. "Microcontent: How to Write Headlines, Page Titles and Subject Lines." Useit.com, September 6, 1998. www.useit.com/alertbox/980906.html.

Scanlan, Chip. "Writing Online Rocks." Poynter.org., February 28, 2000. www.poynter.org/centerpiece/022800-index.htm.

Scanlan, Christopher. "As We May Write: The Web and the Future of Writing." Poynter Reports. http://legacy.poynter.org/centerpiece/CAN=ChipBook.htm.

Stovall, James Glen. *Writing for the Mass Media* (5th ed.). Boston: Allyn & Bacon, 2002. www.abacon.com/stovall.

Walker, Leslie. "A Day-by-Day in the Life." *The Washington Post,* May 17, 2001, p. E-1. www.washingtonpost.com.

Wendland, Mike. "Bob Greene: E-mail Changes Everything." Poynter.org, February 8, 2000. www.poynter.org/centerpiece/020800-index.htm.

WEB SITES

Many of the web sites referred to at the ends of earlier chapters are also useful to those interested in learning more about writing for the web, particularly Cyberjournalist.net (www.cyberjournalist.net) and Jakob Neilson's UseIt.com (www.useit.com).

Contentious.com (www.contentious.com)

This is a web site for web writers and editors, not just journalists. In its own words, Contentious wants to reach "people (who) view online media not simply as a new way to practice their skills, but as a way to make a living. Also, they primarily are concerned with what online venues have to say, and how well they say it. The design, coding, and technologies used to present information online are, for these readers, of secondary importance (although often these topics are closely related to content)." The site has useful and up-to-date material for the web writer.

■ ■ ■ ■ ■

CHAPTER 6

EDITING

MAJOR THEMES

■ Editing is at the heart of the journalistic process, no matter what the medium.

■ Web editors must know the language first; they must understand words and their power.

■ A complete and diverse set of skills, including some technical skills, must be at the editor's disposal if he or she is to be successful in managing a news web site.

■ The web editor will face special problems as the medium continues to develop.

Editing constitutes the vital center of the journalistic process. Despite its romanticized image of the single reporter challenging massive institutional forces, journalism is not a solitary activity. It is a social profession that requires the hands and minds of many people. The process begins with reporting, but if journalism is to complete its mission of gathering, processing, and disseminating the new, the most important person in the entire process is the editor.

Reporters, photographers, graphics journalists, and others are the foot soldiers of journalism. Editors are the officers. They are in charge. They determine the content of the publication or web site as well as its procedures and direction. They are the ones who are responsible for what the publication is and what it does. They have the authority to organize a staff and to decide what stories will or will not be pursued.

To do their jobs well, editors must possess wide knowledge and a wide range of skills. They must know the language and the media environment in which the language is used. They must be able to manage the people who work in the news organization. They must be able to make immediate, sound, and ethical decisions, often without much time to consider their implications. Above all, they must be willing to take the responsibility for what the news organization produces.

Editors must understand context. They must be sensitive to the nuances of how information fits together. They must have enough memory about recent and ancient events that they can judge the nature, credibility, and legitimacy of the information they present.

Editors must be steeped in the culture of journalism. As a part of their nature, they must understand the importance of accurate information and the generally accepted procedures for assuring accuracy. They must value the faith, trust, and intelligence of their audience. They must know that hard work is the norm—something the profession assumes but also rewards.

And editors must lead. They must have the highest standards and expect others in their environments to meet those standards. Their very attitudes and approaches to the daily routine of editing should tell all those around them that honesty, integrity, hard work, devotion to accuracy, intelligence, and humanity are the norm.

The job of the editor is more than just fixing copy and designing a coherent web site. The editor sets the standard and tone for the kind of journalism that is practiced at a news organization. That is why the job of the editor is so important.

Every place that handles information and puts it into some form for distribution needs an editor, a person who understands the information, the procedure by which it will be processed, and the medium through which it will be disseminated. We may traditionally think of editors as working for newspapers or magazines, but editors—no matter what their job titles—are everywhere. This Information Age cannot do without them.

EDITING FOR THE WEB

Many of the good practices and procedures described and prescribed in this chapter are fundamental journalism, applicable to newspapers and broadcasting. However, the Web is a fundamentally different medium from print or broadcast, and it requires different things of both a writer—as we noted in the previous chapter—and the editor. The special characteristics of the Web—capacity, flexibility, permanence, immediacy, and interactivity—weigh constantly on the web editor.

What gives rise to many of these characteristics is the notion of hypertext. The idea of hypertext is that information can be presented in a nonlinear fashion, and this nonlinearity makes a great difference in what a writer and editor does with the information. A good example of nonlinearity is a large art museum, such as the Metropolitan Museum of Art in New York City. At the Met, there is no beginning and there is no end. When you walk into the Met, you can go right, left, straight ahead, or up the stairway. Most people who enter for the first time get a floor plan brochure, find what they want to see, and head in that direction. They may pick out several areas they want to find before their visit is finished. In doing so, they create their own linearity for their visit; it is not imposed on them.

In traditional media, the structures used for presentation of information are mostly linear, though not entirely. A newspaper is divided into sections, and a reader can start with the sports or classified section if he or she chooses. The news and feature stories themselves are linear. They are designed for readers to start at the beginning and read through to the end. A reader would not start in the middle of the story because it is unclear what is there.

Hypertext means that information is broken into chunks or bits, just as in the museum nineteenth-century American art is in one room and Chinese pottery from the Ming dynasty is in another room. The museum does not assume there is much connection between these two forms of art. Consequently, its floor plan will not place these two rooms together. A museum visitor might feel differently, however, and might want to visit one just after visiting the other. The visitor could do so by walking from one room to another without paying much attention to what is in between.

On the Web, information can be broken into chunks and made available to readers through a logical and visible navigation system. Readers can then make their own connections and create their own linear trail through the information.

The concept of hypertext is more complex than simply being able to move from point to point among pieces of information. Not all information is equal or of equal value to the reader. When we page through a newspaper or magazine, most of us will read most of the headlines but few of the stories. The headlines give us some information, and that is enough for us to decide whether we want to read the story. When we choose to read a story, we may or may not read the story all the way to the end. The lead paragraph may give us all the information we want about that subject.

This idea is called layering information (a concept discussed in previous chapters), and because of the environment of the Web (a computer screen), it is how information is presented. A headline gives some information; a summary gives more. Clicking to the story page produces even more information. At that point, the reader has just additional details in the form of text. There may also be pictures, graphics, audio, video, and links to more information. The reader may have stopped with the headline, deciding this was not a story that interested him or her. Or the reader may have stopped with the summary, believing that it contained all of the information necessary to satisfy him or her. Or the reader may have stopped on the story page, deciding not to spend the time to delve more deeply into the story.

The concept of layering information is an important one for web journalists, particularly for editors. They have to decide how the information is to be divided into chunks and then how the information is to be organized and presented. Editors must develop styles of layering that are consistent, so that readers who visit the site regularly can get used to these styles and learn to depend on them.

Web editors, at this point in the development of the Web, have few guidelines to use in formulating these ideas and styles. They need to depend on research that is done into their audience, but they also have to call on their own logical assessments of information and how it can best be understood by a mass audience.

As the Web is constituted today, readers are finding a mixture of linearity and nonlinearity in news web sites. They begin at the front page as they would in the lobby or rotunda of an art museum. From that point, however, they have many choices about where they might go, and they begin to make decisions. This decision-making process and the interplay between the editor and the reader is a critical factor in how the site will grow. Setting up and managing this process is among the most important jobs of web editors.

UPHOLDING STANDARDS

Editors are the chief arbiters and enforcers of standards of behavior in a news organi-zation. They preserve the journalistic culture that should pervade the organization. Many publications and web sites do this by formulating a written code of ethics. Ed-itors are the ones who interpret the code on a day-to-day basis.

Most of these codes are directed toward one goal: accuracy. Accuracy is the most important consideration of an editor. Accuracy is the central reason for much of what an editor does. In the pursuit of accuracy a word of doubtful spelling is checked, one last fact in the story is looked up, or a source is called again when some part of a story is in question.

A reputation for accuracy is a news organization's most valuable resource. Not only does such a reputation inspire the confidence of readers, but an obvious willingness on the part of editors to strive for accuracy opens up new sources of information and often helps the organization avoid embarrassing and dangerous legal entanglements. This rep-utation for accuracy may be the surest way to ensure the survival of the publication.

Such a reputation is particularly important for a web site. Because it is a new medium, many professionals and nonprofessionals do not believe that it has the same culture or standards as a traditional newspaper or broadcast station. They see the web organization as populated by computer geeks who know nothing and care little for the customs of journalism, particularly the hard work that it takes to achieve accuracy. And when a web site makes a mistake (as all news organizations, traditional or new media, do), their beliefs are confirmed.

This is where a strong editor has to step in. An editor has to permeate the orga-nization with one concept: there is no substitute for accuracy. Readers are notoriously unwilling to accept the very reasonable excuses that a reporter was inexperienced, the publication is understaffed, or the paper was having a busy news day. Few readers have any concept of how difficult it is to do good reporting or editing. What they un-derstand is that a headline did not accurately reflect the content of a story, that the cap-ital city of their home state was misspelled, or that their child was misidentified in the cutline of a picture that included several other children. Readers will not easily for-give such mistakes, nor will they forget them. Just a few errors are enough to get a news organization in trouble, damage its credibility, and demonstrate to readers that it is unworthy of their attention. Like weeds in a garden, a bad reputation needs no cul-tivation: all it needs is a start.

For an editor, the pursuit of accuracy is a state of mind. An editor must be will-ing to check everything in doubt and must be willing to doubt anything. An editor must cast a cold eye on the work of the reporters, even those with the most experience and best reputations; the editor must demand an accounting from them as much as from novices. The editor must even be willing to doubt his or her own knowledge and experience and must occasionally recheck what he or she knows to be true. Such ed-itors may make life hard on themselves and those around them, but their efforts will pay dividends for the good reputation of the publication.

All of these difficulties are compounded by the immediacy of the Web and the speed at which information can be posted. When a web site covers a big story—

■ ■ ■ ■ ■ ▬▬▬▬▬▬▬▬▬▬▬▬▬▬▬▬▬▬▬▬

SIDEBAR

JOURNALISTIC STYLE: RULES OF THE ROAD
ON THE INFORMATION SUPERHIGHWAY

Journalistic style may be divided into two types of style: professional conventions and rules of usage. Professional conventions have evolved during years of journalistic endeavor and are now taught through professional training in universities and on the job. The rules of usage have been collected into stylebooks published by wire services, news syndicates, universities, and individual print and broadcast news operations. Some of these stylebooks have widespread acceptance and influence. Others have remained relatively local and result in unique style rules accepted by reporters and editors working for individual publications.

For example, a publication may follow the Associated Press Stylebook and say that AM and PM should be lowercase with periods: a.m. and p.m. The writer will know that a reference to the President of the United States is always simply "president," lower-cased, except when referring to a specific person, such as President Lincoln.

Likewise, the reader will not be confused by multiple references to the same item. Unconsciously, the reader will anticipate the style that the publication uses. Consequently, if the reader follows a college newspaper regularly and that paper always refers to its own institution as the "University," upper-cased, the reader will know what that means.

Similarly, a reporter may follow the usual convention in newspaper writing and write the sequence of time, date, and place of a meeting despite the fact that it may seem more logical to report the date before reporting the time.

Having a logical, consistent style is like fine-tuning a television. Before the tuning, the colors may be there and the picture may be reasonably visible. Eventually, however, the off-colors and the blurry images will play on the viewer's mind so that he or she will become dissatisfied and disinterested. That could cause the viewer to stop watching altogether. In the same way, consistent style fine-tunes a publication so that reading is easier and offers the reader fewer distractions.

Beyond that, the question may still remain: does style really matter? The answer is an emphatic "Yes!" Many young writers think of consistent style as a repressive force hampering their creativity. It isn't. Style is not a rigid set of rules established to restrict the creative forces in the writer. Style imposes a discipline in writing that should run through all the activities of a journalist. It implies that the journalist is precise not only with writing but also with facts and with thought. Consistent style is the hallmark of a professional.

Editors are the governors of the style of a publication. It is their job to see that style rules are consistently and reasonably applied. If exceptions are allowed, they should be for specific and logical reasons and should not be at the whim of the writer. Editors should remember that consistent style is one way of telling readers that every effort has been made to certify the accuracy of everything in the publication.

▬▬▬▬▬▬▬▬▬▬▬▬▬▬▬▬▬▬▬▬▬▬▬▬

particularly a breaking news story—there is little time for the diligent fact checking that most editors would prefer. An editor does not want the site to have a reputation for being slow, especially if the site is competing with other sites to post the news first. It is at these times that the attitude toward accuracy that an editor has established will make a real difference to the organization. Editors must depend on their reporters and subeditors in these situations to understand the importance of accuracy and to take special care with the information they acquire.

FIRST DUTY: KNOW THE LANGUAGE

The first duty of any editor is to be a master of the language. No matter what position in the news organization the editor holds, he or she has to read copy at some point and has to evaluate it from its most basic level. Consequently, an editor must know the fundamental rules of using the language and must understand words in both their abstract and contextual meanings. The editor must understand the structure of sentences and how words work.

Editors must be keepers of the language. They should be students of the use and dynamics of the language. They must understand the use of the language in a media context and ensure that it is used accurately, clearly, precisely, and efficiently.

The following considerations are a few of the most important things that an editor should keep in mind in reading copy.

Grammar, Spelling, and Punctuation

Knowledge of grammar and punctuation and how to use a dictionary are basic for an editor. No editor can survive without them. Words must be spelled correctly, and grammar and punctuation must conform to standard rules of English. The editor who consistently allows incorrect grammar and misspelled words onto a web site is failing at the most basic level, and there is no way such a site can maintain credibility.

Style

Every web site and publication should have a set style, and every editor should see that the news organization conforms to that style. Most newspapers and web sites use the *Associated Press Stylebook* and supplement this with a local stylebook. Style should not be a straitjacket into which an editor forces all copy; rather, it should be a help to writers and editors in achieving accuracy and consistency.

English is an extremely diverse language, giving the user many ways of saying the same thing. For instance, 8 or eight o'clock, 8 a.m., 8 A. M., eight a.m., and eight in the morning may all refer correctly to the same thing. A reference may be made to the President, the U.S. president, the President of the United States, and so on. All of these forms are technically correct; which one should a journalist use?

The answer to the question is governed by journalistic style. Style is a special case of English correctness that a publication adopts. It does so to promote consistency among its writers and to reduce confusion among its readers. Once a style is adopted, a writer does not have to wonder about how to refer to such things as time.

Names and Titles

Journalists should be particularly careful in the handling of names and titles, and editors must make every effort to ensure their accuracy. Names that have unusual spellings should always be checked. Editors must remember that even the most common names may have uncommon spellings (as in Smith, Smyth, and Smythe). Nothing should be taken for granted when dealing with a person's name. There is no quicker way for a web site to lose credibility than by misspelling a name.

Titles, too, need extra attention. Formal titles should be stated correctly; they are extremely important to the people who hold them. Titles should also be descriptive of the jobs people have. If they are not, editors may consider adding a line of job description in the story if this will clarify things to the reader.

Attribution and Quotations

Journalists should make it clear to readers where information has been obtained. All but the most obvious and commonly known facts in a story should be attributed. Editors should make sure that the attributions are helpful to the reader's understanding of the story but that they do not get in the way of the flow of the story.

Journalistic conventions have grown up around the use of indirect and direct quotations. First, except in the rarest instances, all quotes must be attributed. The exception is the case where there is no doubt about the source of the quote. Even then, editors should be careful. Second, journalists disagree about whether a direct quote should be the exact words, and only the exact words, a person speaks, or the exact meaning the quoted person intended. Most of the time, people's exact words will express their meaning accurately. If they don't, paraphrasing them and removing the quotation marks is the best approach.

Sometimes, however, a journalist must choose between accuracy of words and accuracy of meaning. People misspeak. When we know they misspoke and know what they meant, should we crucify them on their own words? Generally, no.

Finally, direct quotes in news stories rarely include bad grammar even if the person quoted used bad grammar. Quoting someone who uses English incorrectly can make that person appear foolish unnecessarily and can distract from the real meaning of the story. In a news story, a journalist usually cleans up bad grammar in a direct quote. (Feature story writers may choose not to follow this practice.)

SECOND-LEVEL EDITING: FORMULATING THE LANGUAGE

Writing is more than technical; it is also technique. Editors must make sure that writers move beyond merely using complete sentences and getting the punctuation right. They must do more than enforce the rules of grammar. Editors must exercise critical judgment about the way the language is used. They must pay particular attention to the following points.

Clarity

Clarity must be one of the chief goals of an editor. Facts that are presented unclearly are of little use to the reader. The English language is extremely versatile, but that

■ ■ ■ ■ ■

SIDEBAR

THE FIVE COMMANDMENTS OF COPYEDITING

Complete editing demands that editors observe five general commandments in helping writers and reporters produce their best work.

I. THOU SHALT NOT ACCEPT BAD WRITING.

Attitude: That's what we're talking about here. An editor should be a good guy (or gal). An editor should understand the pressures and difficulties that a reporter faces. An editor should be sympathetic when a writer tries hard.

But an editor should never read a piece of copy he or she thinks is inferior and say, "Well, I guess that's the way the writer really wanted to say it." Nor should the editor justify bad reporting by saying, "I guess the writer knows more about this than I do." And the editor should not disclaim responsibility by saying, "It's the writer's story, not mine."

An editor must take responsibility for the copy that he or she reads. An editor must develop high standards of reporting and writing and then expect writers to live up to them. And, finally, an editor should reject copy that does not meet those standards.

II. THOU SHALT NOT TOLERATE POOR LANGUAGE.

Precision: We have discussed this to some degree already in this chapter and earlier in the book, but this part of editing is so important that it has to be elevated to the level of a commandment.

Any editor of any publication is a guardian of the language. Not only should the editor know the rules of grammar, punctuation, style, and usage—and enforce those rules—but the editor should have a keen interest in the state and dynamics of the language. The editor's bookshelf should be filled with books about the language, and the editor should have several language references at hand—in addition to a dictionary and the AP Stylebook, of course.

A good editor does not tolerate "near misses" in the use of words (for example, "noisome" when the writer really means "noisy") and does not give in to language fads or clichés. The good editor is slow to accept change in the language.

And the good editor is someone in whom the writer—often secretly and sometimes begrudgingly—has confidence as an expert in the language.

III. THOU SHALT NOT HAVE TO FIGURE OUT WHAT THE WRITER IS SAYING.

Clarity: An editor must make sure that writing is as crystal clear as possible.

Most writing is not so incoherent that it cannot be understood. Suppose the story the writer wrote is terrible, but with careful reading it can be understood. Should the editor let that copy go with the thought, "Well, I know what the writer was really trying to say, so I guess the reader will be able to figure it out, too." Absolutely not.

Clarity is often lost when the writer has too much information and too many ideas. Too many facts get rolled into a sentence, and the sentences themselves run on too long. The editor should sift through the facts and parse out the sentences so they will make efficient sense to the reader.

IV. THOU SHALT NOT FORGIVE FAULTY LOGIC
OR CONTRADICTORY INFORMATION.

Thinking: The chief goal of the journalistic process is to present accurate information. But what if a reporter presents information in one part of a story that contradicts information in another part of the story? What if a writer says something in a paraphrase that seems to be contradicted by a direct quotation? And what if information in a story is irrelevant and serves to confuse rather than enlighten the reader?

All of these conditions make it into print far too often, and when they do, it is the fault of the editor just as much as the writer. An editor should always be questioning the assumptions and information the writer is presenting. An editor should read the words the writer uses for what they mean literally. (Journalism has little tolerance for figurative writing.) Editors should always be constructively critical of the copy that comes to them.

V. THOU SHALT DO THE MATH.

Details: By all means, do the math. Make sure that things add up. Make sure the percentages make sense. Make sure that you as an editor understand the mathematics in a story, even if the writer doesn't seem to.

Pay attention to the details in a larger sense, too. Journalism is not a profession that tolerates loose ends, unanswered questions, contradictory information, or faulty logic. Lapses have a way of getting into print or onto the air or on the Web and will be duplicated many times. And readers and viewers will notice.

And the editor shall bear the responsibility for it all.

Source: Adapted from *The Complete Editor* by James Glen Stovall and Edward Mullins. Kendall Hunt, Dubuque, 2000, pp. 174–176.

---

versatility can lead to confusion when the language is in the hands of amateurs. Editors must be experts in the language and in the proper and clear organization of a story. Editors must be on constant guard against writing or story structures that could be confusing to the reader.

Web sites, especially front pages and section fronts, are often viewed as "quick reads" for readers; that is, readers do not expect to spend much time with them. As we discussed in the previous chapter, they often scan these pages rather than reading them closely. Consequently, the words, phrases, and sentences used to convey the information on these pages must be accurate, straightforward, and efficient.

Like the pursuit of accuracy, the pursuit of clarity is a state of mind for editors. It must be constantly with them, and they must make sure that everything they do in some way promotes the clarity of the copy with which they are working. Editors must look at a story with a fresh mind—one that is loaded with facts but at the same time unencumbered with too much knowledge of the subject. An editor must approach a story just as a reader does—as one who was not at the scene of the event and did not see it happen and who has probably not discussed it with anyone. This approach is doubly difficult for an editor who may know a great deal about the story's subject. Editing for clarity demands a rare degree of mental discipline on the part of the editor.

The opposite of clarity is confusion. Confusion can infiltrate a headline, summary, or story in many ways, and it is the editor's responsibility to eliminate this confusion. A common source of confusion is the reporter who does not understand what he or she is writing about. If a writer does not understand his or her subject, it is highly unlikely that he or she will be able to write about it so that other people can understand it. Reporters rarely recognize this shortcoming, however, and it is up to the editor to point it out and to make any necessary changes, assisted by the reporter.

Wordiness

Using unnecessary words is a cardinal writing sin in any medium, but it is especially serious on a web site. A story should not be one word longer than necessary in order to maintain accuracy and clarity. Most reporters, especially novices, use too many words. Editors should be on the lookout for such expressions as "a total of," "in order to," "as a result of," and "at this point in time." The vigil against wordiness is a constant one for an editor.

Repetition and Redundancy

Speakers who use the same words over and over quickly become boring, and so do writers. English is a language with a large variety of words easily understood by most people. Reporters and editors should take advantage of this variety and make sure they don't repeat major nouns, verbs, or adjectives in one sentence or paragraph.

A redundancy is a phrase or set of words in which the same meaning is transmitted twice. Some redundancies make writers and editors look foolish. "A dead corpse," "we should not forget to remember," "apathetic people who don't care" are phrases in need of editing.

Triteness and Clichés

Even the most common news stories should have some freshness about them. Editors need to be sensitive to the fact that some words and phrases are being overused in their respective publications, and periodically they should attempt to change their habits. "Dead on arrival," "straight as an arrow," "very," "basically," "quite," "mainly," "really," and "actually" are all words and phrases that can easily show up too many times in a publication.

Taste, Tone, and Mood

A hilarious story about a car that flips over and bounces around a road is not so amusing if two people were killed in the wreck. Editors should make sure that their stories convey the proper tone and mood and reflect the facts accurately. In deciding about taste, an editor often has to weigh the importance of the facts and the people in the story. For instance, if the President goes to the hospital for an operation on his hemorrhoids, an editor will have to decide whether that situation is important enough to merit a story. There are no iron-clad rules governing taste, tone, and mood; there are only editors who have the sensitivity to make thoughtful and logical decisions.

Offensive Language

Different publications maintain different policies on printing offensive language. Not too many years ago, "hell" and "damn" were regularly expunged from a story. Today much stronger language finds its way into many publications. Web sites, often thought to be the purview of younger readers, can sometimes venture too far into the gray areas of language impropriety. The site should have definite and well-considered policies on what kind of language is acceptable, and the editor's job is to see that these policies are carried out.

HEADLINES, SUMMARIES, AND LINKS

Headlines

One of the first things an editor may be called on to create for a news web site is a headline. Headlines may also be a writer's responsibility, depending on the expectations and procedures of the site. As such, they were discussed to some extent in the previous chapter. Whether they originate with the writer or not, they will undoubtedly come under the scrutiny of an editor.

Headlines are an important first layer of information readers. For many readers the headline is the only information they will have about a story. Although every news organization will develop different styles for headlines, those styles should observe the following guidelines.

Headlines should be accurate. They should accurately reflect the content of the information that is presented about the topic or event. A headline has failed as a journalistic endeavor when the reader reads it and then is surprised or disappointed by the information in the article.

Headlines should emphasize the most important information. The headline should tell the essence of the story, not some interesting sidelight. A headline must get to the point, quickly.

Headlines should express a complete thought. Most headlines on web news sites follow newspaper style in this regard. That is, the headlines have a subject and a verb (sometimes the verb is understood rather than stated), and they simulate a complete sentence. Thus, an appropriate headline would be

Summer internship teaches professional values to students

rather than

Holding a summer internship

Headlines should be as specific as possible. Even though the headline writer is trying to summarize, he or she should still attempt to deliver specific information. In general, more information makes for a more interesting headline and increases the likelihood that the reader will read the story. So, rather than

> Senator speaks to students about many issues

the headline should read

> Sen. Smith advocates new student loan program

The second headline has just as many words as the first, but it has far more information.

Headlines should be short, usually no more than eight to ten words. Web headlines are not as difficult to write as newspaper headlines because there are no space and line restrictions. Still, headlines are not easy to compose, because they require brevity. The headline is not a full summary; it should be just an indication of what is in the story.

This brevity can be achieved in a variety of ways. One is leaving off articles (a, an, the) unless they are necessary to the clarity of the information. Another is using active and descriptive verbs. Look at the two headlines immediately above, and compare the verbs. The verb in the second headline, "advocates," carries far more meaning than the one in the first.

People who have never written headlines often believe that it is an easy task because headlines are so short. Nothing could be further from the truth. Headlines are difficult and taxing. Finding just the right few words can be a struggle and takes skill and practice.

Summaries

Much of what we have just said about headlines can also be said about writing summaries (also discussed in Chapter 5). A summary is a two- or three-sentence description of an article or package of items. It contains more information than the headline, of course, and its purpose is to add another layer of information to the reader's knowledge about the story. A summary can be written simply to inform or to encourage the reader to click into the story package. For instance, the following summary is written to inform:

> Three Midville men are sitting in the county jail charged with attempting to rob the First National Bank. Despite being heavily armed, the men gave up without a fight when their car was surrounded by police. They failed to get away because the battery of their getaway car went dead.

This summary is written to encourage people to read:

> Three Midville men, armed with various rifles and handguns, thought they could power their way through a robbery of First National Bank. They were wrong. The one thing they really needed lacked power.

The second summary has information, but it tries to raise a question in the mind of readers that will make them go into the article to find the answer.

Neither kind of summary is easy to write. Summaries require writers to boil a lot of information down into just a few words, usually between fifty and seventy-five. If they are written for an inverted-pyramid news story, they should give more information than is found in the lead paragraph, and they should try to draw out some interesting facts of concepts within the story itself.

Links

The real power of hypertext is found in links. Ideally, links allow readers to gain more information than what they are getting on their screens. However, links require a great deal of consideration at several levels on the part of the editor.

First, deciding what links should be included in a story package demands some disciplined and logical thinking. The depth and variety of information on the Web has grown to such an extent (and continues to grow) that the problem for the editor is often in deciding which links should be established and which should be ignored. Too many links in a story package can be confusing and nonproductive; two few can shortchange the reader and reduce the depth of the information the site offers. An editor must determine what will be useful to the reader and what would be overkill.

Another consideration of linking is that their production requires time and effort on the part of some member of the staff. How much of the news site's resources does the editor want to invest in coming up with links for a story package? Usually, an editor will want links to previous stories that the site has posted about a topic if they are relevant to the current article. Beyond that, links should be considered carefully and should not be included unless they are productive—that is, unless they can provide readers with additional quality information quickly. For instance, a story about lung cancer might link to the front page of the National Cancer Society. That would be a productive link if the reader wanted to start finding information about cancer in general or other types of cancer. It would be nonproductive if the reader were looking for immediate additional information about lung cancer. For that, the editor or writer would have to dig deeper into the National Cancer Society's site, and such digging would require time and effort.

How links are presented to the reader is yet another important decision that an editor must make. Some news web sites list links at the end of the articles they present. These links may be organized into categories that are appropriate for the subject matter. Some even carry descriptions of what the reader is about to link to—a practice that shows the site is going to some lengths to help out its readers. A variation on this practice is to put a links box at the top of the story page so that readers will know immediately that there are additional links and they don't have to scroll to the bottom of the page to find them. News sites that group links outside the article are sending a message to readers that the information in their articles should be read and considered first, before the readers seek additional information. Still another variation is to insert a box within the copy at the appropriate paragraph, which contains links to subjects referred to in the paragraph.

Another approach to linking is to embed the links in the article itself. For example, a story might contain the following paragraph:

> The history conference will include a panel on the character of American presidents. Leading that discussion will be William Lee Miller, author of the book **Lincoln's Virtues**. Miller is a **professor at the University of Virginia**.

The phrases that are boldfaced and underlined are links to additional information, the first to the web site for the book and the second to the university's information on the professor. This method of linking is efficient and effective and avoids the clichéd approach of "Click **here** for more information." It also avoids the inelegant practice of using the URL address as a link, as in "Go to **www.uva.edu/professors/wlmiller.html** for information." This approach gives readers the choice of going to a link immediately or reading through the copy without a great deal of distraction.

Whenever links are established and whatever style of linking is used, it should be clear to the reader what they are linking to and what they are likely to find if they go to that link. Let's say that in the paragraph above, the phrase "character of American presidents" were made into a link. It would not be at all clear what information would be at that link or where it would take the reader. The same can be said for links that use the words "resources" or simply "additional information." Editors, as always, should put themselves in the place of their readers and try to answer as many questions for them as they can.

THE EDITOR–REPORTER RELATIONSHIP

As the Web develops as a news medium, one of the differences we are likely to see is that stories will require a number of people to cover them, rather than a single reporter. The flexibility of the Web in handling various types of content (see below) means that people with a variety of skills will bring those skills to bear. Editors, as leaders of these teams of reporters, will need to understand the dynamics of this kind of coverage and will need to develop skills that will allow members of the team to work together. The editor's relationship with the reporter—whether a writer, graphics reporter, photographer, or video reporter—will become increasingly important if this system is to work.

Editing is a partnership into which an editor enters with the reporter. Professional reporters understand that in most situations they will rarely be on their own. The editorial process demands that the writer's products come under the scrutiny of some other person. That person, or persons, must then take as much responsibility for the writing as the writer. At the reporting and writing stage of journalism, the reporter is the senior partner in the relationship with the editor. At the editing stage, the editor becomes the senior partner. *Partner* is the key word.

A good way to operate in this relationship is for both the reporter and editor to recognize the strengths that they bring to the process. The reporter should be the expert on the subject and substance of the reporting. He or she should know the sources of information about the subject and should have a means of assessing their completeness and credibility. Good reporting means that the reporter knows far more about the subject than he or she is able to put in an article.

The reporter should also be an "expert" in the approach the story takes. He or she should understand the material thoroughly and should have considered a variety of tacks the reporting could take. The reporter should also be an expert in the tools and means of reporting, whether it is writing, graphics, photography, or video.

The editor's strength in this relationship lies in both ignorance and expertise. On first reading or viewing the work of the reporter, an editor can simulate the position of the readers—someone who knows nothing or very little about the subject. An editor can ask the same questions that a reader would ask, mainly, "Does this story (photo, graphic, video) make sense?" Here, the editor is acting as the reader's representative.

That representation should be active rather than passive. In other words, the editor should—indeed, must—recognize instances of lack of clarity. The editor must point out legitimate questions that the writer has failed to address.

This "ignorance" is not the only strength that an editor brings to the editing partnership, of course. An editor should be an expert on the web site for which both are working. The editor must know what the site's standards are, what it will accept and not accept, who the audience is, and the possible effects any story will have on any member of the audience and on the site's reputation.

Another area of strength that an editor is likely to have is a broader range of experience in the field of journalism than the reporter. Editors usually get to their position through the reporting process. At some point in their careers, they should have been doing what the reporter has done, and that experience should have imbued them with some empathy for the difficulties of the reporter. In addition, editors will probably have worked with a variety of reporters. Having seen the approaches of different reporters, they may be able to offer suggestions and approaches to a reporter based on the experience of others.

In this same vein, a good editor will probably have a broader view of the field of journalism than the reporter. The editor will have seen a greater variety of publications and web sites, will have studied other journalistic environments and situations, and will have discussed the care and feeding of reporters with other editors. This broad view of the field should add a source of stability to the reporter–editor relationship.

Finally, the editor should be a confident wordsmith. Editors should know and understand the application of standard rules of grammar, punctuation, and style. They should be aware of trends in the language, the changing meanings of words, and the development of jargon and clichés. Good editors maintain a keen interest in the language.

Ideally, the editing process works because both the reporter and editor believe that they are trying to produce a good piece of writing. Both realize that they have a stake in making the writing good. They should both be sensitive to the pressures of the other's job and sometimes even of their personal lives. Their relationship should be one of respect and good faith.

CONVERGENCE: WHERE MEDIA MEET

Writers are word people. Editors, who probably started out as writers, are also word people. But such self-descriptions may be too one-dimensional for the Web environment. The flexibility quality of the Web allows it to handle many forms of information. Some writers may try to remain simply "word people" (although it is doubtful that they can), but editors will probably not have that luxury.

Much has been said and written in journalism during the last generation about "convergence." The term can mean a couple of things. In Tampa, Florida, Media General owns the Tampa *Tribune* and one of the major television stations, WFLA-TV. Once operated completely separately, the corporation has put both news operations, plus its combined web site, TBO.com, into one building. The television news and newspaper staffs still operate independently, but they share resources and communicate with one another. They also cross-promote; that is, the television station often mentions what is going to appear in the *Tribune* and vice versa. The web site has its choice of content from both the newspaper and the television station, and the web site staff can create its own specialty packages. *Tribune* reporters are sometimes interviewed by the television station for its newscasts, and television reporters contribute information to newspaper reports. Reporters and editors from both operations may participate in forums or chat sessions set up by the web site. A liaison editor for all three media shuttles from news meeting to news meeting and talks constantly with reporters and editors from all news operations to make sure that each knows what the other is doing. (See Figure 6.1.)

That is one meaning of convergence. Another meaning emerges on a more individual level. In some news organizations, reporters and editors are expected to operate as both television and newspaper journalists. They must understand and be able to deliver content for both media. At the reporter's level, they must know how to shoot video as well as write in the inverted-pyramid structure. At the editor's level, they must edit video and enforce Associated Press style rules. These journalists can produce the multimedia packages—words, pictures, video, graphics—that are the content of a news web site.

Some people see convergence, whether at a corporate or an individual level, as inevitable in the future of journalism. It makes economic sense, they say, for more people to be able to do more things, and the Web will demand multiple skills. Jane Stevens, a self-described "backpack journalist" writing for the *Online Journalism Review,* says that multimedia provides the context for stories that print and broadcast by themselves cannot:

> Two of multimedia's most important characteristics are context and continuity, characteristics that television and print don't have to multimedia's degree. For example, many news organizations created specific sites for the continuing developments after the September 11 terrorist attack. These sites contain the stories of the day. Wrapped around them, in a "shell," are archived stories, including slide shows and/or video of the events of Sept. 11; information about Afghanistan, Pakistan, the history of terrorism, etc.; and other resources in the forms of links. Print and television simply can't provide that much information around each story. Many news organizations' business and sports sections

FIGURE 6.1   Tampa Convergence. Ken Knight, the editor at the
Tampa Tribune in charge of making sure that the *Tribune,* WFLA-TV,
and TBO.com work together, spends much of his day on the phone.
All three media are owned by Media General and housed in the same
building in Tampa. The web site, TBO.com (Tampa Bay Online),
processes newspaper stories and televisions reports, and also creates
its own original content.

are already using this approach. These characteristics of the medium will change how
beats are covered and expand local news coverage.

So, in a few years, backpack journalists—or at least those who are familiar with
backpack and converged journalism—will not only be the rule, they'll rule. And rock.
(Stevens, "Backpack Journalism," 2002)

Not everyone agrees with the multimedia or convergence trend. Part of the dis-
agreement is philosophical and part is practical. Some argue that the cultures of print

and broadcast journalism are so strong and so different that they will not mix readily or well. Until this generation, when broadcasting and print have existed close to one another, they have tended to compete—sometimes fiercely—rather than cooperate. In addition, the cultures often do respect each other; print journalists in particular have heaped contempt on their broadcast brothers and sisters, citing them as shallow talking heads with few abilities to investigate and conduct real journalism.

Another argument against convergence is that it will be the rare reporter and editor who can do both media well. Many people spend their entire careers in one medium, honing their skills for that medium. How can anyone expect that these people will become good at two media rather than just one? Training and practice in multimedia skills is a heavy burden to place on both the individual and the news organization itself.

Convergence critics also say that there simply is not time enough during the day for a single journalist to put together good stories for print and broadcast media, in addition to meeting all of the other demands of the organization. All of these factors—if forced on journalists—will lead to mediocrity rather than excellence. As Martha Stone writes in a counterpoint to Jane Stevens' article (quoted above):

> While some multimedia journalists can handle a variety of tasks efficiently and professionally, most will only deliver mediocre journalism. While some may excel at writing the story for print or broadcast, they may produce poor-quality video or still pictures. Specialization as the prevailing employment strategy has stood the test of time with other forms of journalism. In time, the message that quality comes from those journalists who practice a defined job, be it writer, videographer, photographer or editor, will be clear. (Stone, 2002)

Critics of convergence, backpack, or multimedia journalism have strong arguments. However, these arguments are largely overcome by the reality of the Web. Because the Web can handle text, images, video, and graphics—and can handle them in ways never possible in traditional media—journalists will find ways to use all of these methods to present their information and tell their stories. Audiences, then, will come to expect that kind of presentation.

Not only will editors have to understand how to edit and improve text, they will also have to understand various forms of visual presentation, such as pictures and graphics. Editors need to know visual logic (see Chapter 9), not only for their site as a whole but for the various parts of the site.

Web editors will also have to understand the concepts and techniques of audio and video editing and how these forms can be divided and put together so they can be accessed by readers. They will need to learn about the kinds of shots, sound bites, and voice-overs that work best in a Web environment (see Chapter 8).

SITE DESIGN AND ORGANIZATION

The design of a web site is discussed more fully later in this book (see Chapter 9), but it should be noted here that it is an editor's decision how the site should look, how it is organized, and how a reader is able to navigate through it. While esthetics are important, the major goal of a site designer should be simplicity and efficiency. A reader should be able to discern quickly the way a site is organized, by looking at the navigational bars. The reader should have no problem figuring out how to go from one section to another on the site.

Simplicity and efficiency in design are elusive goals. A news web site deals with a variety of information and a variety of forms. Originating the proper set of inclusive yet discrete categories into which to place this multiplicity of information is difficult. Continuing to use these categories and refine them requires a high level of intelligence on the part of the editor.

Site organization and navigation should be not only easy to understand for the reader, they should also be easily visible. Too many sites obscure their navigation behind funky bars or buttons, so that design itself, rather than usefulness, becomes the point of the site. Editors should be the readers' representative, making sure that visibility and visual logic govern the design and placement of the navigation aids.

ENCOURAGING AND MANAGING INTERACTIVITY

Interactivity carries great value for a news web site, but it can also be costly, particularly if a web site is not prepared to handle it. Interactivity can require a great deal of staff time and resources. If staff members are expected to handle interactivity as part of their jobs—without any reduction in other duties—it can become frustrating and demoralizing.

Well-considered policies on the part of the site and good planning among the editors can relieve or prevent much of this frustration. A news site should have continuing discussions about the type and level of interactivity that it wants to encourage from its readership, and it should develop sound policies that are articulated clearly to the staff. For instance, it is easy to include the email address of a reporter at the end of a news story, but what happens if a reader sends an email to the reporter? Is the reporter obligated to respond? Many stories will provoke few reactions, but some will generate a great many. How much time should the reporter spend responding to emails? Editors should understand that if a reporter spends two hours responding to emails about a story, that is two hours the reporter will not have to spend covering other news.

Another seemingly benign technique to encourage interactivity is the web poll. Some editors look at these polls and believe that the process can be completely automated. A web program can receive the responses and put them into a graphic format that readers can view. Much of this activity can indeed be automated, but writing good questions and good responses is no easy task. Any survey researcher will tell you that. The questions must be clear, and the responses that are offered must give readers choices that match their attitudes, behaviors, or feelings about the subject. Web polls also need to be changed at least every few days, if not every day. All of this requires time and effort—not to say skill—from the staff. And what if a reader decides to email a longer response to the poll question? How is that handled? Who handles it? Again, editors need to think through these issues before sailing out onto the sea of interactivity.

The whole issue of interactivity represents a sea change in the culture of traditional journalism. Journalists have always claimed that they have been responsive to their audiences, but this has been true in only a very limited sense. Except for the institutionalized letters-to-the-editor columns on editorial pages and some short corrections notices that newspapers run, journalists have not felt much obligation to deal directly with readers or viewers, especially not within the medium itself. The claim of journalists has always been that their job is to report the news, not to have contact or satisfy individual readers. That journalistic demeanor does not have to change with the Web, but it certainly can. And readers themselves are likely to expect such a change. The great benefit to news web sites of interactivity is that it engages the audience and gives the audience some feeling of ownership of the site—a feeling that journalists have claimed to value. The Web will give editors a chance to test how seriously they take that claim.

PRESERVING THE SITE

A web site is never finished in the sense that an edition of a newspaper is printed or a newscast is completed. A news web site is a dynamic structure that is always expanding its content and often changing its look. To have editorial and conceptual integrity, however, it must be seen to have some stability. That stability can be derived only from the consistency of the editors.

Editors must maintain the site's style, tone, and standards. To do this, they must have a clear idea of what those elements are, why they exist, and how they concern the purpose of the site. Constant discussion about them may not be necessary (in fact, it may be counterproductive), but these things should never be neglected.

Editors must ensure the technical integrity of the site. A dead link—a link that gives a "not found" or error message—is as much of an embarrassment to a news web site as a misspelling in a headline is to a newspaper. Editors are responsible for maintaining a robust, operating site with sensible, reliable, and consistent navigation and satisfying content.

Additions to the site—new sections and new functions—should be consistent with the look and feel that the site has established. Readers should not be jolted by a portion of the site that looks completely different from other parts, or by content that violated the standards and tone of what is already there. Changes and variations in the site will naturally occur as the site grows, but these changes need to be made within the overall limits of the policies of the site.

All of these things are the responsibility of the editor. The attention or neglect that an editor gives to a news web site will determine its direction and success.

COOL IDEAS

Comics, Your Way

Talk to just about any newspaper editor, and he or she will tell you how hard it is to change the paper's comics page. Drop a comic, and you'll get a flood of mail and phone calls. Try to add a new comic, and readers will get disturbed that you're changing the page around.

What if individual readers could get just the comics they wanted? That's the thought behind uclick, a sibling company to Universal Press Syndicate, the firm that handles comics for many newspapers. The site (www.mycomicspage.com) gives users a choice of more than a hundred comics and editorial cartoons at a cost of $9.95 per year. Users can customize their comics pages and read just what they want to read. The site will email the comics to them if the user chooses that option.

Would that be a way for newspaper web sites to make some money?

DISCUSSION AND ACTIVITIES

1. Read the two articles on backpack journalism listed in the bibliography below. What are the major issues here? How do you feel about it? Is backpack journalism the wave of the future?

2. For a story in your local newspaper, set up a layering chart. What are all the layers of information that are presented to the reader? How does the reader get from one layer to the next? What are the visual cues?

SELECTED BIBLIOGRAPHY

Arant, M. David, and Janna Quitney Anderson. "Newspaper Online Editors Support Traditional Standards." *Newspaper Research Journal* 22:4, Fall 2001, pp. 57–69.

Gahran, Amy. "Context: Web vs. Print Writing." Contentious.com, May 18, 1999. www.contentious.com/articles/v2/2-2/editorial2-2.html.

Lasica, J. D. "Innovation in the Heartland." *Online Journalism Review*, August 28, 2002. www.ojr.org/ojr/lasica/1029874865.php.

Stevens, Jane. "Backpack Journalism." *Online Journalism Review*, April 3, 2002. www.ojr.org/ojr/workplace/1017771575.php.

Stevens, Jane. "TBO.com: The Folks with the Arrows in Their Backs." *Online Journalism Review*, April 3, 2002. www.ojr.org/ojr/workplace/1017858030.php.

Stone, Martha. "The Backpack Journalist Is a 'Mush of Mediocrity.' " *Online Journalism Review*, April 2, 2002. www.ojr.org/ojr/workplace/1017771634.php.

Stovall, James Glen, and Edward Mullins. *The Complete Editor.* Kendall/Hunt, 2000.

Troffer, Alysson. "Editing Online Documents: Strategies and Tips." Contentious.com, August 6, 1999. www.contentious.com/articles/v2/2-4/feature2-4a.html.

WEB SITES

American Copy Editors Society (www.copydesk.org)

The American Copy Editors Society is a professional organization of copy editors and is dedicated "to improving the quality of journalism and the working lives of journalists." Its mission says its main purpose is "to educate our members—and others in the news business—in ways of improving the standards of copy editing and increasing the value the news industry places on our craft." The web site contains a discussion board and some useful information for editors.

The Slot (www.theslot.com)

This web site is run by Bill Walsh, chief copy editor for the business section of the *Washington Post.* Walsh is the author of the book, *Lapsing into a Comma: A Curmudgeon's Guide to the Many Things That Can Go Wrong in Print—and How to Avoid Them* (New York: McGraw Hill, 2000). The site has a number of enjoyable and useful sections, including an explanation of what a "slot" is.

CHAPTER 7

PHOTOJOURNALISM ON THE WEB

MAJOR THEMES

- With the shift from film and chemicals to electronics, photojournalism has been the area of journalism most profoundly affected by the digital revolution.
- The Web's most important quality for photojournalism is capacity; that quality is mitigated somewhat by the size of the computer screen.
- The product and content of the photojournalist are unlikely to change fundamentally because of the Web.

PHOTOJOURNALISM: JOURNALISM, BUT DIFFERENT

Possibly the most stereotyped of all journalists, the photojournalist zooms around in his sports car and torn jeans, unworried about the alimony payments he owes his second wife. Editors don't want him in their meetings because he always looks lost and haggard. Most reporters think the guy is a little weird, mainly because he has spent his professional and leisure life breathing in smelly darkroom chemicals. He smokes so much, he'll probably die of lung cancer at age forty-five. He's not stupid, but he can't write a complete sentence. That's why he's a photographer, of course. Still, occasionally the guy will take a picture that makes a page pop.

As with many stereotypes, bits of truth can be found here and there in this picture, but it's mostly smoke (especially the "he" part, since many photojournalists today are women). Photojournalism today is practiced by men and women who are highly skilled and deeply thoughtful about what they do and what they produce.

Photojournalism is journalism, but with a far different method and outcome than the journalism practiced in other parts of the newsroom. The picture may indeed be worth a thousand words, as the ancient Chinese proverb goes, but to try to equate words and images may be a fool's errand. The picture is fundamentally separate from the word, and its production and effects are certainly different.

Philosophers, practitioners, and consumers have wondered at the power of the still image, particularly since the advent of photography in the 1830s. Before then, the unseen world was, for the most part, a matter of imagination, supplemented only by paintings and other artwork. Words, via books, magazines, and newspapers, helped people form an image of the greater world that they would probably never see. But that formation was slow, something like a slow horse and buggy. Photography brought the world into view at the speed of a lightly loaded freight train.

And the pictures carried with them an aura of accuracy that even the most skilled painter could not match. With photography, seeing was truly believing—and remembering. Images were etched onto the brain with far greater ease than one could remember the shortest scriptures.

The power of the still image is still with us. We carry in our heads, clearly focused, a picture of the overturned statue of Saddam Hussein, an airplane crashing into the World Trade Center, a firefighter carrying a bloody child from the building explosion in Oklahoma City, streams of smoke from the exploded *Challenger* space ship, a Vietnamese general firing a bullet into the head of a Viet Cong soldier, the wonder in the eyes of the Holocaust victim at his survival—and a hundred other images that we did not personally witness. Most of us are living proof that the photojournalist is doing his or her job.

If journalism is the first rough draft of history, then photojournalism is our first impression, and it is often a lasting impression.

LIFE AND TIMES OF THE PHOTOJOURNALIST

Photojournalism is an aspect of journalism that is tied almost exclusively to the print media. Broadcasters, while they take pictures in the form of video, have some overlap with the area, but the work of the photographer varies from the work of the person with a video camera. Consequently, what we are considering here springs from the work of people who operate in the print media. (Video on the Web will be discussed in Chapter 9.)

News publications place great value on pictures. The modern reader expects to *see* news and information as well as read about it. The image is an indispensable part of the information mix that any news publication must offer to its audience. Not only does photography add to the understanding of the words, it also allows the publication to develop a more interesting graphic personality.

Newspapers and news magazines may have from one to scores of people devoted to taking and editing pictures. These photography staffs usually operate as separate units within the organization, but they must cooperate with the other parts of the news department. For most of the twentieth century, photographers and photo editors had such different jobs, skills, and expectations that there was rarely any crossover with other parts of the newsroom; that is, a photographer was unlikely to become a news reporter or vice versa. Both could work a story together, and in an emergency they might be able to do each other's job, but this kind of exchange was rare.

The reasons for this lack of crossover are many and obvious. The photojournalist covering the same assignment as the reporter has many considerations that differ from the reporter. The photojournalist must know the physicality of the scene—the people, the topography, the architecture, the light, and so on. The photojournalist need not be as concerned about the sequence of events, understanding motives of those involved, gathering detailed information, or getting quotes as the reporter. Instead, the photojournalist must understand the camera and other equipment being used. The photojournalist must certainly know a good deal about the scene that he or she is shooting and must get names and information about the pictures that are shot, but that knowledge does not have to be turned into a linear news story.

The photojournalist generally brings two things to a news story: illustration and visual context. Pictures are used to give variety to the printed page, which will make it interesting to look at and will draw readers into the page and into stories. More important, pictures help expand the reader's understanding of a story by giving the reader visual cues. Even a single picture of a newsmaker's head and shoulders (a "mugshot" in journalistic parlance) can give a context to a story that words cannot match.

To provide illustration and context, the photojournalist seeks at least one of three qualities in the pictures he or she takes: setting, expression, or action. Setting gives the viewer an idea of the general area in which a story takes place—a street, a football field, a room. Even when the setting is described in a story (or implied), a picture showing the scene can be a valuable supplement to the reader.

Most photojournalists attempt to go beyond setting to the qualities they consider more interesting to themselves and to their readers: expression and action. Facial expressions can be either subtle or overt. Either way, they are powerful reminders of our humanity and interaction with events anad with each other. Facial expressions can indicate to us how someone is feeling and what his or her reaction is to a particular moment or situation. They can be both interesting and revealing. One of the reasons that pictures of children are so appealing is that adults believe their expressions to be more honest than those of adults. They are not often sophisticated about hiding or altering their expressions, as some adults are.

Expression can be found in more than just the face, however. Hands can be expressive, as can other parts of the body and the body as a whole. In fact, the way two people are pictured together can say much about their relationship at that moment. In the late 1980s, when official statements from Buckingham Palace insisted that Prince Charles and Princess Diana were happily married, one had only to look at a picture of them in public to realize that they were hardly speaking to one another.

Action is a far different quality of photographs, but no less revealing and interesting for readers. Photographs that capture movement show not only expression, they put readers into a moment with the subjects of the photographs. Action shots allow readers to build context around the frozen moment—to think about what came immediately before and after the moment of the shot and to experience in some way what the subjects in the photograph are experiencing. Often, this experience of imagining is more powerful than a video that shows the action but does not let the viewer add his or her own experience to it.

DEVELOPING GOOD PICTURES

Decades of photojournalistic practice and thousands of photojournalists have led to common standards for the pictures they take. These are not rigid rules, but they constitute the physical qualities that most photographers seek in their photos.

Range of Values

Value refers to the intensity of light in various parts of the photograph. Shadows are dark, and items exposed to light will be less so. A good mix of these values can make a picture interesting and easy to look at. A picture that does not have a range of values will lack depth and will tend to lose much of the detail that makes it interesting.

A related concept is contrast. Photographers often seek to have the very dark parts of their pictures next to the very light parts in order to highlight the differences. Good, well-placed contrast in a photograph can enhance its viewability and interest.

Clear, Sharply Focused Subjects

Fuzziness is not a characteristic that most photographers seek in most of their photographs. Photojournalists work hard and spend a great deal of money on equipment to help them produce sharply focused pictures. Cameras are limited in their abilities to bring objects at various distances into focus, and a good photographer understands the equipment and works within its limitations.

Composition and the "Rule of Thirds"

The composition of a picture—that is, where the objects (including people) in the photo appear—is vitally important to the success of a picture. Sometimes a photojournalist can arrange the people and objects he is shooting so that they are interesting to look at because of the arrangement. For instance, a person accepting an award from two other people can be arranged in many ways. The easiest and least interesting arrangement is to stand the three up against a wall and shoot them with the middle person in the middle of the photo. A more interesting arrangement is to have two people sitting and the third person standing behind them. And there are many other variations that you can imagine. When people and object cannot (or should not) be arranged, photographers often try to position themselves so that their angle of view will produce a well-composed picture.

What the photographer is doing in these instances is adhering to a general principle known as the "rule of thirds." This rule is sometimes explained in the following manner: draw two lines horizontally across a picture, dividing it into thirds; then draw two lines vertically, again dividing it into thirds. The lines will intersect at four points in the picture. The focus or action of the picture should be near one of the intersecting points.

The main object of this exercise is to get the focus or action away from the center of the photograph. If this is done, many believe, the picture will be more interesting to look at. While this may be so, there is a deeper reason for drawing the eye away from the middle of the picture. That reason is context, one of the purposes of photojournalism (explained in the previous section). People and events are in an environment, but they are not often squarely in the middle of that environment. Consequently, the rule of thirds or the composition techniques of photojournalism help photographers provide more context for their pictures.

The "Decisive Moment"

Photojournalists want pictures that tell a story, or tell *the* story. That moment is easy to discern for some stories—the final handshake over a peace agreement, the winning field goal at the end of a football game, the pass of the grand marshal of a parade. With other, less climatic stories, a decisive moment may not be so easy to know. The method that many photographers use is to take lots of pictures. They keep shooting, and sometimes they know just as a picture is taken that they have captured the decisive moment. At other times, they need to look at the pictures after they are developed, often to judge the composition and other technical qualities of the photo. Sometimes they need to engage a photo editor or reporter to help decide what photo comes closest to telling the story.

The decisive moment is an elusive and subjective concept. It is a combination of technical qualities, judgments of the photographer and editor, and expectations of the publication.

Words and Pictures

Few photographs can stand by themselves. They need words to back them up and to help the audience interpret them correctly. Most publications have standard requirements for the information that must accompany a photograph, the most common being that everyone in a photo should be identified if possible. The photographer should also have information about the scene or setting of the picture. A batter standing at home plate can look the same whether it is the first inning or the ninth, but the interpretation of the photo will be different if the reader knows the inning. It's up to the photojournalist to provide that information.

THE PHOTO IN PRINT

The most common outcome of a photojournalist's work is a single picture that accompanies a news story. The photo is placed on the page along with the headline and body copy for the story, and it serves to illustrate and supplement the information in the story. Photographs take up a lot of space on the page (referred to as "real estate" in the print media), and because space in any publication is limited, their use must be managed carefully. Some newspapers regularly run two or maybe even three photos with stories on which the photographer has made some investment of time and effort to get the pictures.

The most common frustration for the photojournalist is that the publication does not have the space to run all of the good pictures the photographer has taken. Related to that is the frustration that pictures are reduced in size to the point that the photographer feels the readership cannot appreciate what the photo shows.

Occasionally (and this does not happen at every publication) a photographer is allowed to produce a photo essay. These essays usually appear on a single page (or on two facing pages), and they include a variety of views of an incident or story. The photographer uses a wide range of sizes, shots, and angles—establishing shots, midrange views, and closeups—to give the reader a visual sense of the story. A short article, as well as cutlines, usually accompanies the photo essay. This article may be written by the photographer or by a reporter who knows the story.

Photographers who are able to produce photo essays have a greater opportunity to show off their work, experiment with their equipment, and tell a more complete story. They can achieve great personal satisfaction, and they can have an impact on their subjects and their readers.

The heyday of the photo essay was the mid-twentieth century, when magazines such as *Life* and *Look* gave many photojournalists a forum to display their work. Much of our visual memory from that period comes from photographs that were originally published in those magazines. The economics of magazine publishing changed, however, and when *Life* and *Look* died, they were not replaced with similar opportunities for photojournalists.

Still, the genre of the photo essay lives on through newspapers and, for major news event, news magazines. And the world of photojournalism is populated with thoughtful and enthusiastic practitioners whose work is highly appreciated and impressive to all who see it.

THE DIGITAL REVOLUTION

Print publications underwent a revolutionary, two-stage change beginning in the 1960s, as writing and editing moved from manual to electronic operations. Reporters scanned and later "entered" their stories onto computers rather than typing them on typewriters. Copyeditors retired their copy pencils and pastepots and "called up" on their computer screens the stories the reporters had entered.

By the early 1980s that change had settled in, and the revolution migrated to its second stage: transforming the production operation of the publication. Computers were manufactured (the Macintosh being foremost among them) that could show a page on a computer screen and could allow the operator to manipulate the objects (text, lines, and pictures) on the page without ever having them in a tangible paper form.

The process of journalism changed enormously because of this new technology. Editors took over functions that had been reserved for the "composing" or "paste-up" room of the publication, giving them more control over the publication but placing on them a much heavier production burden than they had ever known.

Through these three decades of the 1960s, 1970s, and 1980s, photojournalism changed relatively little. Cameras became more sophisticated and easier to operate, film became more sensitive and development became faster, but the essential processes of photojournalism stayed the same. Photographers continued to do what they had been doing for more than 150 years: exposing light to film and then developing film and prints with chemicals. Many predicted that photography would always be like that.

But the electronic revolution was not finished. By the 1990s, the adjective "digital" was appearing in front of "camera," and "scanning," converting a print to a digital file, was becoming a common practice. Digital cameras did not need the space or the chemicals that film cameras required, and scanning negatives (if a photographer insisted on using a film camera or the publication could not afford to convert) eliminated expensive photographic paper. Many photographers resisted these changes. Some argued, with good reason, that digital cameras could not deliver the quality of photograph that film cameras could. Others simply did not want to change they way they and their professional ancestors had operated.

Neither of those attitudes could stand up to publishers and editors who viewed the digital revolution in photography as a chance to save large amounts of money and time. Change, they said. Quality will follow, and process is just process.

Now, in the early twenty-first century, the revolution is almost complete. Even though great technical improvements have been made in digital cameras, many photographers are still dissatisfied with the quality of the pictures they produce. A few even miss the hours in the darkroom with their hands in developing chemicals, believing they have lost a valuable part of the process of photography. But a new generation of photojournalists, who never touched a film roller or turned on a safe light, is coming of age, and they are completely comfortable with digital photography.

The digital revolution not only changed the economics of photojournalism—essentially making it less expensive—it changed the process as well. Photojournalists always need to adjust to their equipment, and digital cameras have presented them with a new set of options. What kind of storage medium (in the place of film) does the camera use? How are pictures downloaded and transmitted? What size settings does the camera have, and what is appropriate for a particular shooting assignment?

The major change the digital revolution has brought in the process of photojournalism is speed. Using a digital camera, pictures are produced instantly, and the only delay is getting them from the camera to a computer. What this has meant is that photographers can take more pictures and can stay on the scene longer. They can transmit photographs from the scene of the action. They can even edit what they shoot at the scene, before transmitting the photos. Consequently, a working photojournalist may be called upon to do many more tasks than were once expected.

Another major change has come in editing photographs. The dodging and burning techniques that went into developing a print in the darkroom are now about as useful as the nineteenth-century skills of chiseling line drawings into wood blocks. Enhancing a photo now means calling up a file using Adobe Photoshop, the premier software program for this purpose, and performing an almost automatic set of tasks such as lightening, sharpening, and adjusting the color.

Photoshop allows the editor to go beyond working with the internal content of the photo. An editor can combine two or more photos into a collage or can lay type over a photo or cast a shadow under it. Operations that once took years of practice and hours of work can now be completed in just a few seconds.

Not only has the digital revolution changed photo editing, it has also changed photo editors. In the film-and-chemical days, photographers kept control of the process because they were the ones who had learned the darkroom techniques. Few nonphotographer editors or reporters could go into a darkroom and operate with any skill or efficiency. In this digital age, picture taking and photo editing have become two separate skills that are not necessarily connected. People who have never picked up a camera professionally can learn Photoshop and become highly skilled editors.

Not only has photo editing slipped away from the exclusive grip of the photojournalist, photography itself has become more egalitarian. As digital cameras become lighter and easier to operate, more reporters are taking cameras on their assignments. Though freed from many of the technical considerations of camera operation, they are having to learn about lighting, value, focus, composition, and the decisive moment. They are also being required to gather the information necessary to write appropriate cutlines.

The digital revolution has made photojournalism more economic and more democratic. It has sparked a miniconvergence in the newsroom, so that while photojournalism remains very different from the journalism of the written word, journalists themselves are finding it easier to practice both forms.

So has the real revolution in photojournalism already occurred? Will the World Wide Web as a news medium affect photojournalism less than it has affected other aspects of journalism? Some believe that to be the case, but the changes the Web is bringing to the profession will eventually bring a new set of issues to photojournalism.

A MEDIUM OF ACCEPTANCE AND CHANGE

The World Wide Web seems to be a medium that accepts all aspects and forms of journalism—and then changes them profoundly. How is it treating photojournalism? And what will be photojournalism's future on the Web?

As outlined in the first chapter of this book, the Web has five qualities that make it profoundly different from any of the traditional media. Those qualities are capacity, flexibility, immediacy, permanence, and interactivity. Each of these qualities is changing, or will change, the practice of journalism, but because traditional photojournalism is different from written or spoken journalism, the photojournalism of the Web is also likely to be different. Here we examine what some of those differences might be in light of the peculiar qualities of the Web.

Capacity

The most immediate and drastic change that the Web brings to photojournalism is its seemingly unlimited capacity. The ageless complaint of the photojournalist is that there is never enough room in the publication to hold all of the good pictures that are available; nor is there enough space to run them at the appropriate size. This lack of space can be ultimately demoralizing. Photographers can plan, or they can get lucky. Either way, occasionally, they will return to the newsroom with an excellent set of pictures, only to face any one or all of the following problems:

- The publication has run out of space.
- An editor selects the "wrong" photograph, not the "decisive moment" photo of which the photographer is most proud.
- The photo selected for use is cropped badly.
- The size of the photo is not enough to do justice to the image.

In addition, the photographer's ideas for photo essays are turned aside because the newspaper or magazine simply is not big enough or because the advertising department did not sell enough ads to increase the page count (which probably would not have helped them anyway).

The Web solves these problems and frustrations at a stroke. The Web, as we discussed in Chapter 1, has enormous capacity to hold and display material in a variety of forms, including pictures. Early in the Web's history, images were considered a problem because they were so much larger than text files. That problem has faded somewhat because of software that can compress images and because servers and hard drives are so much larger than in the first years of the Web. (See Figure 7.1).

Downloading time (the amount of time it takes for a web page to appear on a computer's screen) is still an issue, however, and images generally increase loading time for the visitor. Those who work with pictures need to design pages that do not frustrate readers because they take so long to load. This problem, too, will fade as more people have computers with increased speeds and broadband connections.

With the Web's seemingly infinite capacity for storing and displaying pictures, the photojournalist's problem turns from what one or two *can* be shown to which and how many pictures *should* be shown. Photojournalists and their editors have to decide how many pictures they need to tell their stories, not how few they are limited to. This shift relieves the pressure on the photojournalist from having to produce the one "decisive moment" picture. It deemphasizes the single photograph and allows photo staffs to think in terms of showing multiple images.

Of course, while the capacity of the Web may relieve the frustration of photojournalists limited by print, it will undoubtedly increase their workload. Not only can the Web hold more pictures, the Web—and its users—will demand more pictures. Those pictures will not go straight from the camera to the Web. As with anything else in journalism, they will need to go through an editing process that selects and prepares them for posting. That process is not automatic, and it is sometimes difficult. People who have worked with Photoshop know what a powerful program it is for processing pictures, but they also know that it takes time, skill, experience, and judgment to produce a good picture.

The Web even allows the "nonediting" of a photograph. That is, in some rare cases of news presentation, it may be important to show both a cropped version of a photograph at some point in the story and a noncropped version. Such a situation

FIGURE 7.1   Photo Galleries. Many news web sites group photographs about the same topic in a photo gallery that is somewhat interactive. Although these galleries have a variety of designs, they usually show only one picture at a time and provide some means for the user to go from picture to picture. Here, the "Previous" and "Next" buttons above the picture to the right serve that purpose.

would never be considered in print journalism (unless the cropping itself had become an issue), but it could very easily be done on the Web. For instance, an editor might want to show a small, cropped version of a picture on the initial page of a story to increase its downloading speed. A larger, less tightly cropped (or noncropped) version of the photo would be available to the reader in case he or she wanted to view it.

Suffice it to say, at this point, that despite its increased capacity, the Web will not make the decision making for the photographer or the editor any easier.

Flexibility

The Web's ability to handle a variety of media forms will also render an enormous change in photojournalism. The photographer and editor must not only shift their thinking from single to multiple pictures (as we discussed above), they must also consider an ever-broadening expanse of story-telling forms.

No longer confined to the single picture, photojournalists have to think in narrative terms; that is, having a beginning, middle, and end to the stories they tell. They may even have to consider, as reporters often do, whether there are sidebar stories to tell in addition to the main story.

More pictures, various sizes, multiple stories—all of this is only the beginning of the new world that photojournalists will face on the Web. Because the Web can support various forms of presentation, photojournalists need to consider whether they should use audio, video, animation, and text to support their still pictures and to tell their stories. In fact, some photojournalists have found that audio is one of the things they can most easily adapt to their stories. Photographers from some of the major news organizations (including the *New York Times*) now regularly make sound recordings that can be heard while their pictures are displayed. These recordings may include more than the photojournalist talking about his or her pictures. They can also include sounds from the scene of the picture or recordings of interviews the photographer has made while taking the photos.

Obtaining audio material, of course, means that the photographer has a tape recorder or a digital audio recorder along with the standard equipment in the camera bag. The audio recorder is another piece of equipment that requires training and experience for good use. And once recordings are made, they must be edited and placed so the sound comes in at the right moment.

Video, too, is another means of storytelling that is open to the photojournalist, and it has the same requirements as audio—training, experience, and skill. Few traditional photojournalists try to shoot video at the same time they shoot still pictures, however, for a variety of reasons. (We will examine video news on the Web in Chapter 9.)

Text is yet another tool that photographers must learn to use to tell their stories. Photojournalists have always been required to produce some text along with their pictures, as we discussed above. Formerly, those requirements were confined to cutline information and short articles to support photo essays. Because it can accept more text than print can, the Web may now require more text in addition to the pictures the photographer wants to present.

Photographers may also want to integrate nonphotographic images, such as maps and other graphics, into their stories. Most of these images can be handled through Photoshop or similar editing programs, but their acquisition and use will require photojournalists and their editors to think beyond their cameras. Animated images require yet another set of skills, but they too may be necessary for the photojournalist to tell the story properly.

Just as Photoshop has become the standard software for editing images, Macromedia's Flash has emerged as the program of choice for integrating text, pictures, graphics, animation, sound, and video into a coherent presentation on a web site. The photojournalist who can handle these various tools with confidence and skill will be highly sought after. Technical skill, however, is not enough. Understanding storytelling and presentation of information will also be required if photojournalists are to take full advantage of the flexibility the Web has to offer.

Immediacy

One of the most obvious qualities of the Web is the immediacy with which information can be posted and made available to the public. Although information, including pictures, must be produced through an editorial process, however abbreviated, the Web can display that information quickly. The public has amply demonstrated a demand for immediate information—stories, pictures, video—whenever any major news event occurs.

One of the effects that this quality of the Web is likely to have on all journalism, and especially photojournalism, is shortening the decision-making process about what information to present to the public during breaking news situations. In print media, photojournalists and photo editors usually have some time, often hours, to process and edit—that is, to decide what photos are best and most appropriate. The demands of the Web will lessen that time to minutes at most. Pressured by television's live and continuous twenty-four-hour news broadcasts, news web sites will be expected to post whatever they have whenever they have it.

And the Web, like broadcasting, is continuous—although in a somewhat different way. The Web is always on and always available to post new information. That means that a photojournalist may have to begin telling a story before the story itself is finished and will have to continue telling the story as it is unfolding. Or stories may be told in one day, lay fallow for several days, and resume on another day. As we have discussed in earlier chapters, deadlines and publication cycles do not apply to the Web, and journalists—including photojournalists—may have to stay with and add to a story over an extended period of time.

Permanence

The fact that what is produced for the Web does not deteriorate, can be easily copied and stored in other locations, and can be quickly retrieved may have little immediate effect on photojournalists. But as Web archives grow—and photographic archives with them—photojournalists will find it easier to go into their files to produce stories that have a longer reach than just yesterday's news.

One does not have to have a great imagination to think of many stories that would be enriched by previously published or posted photographs. When development of a city block is announced, it would helpful to know what that block has looked like over the years. When a new home-run king is crowned, baseball fanatics might like to see pictures of all of the homers he has hit during the season. Physical archives are difficult to access, and print limits a photojournalist's ability to retrieve and display previous pictures. The Web can make this process relatively quick and easy.

Interactivity

How will photojournalists interact with their audience? The world of photojournalism has heretofore been one of technically trained and highly skilled professionals who have created a subculture that has been walled off from even their own colleagues in other parts of the news media. How can the general public, most of whom have never taken more than photos of a family vacation, break into that work—even through the Web?

At this point in the Web's development, it is difficult to see how interactivity will make a difference in the job a photojournalist does. Still, interactivity is worth brief consideration, if for no other reason than the profound effect it is having on other parts of journalism.

One practical side of interactivity is the choices that it gives to the audience in what they will read and see. Occasionally, editors and photojournalists have pictures that give them pause as to whether the pictures should be published. People in extreme grief, dead bodies, people in difficult situations not of their own making—all of these (and many more) situations have elicited much comment from the public when they see published pictures of them. With print, the decisions in these situations had to be all or nothing—either print or don't print. With the Web, a potentially offensive picture can be posted, but a web page can be set up as a buffer, explaining that clicking at a certain point will show a picture that may be upsetting or offensive. Visitors can then choose whether to view the picture. Thus the journalists can fulfill dual responsibilities of telling a complete story and protecting or warning those who may be offended by the content.

Also in those cases, the Web can keep track of the number of people who go on to view the material and those who do not, thus receiving some guidance from the audience about what it considers offensive.

Another aspect of interactivity is accepting photographs from people who are not part of the news organization. Some news web sites have done this, and it has proven to be a popular and often interesting part of the content of the site. Occasionally, a news organization has accepted photographs of a breaking news event that were taken by people who were not part of the staff. Such photos must be treated more circumspectly, given the ease with which photographs can be digitally manipulated. News organizations will be wise to develop some guidelines for this kind of situation.

ETHICAL CONSIDERATIONS

Photojournalism is heavily laden with ethical concerns. Few discussions about the field in general can develop without dealing with some of the difficult questions that surround the impact photos can have on the individuals in them and on those who see them. Photos have the power to go beyond text in entering our psyche and making an impression. How they are taken, processed, and displayed is always a matter of the utmost concern to professionals and audiences alike. What effect will the Web have on these considerations and decisions?

Ethical questions in reporting and photojournalism generally revolve around one major theme: when should a photojournalist raise the camera, and when should he or she put it down? This question involves both the individuals who may be photographed and the effects the content might have on the audience. Legally, anything that occurs in public and in plain view is fair game for the photographer. But should some pictures be taken? Should a member of the British royal family be photographed when the wind catches her skirt and reveals the color of her underwear? Should the President be photographed when he becomes sick and throws up at a state dinner? Should a person who has just learned that a relative has been killed in a mining accident be photographed? Should a photographer who could relieve someone's pain or discomfort continue shooting photographs instead?

And what about situations and subjects that are not in plain view but are still part of the public record? What rights do photographers and editors have to obtain pictures? For instance, should they demand the autopsy photos of a dead race car driver? Should they publish or post pictures of the murder of a U.S. journalist in a foreign country?

All of the questions raised above have been dealt with many times by members of the traditional media, and the existence of the Web is unlikely to change the basic assumptions and considerations they involve. Where the Web may make a difference is in the speed with which decisions will be made. The immediacy of the Web and the competition among web journalists will shorten the already brief time that photojournalists have for reflection and consultation on these questions.

In addition, there is a growing feeling that anything and everything will eventually appear somewhere on the Web. The brutal murder of *Wall Street Journal* reporter Daniel Pearl in Pakistan in 2002 was recorded on videotape by his murderers, and its most horrendous portions eventually were posted on a number of sites. Journalists are sometimes pressured to publish questionable material not only because they want to be first but also because they want to avoid accusations that they have withheld what they have from their audience. The ubiquitous quality of the Web may increase those pressures.

Processing pictures presents another set of ethical dilemmas for photojournalists. These dilemmas existed long before the digital age, and modern technology has exacerbated them. The major question is how much should a photograph be changed? Photographs are thought to represent a visual reality that can be shared among those who see the photograph. The assumption behind a photograph is that you would have seen the same thing the photographer saw had you been there when the picture was taken. That assumption is supported when we see a picture of someone we know, and we recognize that person. The size, shape, and proportions of the person in the picture fit closely with our visual memory, and consequently, we are likely to feel that the camera can come close to telling a visual truth.

With that assumption in place,* there is a strong tenet of photojournalism that photographs presented in a news context should not be altered so they represent something different from the original image. Darkroom techniques that enhance the technical qualities of the picture are acceptable, but those that change the substance of the picture (adding or subtracting objects, disproportionate scaling, flopping†, changing colors, etc.) are not acceptable enhancements.

---

*Many have challenged that assumption, on both physical and philosophical grounds.

†Flopping is reversing a picture horizontally. A picture of people walking to the left would become a picture of people walking to the right. Photojournalists consider flopping a violation of the photo's accuracy.

So far, so good. As long as photographs were coming out of a chemical dark-room, manipulating them was difficult and usually detectable. The digital age, however, has given us tools that make manipulation of photographs easy and almost unde-tectable. While these tools allow editors to effect appropriate enhancements (such as adjusting contrast or sharpening) with relative ease, it is also easy to eliminate objects or add them to a photograph. As always, a person with technical skill but little under-standing or few scruples can damage the credibility of a news organization by manip-ulating photographs.

Will the Web make any difference in this area? Probably not, for the foreseeable future, except that it might offer more chances and more temptations for unacceptable manipulation to occur. The culture of photojournalism remains in the hands of editors and practitioners who enforce, with varying degrees of success, their own rules and cus-toms. The Web will probably not change that; nor will it change the basic debates that those interested in this area have concerning manipulation and alteration of photos.

The third area of ethical consideration is presentation, something we have deal with in part in earlier sections of this chapter. As we noted, for breaking news, the Web may shorten the time available to make decisions and consider the consequences of showing photographs. The worldwide reach of the Web may also have some effect on a local news organization's decision making, possibly making editors more wary of what they decide to post. However, as we noted above, the Web will offer more pre-sentation options than print so that difficult photographs can be shown at different sizes or with different cropping, or they can be filtered so that users can be forewarned before they choose to view them.

PHOTO WEB SITES

Web sites devoted solely to the work of photojournalists—either as part of a news organization's larger site or as stand-alone sites maintained by photographers and ed-itors themselves—are beginning to emerge on the Web. Many individual photojour-nalists have sites to display their work; others are collaborations among photographers who share the same area of interest. These sites point toward the possibility of another golden age of photojournalism like the one that occurred in the middle of the twenti-eth century.

A photojournalism web site gives the photographer virtually unlimited space to display his or her pictures. The photographer can work without the pressure of publi-cation or distribution deadlines and can even add to a work that has already been posted. The Web presents the possibility of new forms of storytelling that use words, sound, and animation.

As of this writing, however, these sites generally have yet to take full advantage of the Web's tools or develop its possibilities. Some established news organizations—most prominently, the *New York Times,* the *Washington Post,* and MSNBC—have de-voted time and resources to allowing their photographers to see how the Web can be used to relate news through photography. At these and a few other sites, visitors can find photo presentations that use audio, text, and even animation in restrained and insightful ways. Other news sites have ignored photography almost completely or treated it simply as a difficult add-on at best.

Independent sites devoted to photojournalism have so far failed to deliver on the promise of the Web. Many are burdened by too much emphasis on music or other sound and movement, often obscuring the story and strength of the still photographs. Many of these sites want to control the pace and sequence of viewing rather than allowing the user to do that. They also carry funky designs that do not enhance the quality or content of the photographs.

Web sites that emphasize photography carry two technical burdens. One is load time; photographs can be notoriously slow to load and can try the patience of the viewer. When sound or animation is added, load time is increased further. Another technical problem is screen size. Photographs are limited to the size of a computer screen if they are going to be convenient to view. Although even the smaller screens can handle most photographs, most of the time, a photographer will occasionally want to display a picture at a very large size or at a vertical or horizontal size that does not allow full viewing at one time. Downloading photos by the user to an individual computer is a partial and unsatisfactory solution to this problem.

Another problem may be one that seemed like a solution at first glance. For generations, photographers have complained of a lack of space to show their work. With that complaint eliminated, photographers are reminded of the work and energy involved in producing a good picture. Now that more than one picture can be displayed, many photojournalists are finding that they are expected to produce more. Despite modern technology, it still takes great human effort to take a good picture and produce it for the Web. Having unlimited space to do that may turn out to be the blessing photojournalists should not have prayed for.

THE PROMISE OF THE WEB

Photojournalism is one of the areas of web journalism in which relatively little development has taken place. Some visionaries can see great possibilities for the professional in this new medium, and speculating about the future of photojournalism on the Web can tax a person's creative powers. In this chapter, we have tried not to look beyond what is likely to happen in the near future. Still, what we have discussed are promises that, for the most part, remain unfulfilled. A new generation of photojournalists—people who never touch chemical developer or photographic paper—will be needed for the Web to become what it promises to be.

COOL IDEAS

One More Medium

When the first anniversary of the September 11 attacks rolled around in 2002, many newspapers put together special sections for both their print and web site editions. The print editions carried articles, pictures, and graphics, while the web sites added sound, video, and animation.

The *Chicago Tribune* went one step further by gathering their three hundred pictures and six hundred articles and other material together on a CD and stuffing it into the newspaper on the Sunday before the anniversary.

Journalists at the *Tribune* worked for several weeks to put the material together. Their biggest problem, however, was figuring out how to package the disk so that it could be stuffed automatically into more than a million Sunday papers, according to Senior Editor Tony Majeri.

The newspaper put the disk into a sealed plastic and cardboard envelope about four or five times the size of the disk itself. That made it large enough to be grabbed by the stuffing machines.

The *Tribune* received requests for the disk for many weeks after it was originally distributed. (Much of what was on the CD can be seen at (www.chicagotribune.com/news/specials/911/showcase/chi-911intropage.htmlstory).

DISCUSSION AND ACTIVITIES

1. What news photos have stuck in your mind? Describe them or find copies of them to share with your colleagues. Why have these made an impression? What are the technical aspects of the photo that enhance the impact of the photo?

2. With a digital camera, take pictures of a large, inanimate object, such as a tree. Try to "tell the story" of that object. Download the photos onto a computer and try to sequence them so that they present the story you want to tell.

3. Photo galleries are a means that many news web sites use to display multiple pictures of a subject. Each member of the class should find a photo gallery style, study it, and make a report to the class. How are the photos displayed? How does the user go from one photograph to the next? How is text displayed? Does the gallery give the viewer an overall sense of the subject as it is displaying the photos? Compare the photo gallery designs of various web sites such as the *New York Times,* MSNBC, the *Washington Post,* the *Chicago Tribune,* etc.

SELECTED BIBLIOGRAPHY

Dorow, Alan. "The Internet and Online Publishing." *The Digital Journalist,* March 2002. http://digitaljournalist.org/issue0203/dorow.htm.

Halstead, Dirck. "The Digital Journalist: Looking Back and Looking Forward." *The Digital Journalist,* March 2002. http://digitaljournalist.org/issue0203/halstead.htm.

Hoy, Frank. *Photojournalism: The Visual Approach* (2nd ed). Englewood Cliffs, NJ: Prentice Hall, 1986.

Meyer, Pedro. "Bridging Art and Technology at ZoneZero." *The Digital Journalist,* March 2002. http://digitaljournalist.org/issue0203/meyer.htm.

Pavlik, John. "A Three Dimensional Depth." *Online Journalism Review,* July 15, 2002. www.ojr.org/ojr/technology/1026801335.php.

Rosenberg, Jim. "The Future of News Photography?" *Editor and Publisher,* March 11, 2002.

Storm, Brian. "Made for the Medium: Photojournalism at MSNBC.com." *The Digital Journalist,* March 2002. http://digitaljournalist.org/issue0203/storm.htm.

WEB SITES

Souleyes (www.souleyes.com)

> Terrence Antonio James, photojournalist for the *Chicago Tribune,* runs this interesting web site that gathers pictures from around the world. This web magazine has "a commitment to documenting communities of color through single images, photo essays, and works-in-progress, with a strong preference for photographers' personal projects," according to its founder.

Musarium (formerly Journale) (www.journale.com)

> Musarium is in partnership with MSNBC and describes itself as a "laboratory for modern storytelling, . . . a place where stories are told in interesting and powerful ways." The site encourages people to contribute words, pictures, video, audio, and any storytelling forms they have.

Pixel Press (www.pixelpress.org)

> The intent of PixelPress, according to its mission statement, "is to encourage documentary photographers, writers, filmmakers, artists, human rights workers and students to explore the world in ways that take advantage of the new possibilities provided by digital media. We seek a new paradigm of journalism, one that encourages an active dialogue between the author and reader and, also, the subject."

News Web Site Photo Galleries

> Two of the best, and the two to which most people in journalism look as the most innovative, are the *New York Times* Photo Gallery (www.nytimes.com/pages/multimedia/index.html) and the *Washington Post* Camera Works (www.washingtonpost.com/wp-dyn/photo).

■ ■ ■ ■ ■

CHAPTER 8

GRAPHICS JOURNALISM
WORDS AND PICTURES TOGETHER

MAJOR THEMES

■ Graphics journalism is a vital but underdeveloped part of journalism in all media, particularly on the Web.

■ Forms and techniques of graphics journalism can be extended by the technical characteristics of the Web.

■ Coverage of breaking news, particularly planned events, can be enhanced by graphics journalism in ways that text, photography, and video cannot match; because of restrictions on broadcasting some live events, especially sports events, graphics reporting can bring these events to a wide audience.

Graphics journalism combines words and images to present ideas and information in ways that cannot be accomplished by text or illustrations alone. The best graphics journalism helps viewers understand—and picture—the information. It gives insights into the topic. And it opens up the possibility that viewers will find meanings and interpretations beyond those intended by the journalists.

To date, graphics journalism has not fulfilled its promise in print journalism. Much good work is being done, to be sure. Newspapers such as the *New York Times,* the *Chicago Tribune,* and the *Washington Post,* among many others, produce excellent, informative graphics under the pressure of daily deadlines. News magazines such as *Time* and *Newsweek* fill their graphics staffs with excellent artists and journalists. However, graphics journalism is expensive. It takes time and consumes valuable and always scarce space in the publication. The difficulties of producing good graphics journalism are not always understood or appreciated by a news organization's management. A graphics reporter must have a special orientation to both information and design that is often ignored by journalism schools and misunderstood by top-level editors. These editors do not understand infographics the way they understand reporting, writing, and editing.

Is it any wonder that graphics journalism on the Web remains in an embryonic state? Even the publications that produce the best print graphics journalism have not always done a good job in transferring their work to their web sites, much less in developing ways to allow the Web to enhance it.

Graphics journalism is simply very hard to do. The research that goes into building a good graphic demands concentration and special talents of the journalist. Conceptualizing a good graphic takes not only good information but also a thorough understanding of visual forms of presentation. In addition to the visual forms, graphics journalists must be experts in the language because they have so little space and consequently so few words to use. They have to make every word count. Graphics journalists are required to perform intellectual multitasking that rarely occurs anywhere else in the newsroom. A good infographic is easy to look at. It presents its information in a way that is easy to understand. However, there is nothing easy or quick about graphics journalism.

Graphics journalists sometimes describe what they do as narrow and deep, comparing it to news reporters, who write stories that are wide and shallow (though not in a pejorative sense). That is, graphics journalists home in on a part of the larger story and explore that part in depth. In print, exploring or extending a part of the story with graphics is usually all that can be done, given the limitations of time and space.

The Web, as we shall see, greatly extends the possibilities of graphics journalism. As in no other area of the profession, graphics journalism holds the promise of discovering new storytelling forms. The graphics journalist has more room to be creative and yet remain within the traditional bounds of journalistic accuracy than any other type of journalist. The graphics journalist can both tell and show in powerful and enlightening ways.

THE GRAPHICS REVOLUTION

A graphics revolution in the print media began in the 1980s and gained momentum in the 1990s. Newspapers, magazines, and other media took on new looks, with color, charts, illustrations, maps, and other visual presentations. Graphic forms became part of the norm for the reader of news.

A number of factors worked in concert to help journalists see that the paragraph was not the only—or sometimes not the best—way to present information.

One factor was *USA Today,* the national newspaper published by Gannett. When the paper began publication in 1982, it splashed onto the field of journalism, spilling color and graphics everywhere. The newspaper demonstrated the extent to which the graphic forms could be used to present information. It put a cartoonish chart in every section. The paper used an enlarged weather map and surrounded it with related information in outsized proportions. Because readership surveys had shown weather to be a high-readership item, *USA Today*'s editors explained weather with pictures and process graphics. In many other areas—particularly sports—the paper's use of informational graphics was extensive and often controversial, but its influence on other newspapers was undeniable. Many editors, at the same moment they were sneering at *USA Today* as "McPaper," copied its colorful weather maps and began a silent "me-too" campaign by developing more illustrations and charts.

USA Today was not the first newspaper to use these forms, of course. Others, notably the *Chicago Tribune,* had pioneered the use of infographics to present information. But *USA Today* took graphics beyond almost any other publication at the time. Its unique look, national circulation, and expensive start-up shook an industry that had been timid and moribund—and, in the areas of design, very much look-alike. *USA Today* was not only different, it looked different. And it justified its look by saying that it was giving readers what they wanted and in the form they desired. The paper had extensive readership surveys to back up its decisions.

The idea that readers expected something different also contributed to the graphics revolution. Partly because of *USA Today,* a feeling developed among many journalists during the 1980s that readers—particularly those who had grown up with television—expected publications to be more visual and for information to be presented in smaller and more digestible bites. This feeling was reinforced by the fact that newspapers were failing to gain the loyalty of young readers.

That feeling was reinforced by the movement toward computers, especially by young people, in the 1980s, and the development of the Internet and the World Wide Web in the 1990s. As we observed in the previous chapter on photojournalism, the 1980s was also the decade of the computer revolution in journalism. The development of technology that would put the equivalent of mainframe computers onto people's desks and into their laps profoundly affected the way that newspapers and other publications were produced. Many of the tasks that had been laboriously done by hand in previous generations could now be done more precisely and more quickly on a PC.

One of these tasks that was made simpler and easier by computers was the building of a chart and the information that surrounds it. What had previously taken the hand-to-eye skills of a surgeon could now be handled by anyone who knew the right buttons to click on. The leader in the development of this technology was the Apple, which produced the Macintosh computer. The basis of the Macintosh was a "graphic interface," and the very name signaled a move away from words and toward pictures and graphics.

Adding to this mix was a heightened graphics sophistication among journalists themselves. Journalists began to reconsider the types of information they were presenting to their audiences and the means they were using to do so. This reconsideration led to the realization that some information could be better presented in charts or illustrations. For instance, how an earthquake occurs is not easy to describe with words and is impossible to photograph. (The effects of an earthquake can be photographed, of course, but not the process that makes it occur.) The best way to present this information is through a drawing, a technique that many newspapers used to "describe" the 1987 and 1989 earthquakes in California.

In the same manner, much information that is based on numbers is better presented in a chart than in a paragraph. A block of type containing categories and numbers is difficult to read and understand. A table is easier to read, but the text itself has little visual impact. A chart can make a simple, easy-to-understand visual statement that delivers the information and allow readers to evaluate it themselves.

While this reconsideration took place on the part of some journalists, many others still resisted any move away from text and the paragraph. That resistance continues in many areas of journalism today. Most working journalists grew into their profession as "word people." Many of them came to the profession because they like to write and use the language. Some continue to act as though the emphasis on graphic presentation is nothing more than a passing fad. Despite this attitude, graphic presentation of news and information will continue to be a major form used by news organizations. Editors of today and tomorrow will need to know how this form should be used appropriately, and they should understand when and why graphics are the best form for presenting information.

The advent of the Web as a news medium makes this necessity even more acute. The difficulties of reading text on a computer screen do not negate text as a form of presentation, but they should spur web editors to seek more visual means for giving readers what they have. In addition, the special qualities of the Web (discussed later in this chapter) open up enormous possibilities for journalists to develop new graphics forms.

INFORMATIONAL GRAPHICS

Good informational graphics, whether in print or on the Web, have the basic characteristics of all journalism: accuracy, clarity, precision, and efficiency.

The two major content principles of informational graphics are accuracy and clarity. Above everything else, an informational graphic should present information accurately. Graphics, like words, are easy to distort. Graphics often present relationships, and the basis of those relationships should be clear to the reader.

Clarity is the second major principle. Clarity begins in the mind of the journalist and editor. They both should have a clear idea of what information is important and of how it is best presented. Although a single graph may show different things, it should be governed by a central idea, much as a good story has a central theme or idea.

A good graphic should be precise, not only in presenting information, but in the use of the forms of graphic presentation. These forms often have specific uses that the graphics journalist must know, understand, and observe.

Informational graphics must also be efficient. They should use the words, lines, and images in a way that helps readers understand the information. All of those elements should enhance the reader's knowledge rather than obscuring it.

To achieve these qualities, graphics journalists often use standardized forms of presentation, just as news reporters use the inverted-pyramid story structure for most of their news stories. Three general types of informational graphics are used in the print media, and they are the three most likely to be transferred to the Web: type-based graphics, chart-based graphics, and illustration-based graphics. Each may use elements of the others, but this classification is a good way to begin to understand graphics.

TYPE-BASED GRAPHICS

Type-based graphics are those in which text, or type, is the major graphic element. Sometimes it is the only graphic element. These graphics use type to draw attention to themselves in addition to providing informational content (see Figure 8.1). The following are some common types of text-based graphics.

■ *Lists.* Some of the best graphics are nothing more than lists, and lists are readable and popular with readers. They are clean, simple, and easy to produce, and they give readers interesting information quickly. A list might be a simple listing of items, such as a movie reviewer's five favorite movies of the year, or it might contain some additional information about the items. As web graphics, lists can be an ideal means of linking to related information.

■ *Refers.* A "refer" (pronounced REE-fer) is short for "reference" in newspaper jargon. In a newspaper or newsmagazine, it is a way of telling the reader that there is another story on the same subject elsewhere in the paper. It is also a good graphic device that breaks up body type.

■ On the Web, a refer becomes a link to some other item, either within the web site itself or on some other site. Such links may be placed within the copy and set off

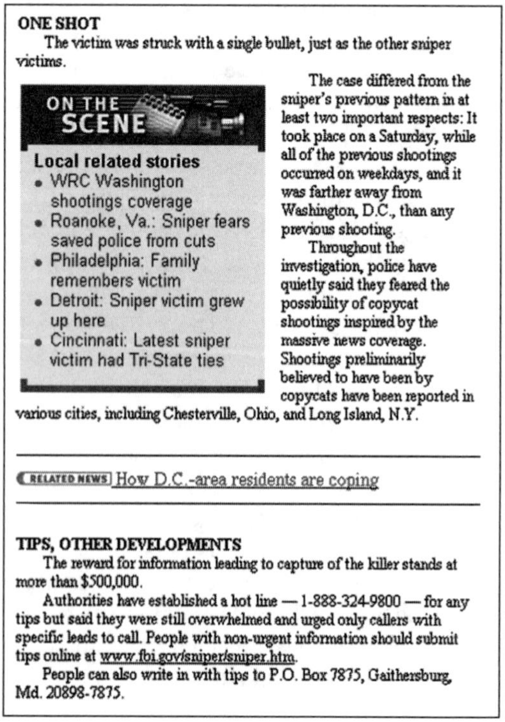

FIGURE 8.1 Type as a Graphic Device. Sometimes all it takes is some well-placed type and a little color as a graphic to introduce some visual variation to the screen and also add to the information for the reader. This is the way MSNBC.com does it, but there are many styles of using type as a graphic.

ONE SHOT
The victim was struck with a single bullet, just as the other sniper victims.

ON THE SCENE

Local related stories
- WRC Washington shootings coverage
- Roanoke, Va.: Sniper fears saved police from cuts
- Philadelphia: Family remembers victim
- Detroit: Sniper victim grew up here
- Cincinnati: Latest sniper victim had Tri-State ties

The case differed from the sniper's previous pattern in at least two important respects: It took place on a Saturday, while all of the previous shootings occurred on weekdays, and it was farther away from Washington, D.C., than any previous shooting.
Throughout the investigation, police have quietly said they feared the possibility of copycat shootings inspired by the massive news coverage. Shootings preliminarily believed to have been by copycats have been reported in various cities, including Chesterville, Ohio, and Long Island, N.Y.

RELATED NEWS How D.C.-area residents are coping

TIPS, OTHER DEVELOPMENTS
The reward for information leading to capture of the killer stands at more than $500,000.
Authorities have established a hot line — 1-888-324-9800 — for any tips but said they were still overwhelmed and urged only callers with specific leads to call. People with non-urgent information should submit tips online at www.fbi.gov/sniper/sniper.htm.
People can also write in with tips to P.O. Box 7875, Gaithersburg, Md. 20898-7875.

by a different color or texture of type, or they may be listed beside or at the end of the article.

■ *Pull quotes.* A pull quote is part of an article that is set off in different type. It generally serves two purposes: it is a good way of breaking up large amounts of body copy type; it also gives the reader some interesting point or flavor of a story.

■ *Chronologies.* Events rarely occur without some significant historical context. That context may be very recent, but it also may be important in explaining to the reader what has happened and why. Chronologies take a good deal of time and care to produce, but they can help heighten reader interest in a story. (Chronologies are sometimes referred to as timelines, but in this text, a timeline has some visual element that accompanies the text. A chronology is simply text.)

■ *Organizational charts.* Organizational charts (also called tree charts) demonstrate relationships within an organization. The most common ones show the relative positions of jobs within a corporation. A standard way of presenting this kind of chart is to have the names of positions within boxes, with lines connecting the boxes that represent reporting channels and responsibilities.

Another type of organizational chart is most often found on the sports page. This chart shows a match-up of teams or individuals playing in a tournament and how they will proceed to a championship. Still another type of organizational chart is the genealogical chart that traces a family's history through several generations (thus the term "family tree"). All of these charts make it easy for the reader to see some relationship of a part of the chart to a larger entity such as an organization or a family.

CHART-BASED GRAPHICS

Chart-based graphics present numerical information in a nontext form. These forms are likely to be proportional representations of the numbers themselves. Chart-based graphics are what many people refer to when they talk about informational graphics.

In addition to the principles of accuracy and clarity discussed above, good informational graphics share a number of other characteristics. The following are some of those characteristics.

■ *Simplicity.* Graphics can be complex, but their appearance should be uncluttered. One of the criticisms of many graphics is that they are "chartoons"—that is, they have too many little figures and drawings that do not add to the reader's understanding of the information in the graphic. A graphic should contain the minimum items necessary for understanding the information and the maximum items for good appearance.

■ *Consistency.* Publications and web sites often develop a graphics style, just as they adopt a writing style. This style includes rules about what kind of type is used, when color is appropriate, how information is attributed, and a variety of other matters.

Like style rules for writing, these rules help both the staff in producing graphics and the reader in understanding them (see Figure 8.2).

■ *Attribution.* Information in graphics should be attributed, just as information in news stories should be attributed. As with other information in a publication, sometimes the source is obvious and does not need to be specified. In other cases, attribution is vital to the understanding of a graphic.

Headlines and Explainers

Oddly enough, one of the most difficult things about producing an informational graphic is writing. Headlines and explainer copy must be written with extreme efficiency because space is at a premium within the graphic. The copy must be clear and to the point. The reader should have no difficulty figuring out what the words mean or to what they refer.

Headlines for graphics do not have to follow the rules of headlines for articles; in most publications, they can simply be labels. They need to identify the central idea of the graphic, however, and this is difficult to do in just a few words. One approach that many graphics journalists use to write a headline for a graphic is to write it before the graphic is constructed. Doing that gives them the central idea to keep in mind while producing the graphic.

Explainer copy in a chart is often the most word-efficient copy in journalism. Every word must add to the information that the reader receives. Words that state the obvious are wasted. Words that fail to clarify or enlighten simply take up valuable space. Graphics journalists must understand the use of words, and they must have the facility to write and rewrite until their copy fits into the allotted space.

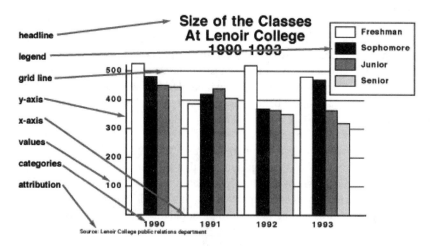

FIGURE 8.2   Elements of a Chart. Most publications and web sites have set styles for how their charts look. Each may require something different. This illustration shows some of the basic elements of a bar chart.

THREE TYPES OF CHARTS

Most mass media web sites and publications use three types of chart-based graphics: bar charts, line charts, and pie charts (see Figure 8.3). Other types of charts are used to present numerical information (for example, scattergraphs), but these are not common in the mass media. Each type of chart is best used for presenting certain types of information and is inappropriate for other types of information. Editors need to understand what charts are appropriate for what types of information.

Bar Charts

The bar chart is the most popular type of chart because it is easy to set up and it can be used in many ways. The bar chart uses thick lines or rectangles to present its

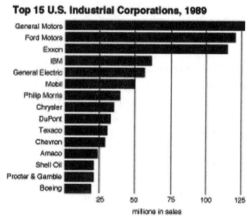

FIGURE 8.3   Types of Charts. Journalism uses three basic types of charts to represent numbers or numerical data: bar charts, line charts, and pie charts. Each has a specific use and can show only certain types of data.

information. These rectangles represent the amounts or values in the data presented in the chart. (There are technically two types of bar charts. One carries the name "bar chart" and refers to charts in which the bars run horizontally. "Column chart" refers to a bar chart in which the bars run vertically. Column charts are more commonly used when time is an element in the data. For the purposes of this text, however, we will not make a distinction between bar and column charts.)

The two major lines in a bar chart are the horizontal axis, known as the x-axis, and the vertical axis, known as the y-axis (see Figure 8.2). Both should have clearly defined starting points so that the information in the chart is not distorted, particularly the axis that represents the amounts in the graph.

The bar chart is popular with many editors and graphic journalists because it is relatively easy to construct. Like all graphics, however, it must contain precise information, something that is not always easy to come by. For instance, drawing a bar chart representing the different classes (freshmen, sophomores, juniors, and seniors) of students at a university might seem to be a simple matter. A graphics journalist would have to define a student precisely (part-time, full-time, night, occasional, probationary, etc.). Then he or she would have to find out who has that information—not always an easy task.

Once the information is obtained, however, and the chart is drawn, a bar chart can help readers understand the information. The reader can draw inferences that may not have been part of the thinking of the journalist who created the chart. Bar charts can show not only relationships but also change, and thus add still another dimension to the reader's understanding.

Another reason that a simple bar chart works well both in print and on the Web is that it can take up relatively little space. The bars representing the data can be almost any size as long as they are corrected in relationship to each other.

Line Charts

Whereas the bar chart may show change over time, the line chart must show change over time. It can also show a change in relationships over time. In some instances, it is preferable to the bar chart because it is cleaner and easier to decipher.

The line chart uses a line or set of lines to represent amounts or values, and the x-axis (horizontal) represents time. One of the standard conventions of the line chart is that the x-axis represents the time element and the y-axis (vertical) represents amounts or quantities of the data.

Line charts can use more than one line to show not only how one item has changed but also the relationship of changes of several items. Data points can be represented by different shapes for each item. The danger with multiple line charts is that too many lines can be confusing to the reader. Graphics journalists should avoid putting more than three lines in a line chart.

A variation on the line chart is the area chart. This type of chart is good for showing how the division of something changes over time. Area charts fill in an area of the graph with a color or design so that the reader can see how the amount fluctuates.

Pie Charts

The pie chart is another popular means of showing data, but its use is specialized. A pie chart shows how an entity or item is divided, and the divisions—or slices of the pie—are most commonly expressed in percentages that add up to 100 percent. Figures also may be used to identify the parts of a pie chart, but it is important that the creator of a pie chart keep the concept of percentages in mind.

Despite the strict limits on the kinds of data that can be shown in a pie chart, this type of chart can be used in a variety of ways. A pie chart can show only one set of data at a time, but several charts can be used together to help compare sets of data, as in the set of pie charts in Figure 8.3 that depict the racial breakdown of populations in three major cities.

Some graphics journalists have found some unusual ways to use the pie chart form. Readers will occasionally see shapes that are not circles but that are divided up like pie charts. This technique can be artful and attention-getting, but care must be taken that the data are not distorted.

ILLUSTRATION-BASED GRAPHICS

Journalistic illustration has a long and rich history dating back to the 1700s. Many nineteenth-century American artists, such as Winslow Homer and Frederick Remington, began their careers in journalism. For much of the twentieth century, illustrators for newspapers and magazines were confined to the sports pages and to editorial cartooning. Still, both of those areas employed some top-notch artists. With the current emphasis on graphics in journalism has come a renewed interest in illustration. The Web is likely to expand that interest. Many news organizations are expanding their art staffs and looking for people who can combine artistic skills with a sense of news and information. They are also looking for people who are adept at using the computer.

As the name implies, illustration-based graphics use illustration rather than type or charts to form the basis of the graphic. An illustration may be hand-drawn or generated by a computer; or it may be hand-drawn and then enhanced by a computer.

Publications use illustrations for two purposes: to draw attention to a story and to make a point about the story. Usually, illustrations do not duplicate photographs. They go beyond the photograph in helping the editors emphasize something about the story or in some way adding to the reader's understanding of the information in an article.

Drawings can illustrate things or events that cannot be photographed. One of the most common uses of drawings in this way is for courtroom pictures. Many courtrooms still do not allow the use of video or still cameras, but most will let illustrators do drawings of the participants.

Drawings may also be used to help explain why things happen. For instance, if a bridge collapses, a photograph can record the aftermath and effects of the event. A drawing can present the structure of the bridge and emphasize the points where the collapse occurred. Both photographs and drawings can help readers understand the event.

One point should be emphasized about good newspaper illustration and especially drawings: they take time to produce; and generally, the better the drawing, the more time it takes. Computers can speed the process, but a good illustration still takes the time of a talented person.

MAPS

One of the most common and useful graphic devices in today's mass media is the map. Maps are quick and easy to read. They provide readers with important information that can be used to help explain events and put them in physical context. In addition, they help to educate a public that many have tagged as geographically illiterate.

Certain conventions should be followed in using maps. First and foremost, a map should always be proportional to the geographic area that it represents; that is, it should be "to scale." Let's say that a country is 2,000 miles long from north to south and 1,000 miles long from east to west. The longitude (north to south) to latitude (east to west) scale is 2 to 1. Any map that represents that area should have the north–south line twice the distance of the east–west line.*

Another important convention of maps is that the northern part of the area represented is always at the top of the map. This northern orientation dates from ancient times and is one of the assumptions that most people make when they look at a map.

A third convention of maps is that they include a distance scale, usually somewhere close to the bottom of the map. Not every map needs a distance scale, because sometimes such a scale is irrelevant. On maps whose area is likely to be unfamiliar to the reader, distance scales are extremely helpful. A distance scale usually consists of two parts: a line that is marked off to indicate units of a distance on the map; and text that tells what the scale is, such as "1 inch = 5 miles."

Many maps on web sites or in print appear with insets—smaller maps that show a larger area that includes the area shown in the map. For instance, a map of Great Britain might include an inset of Western Europe to show where or how large Great Britain is in relation to other countries.

Maps can serve three different purposes: as symbols, as locators, and to display data.

Symbols

The shapes of many states and countries are well known and are excellent graphic devices. They are particularly useful when an article is divided up as a series of reports on different states or countries (or, on a more local level, counties). Although such use does not require that these maps have a distance scale, they should follow the conventions of being proportionally scaled and having the north at the top.

---

*In reality, of course, even a proportional representation is flawed because of the curvature of the earth. For most maps, we have come to accept this shortcoming of two-dimensionality.

Location

Using maps to indicate the location of events is what we think of as the most common and logical use of maps. Here, all of the conventions of map usage should be followed.

Locator maps may be enhanced by a number of devices. Cities, towns, and other locations can be identified. The map may also include buildings or other sites that will help the reader get the point of the map. Hills, valleys, mountains, rivers, forests, and other topographical factors can be included on a map with drawings or shadings. (See Figure 8.4.)

Maps can serve as backgrounds for other information that journalists want to convey to their readers. For instance, to give readers a better sense of a story about a trip by the Pope, the story might include a map with text and arrows pointing to the different locations the Pope will visit and the dates on his schedule.

Location maps do not always have to be of areas that we think of as geographic locations. For instance, the floor plan of a house or other building can be treated as a map if it helps readers understand something about the story. In the general sense, maps are a way of looking down on something and seeing it as a whole rather than seeing part of it from the limits of ground level. Such a bird's-eye view can be both revealing and insightful.

Data

In 1854, central London experienced an outbreak of cholera. In searching for a way to arrest the spread of the sickness, John Snow, a local physician, took a map of the area where the deaths occurred and plotted with dots the residences of everyone who

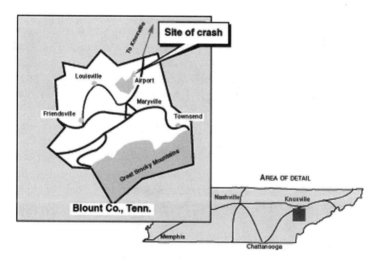

FIGURE 8.4   Locator Maps. A locator map tells readers where events have happened. A standard practice is for a locator map to have an inset or an area of detail.

had died of cholera. He also marked the location of the public water pumps in the area. His map indicated that many of the deaths were clustered around the Broad Street water pump. Upon discovering this, he had the handle of the pump removed and thus ended the cholera that had claimed more than five hundred lives in that area.

Snow used what we refer to as a data map as a life-saving device. A data map places numerical data on geographic locations in a way that will produce relevant information about the data (see Figure 8.5). Data maps can aid our understanding of the data and the areas in which it occurs. Data maps also allow readers to view large amounts of information at a single sighting in an orderly and logical way.

Data maps take time and effort to produce, and they should be created with great care. Data maps that are not carefully thought out can allow viewers to reach superficial or incorrect conclusions. Creators of data maps should be particularly careful that the data they have are, in fact, related to geographic location rather than being distributed randomly.

Maps have become a highly popular graphic device on web sites not only because they carry valuable information cargo, but also because they can be made to be "clickable." That is, links can be embedded into the image file of a map that corresponds to the geographic areas within the map. A reader can click on a part of a map to find more information about that particular geographic area.

Speaking English Some 22 states and many municipalities have declared English as the official language and have limited the use of other languages by the government.

When it happened

FIGURE 8.5   **Data Maps.** A data map combines numerical information with geography, as in this example of states that have passed laws making English the official language of the state. The largest concentration of those states is in the southeastern United States. In this graphic, a timeline is included to increase readers' understanding of the issue.

DEVELOPING INFOGRAPHICS

Large newspapers have multiperson graphics departments devoted full-time to producing infographics, particularly for breaking news. The *Chicago Tribune,* for instance, maintains a staff of graphics coordinators (or reporters) who work on information that will go into a news graphic and a set of artists who will design and execute the graphic.

What these coordinators find is that graphics reporting differs in some significant ways from news reporting. Graphics reporting demands that the journalist focus on a part of the story and find specific, detailed information that a person writing a news story might not need. For instance, a news reporter might be able to quote a source saying that the number of independently owned drug stores had decreased during the last ten years. A graphics reporter, if he or she were going to create a chart showing that, would have to have precise figures for each year of the period.

On the other hand, a news reporter would be concerned with quoting people and getting the quotations exactly right so they could be included in a story. A graphics reporter might talk to many sources of information, but he or she rarely worries about quoting those people.

One skill that a graphics reporter must develop is writing succinctly. Most infographics have an extremely limited amount of space for text, and a graphics reporter must learn to use words with exceptional efficiency. Such honing of language is hard work and takes time. Often it is done with a looming deadline, so the person who becomes a graphics reporter must have confidence in their use of the language.

A graphics reporter also deals in a specialized kind of information, and knowing the nature of this information is important for editors to understand how infographics should be developed. When a news story needs an infographic, graphics reporters and editors tend to think in terms of numbers, location, history and context, and process.

Numbers

Do numbers need to be shown in connection with this story? Will showing the numbers add to the reader's understanding? A newswriter who must handle a substantial amount of numbers in a story will find that an infographic could be a great solution.

Location

Are readers likely to know where a story is taking place? Even if they do, could a map show information more efficiently than a text description? Should the graphic be a simple locator, or does it need to be married to some other information? Is a data map called for—does the geography relate to the numbers? Can the information in a story be divided geographically so that the map can be used to link to that information?

History and Context

How did the events of the story get to this point? Is there a history the reader needs to know about? Chronologies and timelines, as we mentioned earlier, are good ways of showing the events of a person's life or the history of an issue. Another form that this history and context takes is the fact or profile box. Can we add to the reader's understanding of an organization or person that would not be included in a story?

A news organization that has covered an event that has more than a day of history will want to establish links to previous stories and information. Journalists should also be thinking back in order to give their stories continuity and context.

Process

Should we show the reader how something works? Sometimes we can do that with text or text married to pictures. Process items offer good opportunities for animated graphics on a web site if the staff has the skill to create them.

Is there a step-by-step procedure that shows how something happened? Somewhat akin to a timeline, a procedural chart can show how an event occurred. Again, such an item offers an opportunity for a reader-engaging animation.

Most of the print media graphics that we have been discussing in this chapter are easily transferable to a web site. The process involves making them into image files and loading them onto a web site. As simple as this process is, and as much time and effort as newspapers spend in developing graphics for their print editions, it is surprising and puzzling that relatively few newspapers put their charts and graphs on their web sites. The *Chicago Tribune,* historically a leader in graphics journalism and in development of news web sites, rarely places any of its news graphics on its web site. Just why this is the case is not clear, especially when some news web sites do transfer their graphics.

What this has meant for the development of graphics on the Web is clear, however. Graphics journalism, still relatively underdeveloped in print, has only just begun on the web. News organizations have not devoted the creative energy needed to realize its full potential on the Web. Few editors have considered the range of possibilities that the web offers to graphics journalism, and graphics journalists themselves have not had the influence to exert themselves on web sites.

Consequently, much of the rest of this chapter contains examples and discussions of some of the few good instances of graphics journalism on the Web, and much speculation about the possibilities.

GRAPHICS ON THE WEB

The qualities of the Web that we have discussed throughout this book—immediacy, capacity, permanence, flexibility, and interactivity—present many possibilities for graphics journalism. The examples below point to some of those possibilities.

■ Amadou Diallo, a 22-year-old street vendor from Guinea in West Africa, was killed in a hail of bullets on February 4, 1999, just outside his building in the Soundview section of the Bronx, New York. The forty-one bullets, nineteen of which hit Diallo, came from the guns of four New York City police officers. This incident and its aftermath, including a trial of the officers, provoked much interest and response to charges of police brutality in the city.

A month after the shooting, the *New York Times,* in a graphic remarkable for its time, showed the block of houses where Diallo died and placed on the sidewalk in front of the houses all of the shell casings found at the scene. It color-coded the casings to indicate which had come from the guns of the individual police officers. Below the drawing were pictures of each of the officers, and viewers were invited to roll their cursors over each picture. When that happened, windows of information about what each officer did at the scene appeared on the graphic.

The graphic placed the viewer at the scene as no textual information could have done. It also allowed the viewer to control the information presented. The graphic used rollover buttons (buttons that change and cause some action to occur in the graphic when the mouse rolls over them). Rollovers are an accepted and almost ancient technique today, but at the time they were just being developed.

■ A visitor to the Major League Baseball web site (www.mlb.com) can get continuous live updates of every game as it is played. These updates revolve around two static images: one of a baseball diamond, which shows what players are on base, and another of a batter standing at home plate. After each picture, a ball shows up on the second image, indicating where the ball crossed home plate. Text below the image tells whether it was a strike or a ball. When the ball is put into play, an indicator on the diamond shows where the ball went and what happened. Surrounding all of this is information about the pitcher, the batter, the teams, and what has happened in the game to that point.

The National Football League has a similar service during its season. That web site (www.nfl.com) uses a football gridiron to indicate which team has the ball and where the play is located on the field. The screen is updated with each play and with text explaining what happened. Similarly, the NASCAR web site (www.nascar.com) updates its site on a lap-by-lap basis during a race. A graphic shows the position of each driver at each lap.

■ The terrorist attacks of September 11, 2001, spawned many interesting and informative web graphics that went beyond their print counterparts (which were themselves very good). These graphics showed, among other things, the flight paths of the four airliners and the structural reasons for the collapse of the World Trade Center towers. They combined drawings, sound, and pictures to give viewers an understanding of the events and an experience they could not find elsewhere. (A number of web sites have lists and links to many of these graphics, including www.cyberjournalist.com.)

■ Court TV has an interactive survey on its web site called the 13th Juror. This section contains continuous web poll questions (www.courttv.com) about the trials that it is broadcasting and commenting upon. The results of the answers to these questions are then broadcast during the commentary, adding the dimension of viewer reaction to the coverage of the trial.

Many other examples could be cited, although, as pointed out earlier, the development of web graphics is not widespread through the news media. What we have in the examples above are ways in which graphics journalists are using the qualities of the Web (capacity, flexibility, immediacy, interactivity, and permanence) to present interesting and enlightening information to readers.

The Web's capacity is one of its most obvious qualities, and this quality can lift graphics journalism far beyond the narrow confines of print. Earlier in this chapter we discussed the small strictures of space that graphics journalism has for text in many graphics, and how efficient the journalist has to be in using those words. On the Web there is no such limit. A graphic itself may offer limited real estate for text, but the use of rollover buttons and pop-up windows greatly expands the journalist's ability to present information with words.

At the beginning of this chapter we referred to graphics journalism as narrow and deep. The Web's capacity allows graphics journalism to tell stories that are both broad and deep. It ushers in the possibility that a graphic can extend one of its most prominent print qualities—nonlinearity. In print, the entry point for a graphic is usually the largest image in the graphic. Visually, the graphic is often built around that image, and readers can choose the route they want to move through the information. A graphic may have a numbered sequence of items or some other way of indicating some order to its parts, but the reader does not have to follow that sequence because the graphic is spread out as a single unit with all of its parts showing.

A web graphic can extend this quality of nonlinearity in two directions—either back toward linearity or forward toward even more nonlinearity. For instance, a journalist can set up a web graphic with a set of items or windows that a reader must follow; that is, the reader may have only a PREVIOUS or NEXT choice when reading through the items. That setup enforces a linear scheme to the information.

On the other hand, a graphic can be created that is completely nonlinear. A reader can start at any point. Clicking on a part of the graphic takes the reader to another item, where there may be a variety of choices; selecting one of these choices may provide additional information and yet another set of choices; and so on.

The journalist's key concept in handling the Web's quality of capacity is layering. Information is conceptualized and then presented in layers. The journalist should have an organizational scheme in mind that includes all of the categories and layers of information, but this scheme does not have to be sequenced.

Think back to September 11, 2001. Four different airplanes traveling to different locations were hijacked at different times of the morning. For each airplane, there was a different set of circumstances, a different sequence, and a different but tragic ending. Trying to put those four stories together into a single chronological narrative would be senseless, confusing, and nearly impossible.

However, they were all part of the same overall story of a terrible day in U.S. history. That story, and many others that journalists deal with, must be told in a nonlinear fashion. A graphic presentation on the Web gives journalists the tools to do this—tools that journalists have never had before.

The concept of layers, discussed in other parts of this book, is important to graphics journalism because of another of the Web's qualities: flexibility. Because the Web can handle a variety of presentation forms, graphics journalists can take advantage of these forms to present information about their subjects. Images, text, and photographs are the bricks and mortar with which print graphics have traditionally been built. On the Web, the journalist has the ability to use sound, video, and animation (which we will discuss later in this chapter) to lead the reader into a deeper understanding of the information. The reader can experience a subject or event, not just see or read about it. A reader may hear a description of an animated graphic as he or she is watching it. Part of that graphic can morph into a photograph that can then become the beginning of a video sequence. Or text, rather than audio, can scroll beside the animation. Many combinations can be used by the skillful and creative journalist.

That skill and creativity, however, must be grounded in solid journalistic values (accuracy, context, attribution, etc.). The journalist must also be able to think about the items of information and means of delivery as layers in an overall plan for telling the story. The journalist must also possess a "feel" for the information and how it will affect the reader. That is, a journalist might create a graphic that skillfully includes all of the forms of information presentation we have mentioned. The graphic could be a complete failure, however, because the journalist did not understand where there were too many items, choices, and stimuli for the reader; when the pace of the information was too slow or too fast; when the graphic crossed over from being informative and entertaining to being gimmicky; when the information itself went beyond the understanding and interest of the audience.

In other words, having the tools does not mean they must be used, any more than a carpenter must use every tool in the workshop to build a chair.

On the other hand, having the tools does mean that the graphics journalist must learn how to use the tools and when they can provide a means of presentation that will expand the story and lead the reader to a deeper and more satisfactory level of understanding about it.

THE IMMEDIACY OF GRAPHICS JOURNALISM

The Web's ability to deliver immediate information is evident in the examples cited at the beginning of this section. Sports contests are favorite television fare, yet not every college and professional game is carried on television, and relatively few are available to any one individual. And television itself is not always a convenient medium for the viewer to follow a sports contest. (Even the most liberal employers rarely allow television sets in the workplace.) A reader can follow a sports contest on the Web, however, while doing other things and without it being intrusive to those close by. For example, a viewer can watch a pitch-by-pitch account of a baseball with Major League Baseball's Gameday graphics. (See Figure 8.6.)

Beyond sports, however, breaking news offers web journalists a fertile field to plow in developing the tools of their trade. Many important stories have visual components and explanatory needs that go beyond the ability of the television camera to present. Take an earthquake, for instance. An earthquake might last from five to sixty seconds, usually no longer. The aftereffects, including aftershocks, often last much longer.

Assuming that a news organization in the area is able to operate after the quake has occurred, the organization can put a map of the area on its web site within minutes

FIGURE 8.6   Major League Baseball Illustration Graphic. When a last-minute announcement was made in the summer of 2002 that Major League Baseball players and owners had avoided a baseball strike, MLB.com was ready with two illustration graphics that played on famous historical phrases.

of the event. Because an earthquake is a geographic event, the map can become the tablet for providing information about the quake as that information is gathered by the news staff. The map could be clickable—that is, sections of the map could be made into links to other information. Thus, the map could show where the earthquake was centered, what damage was done to buildings and roads, and which hospitals are receiving those injured by the quake. As more information comes in, the map could be subdivided into halves or quadrants, so that a user could click on a section of the original map and find out more about a particular area. Headlines for stories could be listed beside or below the map as more information is compiled. Eventually, there may be pictures that the news organization wants to show, and thumbnails of those could be superimposed onto the map.

The news of an earthquake of this type is a nonlinear event, and its coverage should be nonlinear. The graphic, in this case a map, gives the news organization a means to present breaking information with a central organizing mechanism.

Such a scenario for news coverage requires some planning on the part of the news organization (an intelligent thing to do for a news organization in an earthquake-prone area), and it calls upon the best skills of the organization's graphics journalists.

If we continue with the earthquake example one step further, we find another of the major characteristics of the Web coming into play. That characteristic is interactivity. On the Web, graphics can be not only viewed, they can be manipulated and sequenced by the user. Readers can choose what parts of the story they are interested in and in what order they want their information. In fact, they must go through this process, and their hands-on efforts put them in control of their experience with the story.

Finally, our earthquake story can demonstrate both the permanence and the organic nature of the Web. None of the information that goes onto the map or the web site during the earthquake story need be lost or deleted. Some information may indeed by replaced by later or more detailed information, but it can all remain on the site in some form. Unlike graphics in the print media, however, the web graphic can grow and change as new information is added. It has no deadline and no publication terminus. As long as information comes into the organization, the map can be changed and updated.

The practice of updating, or "write-thrus," for breaking news stories is a standard practice for wire services. The procedure can be a difficult and awkward one because of the linear form that a news story must take. Graphics do not have that problem. They can be established, updated, and added to, but their basic form does not have to be changed.

ANIMATION

The next logical step for web journalists working with graphics is to develop animation techniques. Animation, for our purposes, can be defined as item movement within the web (or HTML) context; that excludes linking to another URL on the low end and video at the high end. Animation can be movement created by scripts, such as rollover buttons and pop-ups. Animation can also be created in its more traditional form, a series of pictures projected at a speed that makes the items in those pictures appear to move.

Movement for its own sake is worse than useless. It is distracting and offputting to the viewer. It's a fairly simple matter to make an animated GIF image—one that flutters, shuffles, or explodes. That kind of movement will certainly attract the attention of the reader, but it will definitely distract from the text and other items around it.

Animation in a news context should expand and explain the information being presented by the graphics journalist. As we noted earlier, the terrorist attacks of September 11, 2001, spurred web journalists to produce some of the most striking and helpful animations to explain the events of the day. In particular, MSNBC put together a set of animations that traced the flight paths of the four airplanes, put viewers on the ground in lower Manhattan with the planes crashed into the World Trade Center towers, showed and explained how the towers collapsed, and described the aftermath of the collapse (www.msnbc.com/news/aaattacks_front.asp). (See Figure 8.7.) The presentation used still pictures, video, audio, and drawings for each of these explanations. It required many hours and many people to produce. MSNBC's multimedia webcast was typical of what a few news organizations attempted in covering that story, and it gives viewers a good idea of how animation can be used in a news context.

The use of animation has also become more popular with the presentation of photo galleries. Typically, these galleries take viewers from picture to picture using fadeouts or some other transitional technique. They may also include an audio to describe the pictures or the story that accompanies them.

The most consistent exploration of animation in journalism to date, however, has come not from graphics journalists or photojournalists but from cartoonists. A

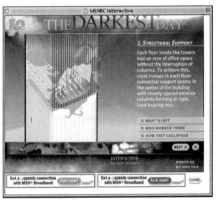

FIGURE 8.7   Animation. Animation is becoming increasingly sophisticated, as exemplified by this MSNBC series of shots of the animation that explains how the World Trade Center towers collapsed during the September 11 attacks.

number of editorial cartoonists, such as Mark Fiore, Pat Oliphant, Bill Mitchell, and others, have developed cartoon sequences and presentations that take their messages beyond the static black-and-white drawings of print. Fiore left his position as editorial cartoonist for the *San Jose Mercury* and set up his own site, where he develops two animated presentations by himself each week. These animations last thirty to forty-five seconds and include from ten to thirty-five drawings each and some audio and sound effects. Fiore's work is picked up regularly by web sites such as Salon and Slate, among others. Fiore is one of a growing number of artists working in journalism who are finding out how effective the Web can be in delivering their messages.

CONCLUSION

Graphics journalism on the Web has many roads to travel, and as of this writing, the journey is just beginning. Graphics journalism requires what all journalism requires—an abiding curiosity, a need to tell and explain to others, and a penchant for accuracy. Beyond that, it calls for skills and a level of creativity that journalism heretofore has not been able to utilize.

COOL IDEAS

Floating in Words

Do you like words—their meanings, their uses, their connections.

If so, you can cast off into a sea of words, courtesy of PlumbDesign.com, which has developed the Visual Thesaurus (www.plumbdesign.com/thesaurus/index.html). There you will find words floating in simulated three-dimensional space, visually connected to words with which they share some meanings.

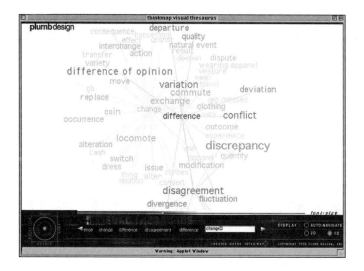

Type in a word and you create a new universe, with that word in the center and related words surrounding it. Click on one of the words you see, and that word floats forward, while the original word recedes. New words related to the one you clicked on appear.

The technology is based on the WordNet database, a publicly available resource developed by the Cognitive Science Laboratory at Princeton University, which contains over 50,000 words and 40,000 phrases. It uses something called Thinkmap, a data-animation program built by Plumb Design.

It's not a speed-demon thesaurus that helps you find the right word quickly. Instead, it can be a relaxing way to make creative associations with words.

DISCUSSION AND ACTIVITIES

1. Find a map of your campus, preferably one on the school's web site. Discuss how useful the map would be if it were included with each local story in your campus newspaper or on its news web site.

2. Discuss the latest major news story on your campus. This chapter lists a number of possibilities for graphics when a news story occurs (see the section "Developing Infographics"). Think in terms of print only: what are the infographics possibilities for this story? Now think in terms of the Web: how do the infographic possibilities increase?

SELECTED BIBLIOGRAPHY

Lasica, J. D. "Let's Get Animated." *Online Journalism Review,* May 14, 2002. www.ojr.org/ojr/lasica/p102140153.php.
Stovall, James Glen. *Infographics: A Journalist's Guide.* Boston: Allyn & Bacon, 1997.

WEB SITES

MSNBC, CNN, *The New York Times, USA Today*
    The best news graphics work is being done by the major news web sites, which often produce highly sophisticated interactive presentations on almost a daily basis.

Society for News Design (www.snd.org)
    The Society for News Design is the chief professional organization for designers and graphics journalists. This group pays attention to the Web as a medium and actively promotes its use.

Cartoons
    A growing number of web sites contain news and political cartoons, often in animated versions. See Slate (www.slate.com), Ucomics (www.ucomics.com), which contains a variety of comics both political and nonpolitical, and Mark Fiore's work on sfgate.com (www.sfgate.com/columnists/fiore).

CHAPTER 9

AUDIO AND VIDEO
SOUND AND LITTLE FURY

MAJOR THEMES

- The Web accepts audio and video in the form in which they are produced for news organizations in the traditional media; it distributes them in the same way—at least in ways that are familiar to the consumer.

- Because the Web was designed initially for distribution of text and images, audio and video on the Web has had to overcome significant technical difficulties in its development.

- Changes wrought by the Web in the use of audio and video as tools of the journalist will be as profound as the changes it is bringing to the print media.

Ask any teenager or college-age student. There is no shortage of sound on the Internet. For some years now, young people have been downloading sounds and exchanging music so pervasively that they have built a language, a protocol, and even a moral code around that activity. The Web's ability to do this exchange is altering the producer–distributor–consumer balance in the multibillion-dollar music industry.

Video is another story—so far. Futurists have envisioned a time when movies, documentaries, or even how-to productions could be downloaded to an individual computer. Videotape would be a thing of the past, as relevant to this future world as buggy whips were to the twentieth century. This video revolution has not occurred yet, but as broadband expands and compression technology becomes more sophisticated, the day when this vision will become reality is not far off.

But all that is entertainment. What about news? Just as the Web accepts text and pictures in the form in which they are produced for the print media, the Web can also handle audio and video in approximately the way they are produced for their media. That is, a text article written for a newspaper can look essentially like that on the Web; an audio story can sound like an audio story on the Web; and a video story can look like a video story on the Web.

Is broadcast journalism, then, facing the same new frontier of change that seems to be confronting print? References have been made earlier in this book to the fact that audio and video are migrating into the hands of nonbroadcast journalists, just as photojournalism is slipping into the hands of nonphotographers. This chapter takes a deeper look at two aspects of this area of journalism. One is the use of audio and video as tools of web journalism. How well do they adapt to the Web? What does the Web do to change them as journalistic tools?

The second aspect is quite different. How does the Web change broadcast news entities? Much of this book has been devoted to the changes that the Web may bring to print journalism, but what happens to broadcast news when it is translated to the Web?

The answers to those questions are occurring daily. A number of major broadcast organizations have devoted huge resources to developing a web presence. Cable News Network, NBC News, National Public Radio, and the Voice of America are just a few that have embraced the Web as an extension of their news distribution. These and others, however, have taken a variety of approaches that, as yet, defy categorization.

THE WEB AND BROADCAST NEWS

The qualities of the Web that have been discussed in other chapters of this book—permanence, interactivity, capacity, flexibility, and immediacy—are certainly present as broadcast news migrates to the Web. Each of these qualities of the medium has the power to reshape the information that broadcast journalists gather and in some cases to change the essential nature of the presentation of that information.

One of the most obvious changes that the Web brings to broadcast news has to do with the Web's quality of permanence and availability. Broadcasting, from the point of view of the consumer, is an extremely linear and ephemeral means of receiving information. Our radios and televisions do not allow us to rewind to the beginning of a news story as it is being presented. A story is presented at a certain time, from beginning to end, and if a consumer is not there to catch it, the story is gone. Only in the last couple of generations has the technology been available to record information easily from the broadcast media. Even then, recording has been up to the consumer. A person has not been able to turn on a radio or television, tune in a station, and tell that station what he or she wants to hear or see.

The Web changes that. It has the potential to transform broadcast news from scheduled presentation to on-demand presentation. On the Web, consumers have the ability to call up stories they missed and to recall stories they want to see again. This change may not have immediate or profound effects on broadcast journalism, but it will imbue it with an air of permanence that it has never had. One of the bases of comparison that print journalists have traditionally used against broadcast news is that it lacks a permanent form that is easily available. The Web gives broadcasting this air of permanence.

More immediately, however, the Web's quality of permanence means that broadcast news no longer has to conform to a structure of linear presentation. Traditional broadcast news has considered story packages as entities, usually measured in the amounts of time they require from beginning to end. The thirty-second dramatic-unity structure (discussed below) is as much a part of broadcasting as the inverted-pyramid structure is to daily journalism. The Web means that broadcasters not only can lengthen their stories but can also consider developing the separate parts of a traditional story package. For instance, a five-minute interview might be reduced to a fifteen-second sound bite for a story package for a broadcast news program. On the Web, the entire interview can be made available to the viewer. Documents that can only be described in a broadcast story can be placed into a web story package and viewed or read by the viewer. Information on a source that might be reduced to a single title line in a broadcast story can be part of a larger story package on the Web. In other words, the same kind of lateral thinking about a story that we discussed in Chapter 2 for print journalists can take place for broadcast journalists.

Another of the Web's characteristics that is likely to change broadcast news profoundly is its interactivity. In traditional broadcasting, audience choice—beyond either watching or not watching (or listening and not listening)—is an alien concept. The advent of remote control (unknown before the 1980s) made it easier for people to switch channels, but the audience could do nothing except select channels.

Not so on the Web. This new media allows users to choose not just programs but segments within programs. As noted above, broadcasting is taken out of its linear confines, and news stories, newscasts, and other programs may be broken into pieces for the audience to select as if they were in a cafeteria. News shows such as the television magazine shows (*20/20, Dateline NBC,* etc.) that depend on sequencing and teasing to hold an audience until the end will no longer be able to do that on the Web. A viewer who wants to go to the end of the story first may do so.

In addition, audiences will be able to respond directly to audio and video stories, and their responses have the potential to change the culture of broadcast news. Broadcasting is the part of journalism that is the most distant from its audience. It is also the medium with the most immediate impact. Distance and impact have produced a culture of arrogance that has many broadcasters operating as if they had no accountability. Broadcast journalists on the Web will be more within reach of their audiences and more accountable to them.

Capacity is another Web quality that will have a great impact on broadcast news on the Web. Every broadcast channel, from a network television system to a local radio station, is limited to twenty-four hours of broadcasting a day. The Web removes that limit. Producers are not confined to a few minutes within a local newscast. They can explore a story as deeply and as thoroughly as they wish, and they can cover as many stories as staff time and energy permit.

As with interactivity, this removal of broadcast limits is also likely to have a profound effect on the broadcast culture. The lack of time is deeply embedded in the minds of broadcasters and has become the major excuse for broadcasting shallowness and lack of substance. It even borders on being an excuse for inaccuracy when broadcasters claim that they do not have time to tell a complete story with full explanations of its nuances. On the Web, no such excuses exist. Broadcasters can have all the time and all they space they need to show and explain a story fully.

The Web, as we have discussed throughout other parts of this book, is flexible enough to handle a variety of forms, not just text, video, and audio. Broadcasters must consider using nontraditional means of telling their news stories. Like print journalists, they have document texts, links, still pictures, graphics, maps, and other forms of information at their disposal. And like print journalists, many broadcasters have never considered using these forms.

Finally, we should consider the immediacy of the Web. Immediacy is the strength of broadcasting. Any major news event will spark a rush to television sets to see the latest news. Broadcasters and discerning viewers, however, realize often they are not seeing the whole story on their screen. The pictures and the voice-overs are finite in their ability to deliver information, and because of the ephemeral nature of the medium, much information needs to be repeated.

Information can be placed on a web site almost as quickly as it can appear live on a television screen. But that information is not ephemeral. It is not lost as over-the-air broadcasting is. On the Web the information remains there until it is replaced by additional or updated information. Visitors to a web site do not "miss" a story, as they might if they were watching television. They can review earlier parts of the story or select the part of the story that is most relevant or interesting to them.

Television is likely to continue to be the immediate, high-impact medium of our age. But whereas television could once dominate a breaking news story for several hours (until a special edition of a newspaper could be published), it will now have to share real-time coverage of an event with the Web. Television is no longer the only source of news that people can turn to when they want the latest on a breaking news event.

REPORTING AND WRITING FOR BROADCAST

No matter what the medium, reporting and writing remain the most salient activities of journalism. Preparing a broadcast story for the Web requires the same skills that traditional broadcasting demands. Broadcast also have to meet some special requirements in their reporting and writing that go beyond those discussed earlier (Chapters 4 and 5) in this book.

Broadcast reporters have to deal with all of the same kinds of stories as print reporters, but because of the qualities of the broadcast media they try to find audio or visual elements to emphasize. Broadcast journalists are rarely satisfied with simply telling a story. They want to have something beyond their own words, such as interviews or visual elements. They are more likely to cover stories when they can get people to talk for a recorder or on camera and when there are sounds or pictures that will help them take advantage of the ability of radio and television to present such information.

The fact that the traditional broadcast media do not show much text (radio, of course, "shows" nothing) does not mean that writing is unimportant, however. Writing is an essential element to any type of audio or video reporting, and the demands of writing for these media are stringent. Web journalism that uses audio and video is also based on good writing—writing that exhibits the essential qualities of all media writing: accuracy, clarity, precision, and efficiency.

The first commitment of the broadcast journalist is to accuracy. Everything a broadcast journalist does must contribute to the telling of an accurate story. Even though the broadcast journalist must observe some strict rules about how stories are written, these rules should contribute to, not prevent, an accurate account of an event.

One of the most admirable characteristics of good broadcast writing is its clarity. Good broadcast writers employ clear, precise language that contains no ambiguity. Clarity is an absolute requirement for broadcast writing. The Web may allow listeners and viewers to go back and re-hear a news broadcast, but the writing of a broadcast story should assure that they do not need to do that. Viewers and listeners should understand what is said the first time. Broadcast writers achieve clarity by using simple sentences and familiar words, by avoiding the use of pronouns and repeating proper nouns if necessary, and by keeping the subject close to the verb in their sentences. Most of all, they achieve clarity by knowing and understanding their subject thoroughly.

Another important characteristic of writing for broadcast is its conversational style. Even the clearest, simplest newspaper style tends to sound stilted when it is read aloud. Broadcast writing must sound more conversational because people read it aloud. Broadcast news should be written for the ear, not the eye. The writer should keep in mind that someone will be saying the words, and others will be listening to them.

This casual or conversational style, however, does not give the writer freedom to break the rules of grammar, to use slang or off-color phrasing, or to use language that might be offensive to listeners. As with all writing, the broadcast writer should try to focus attention on the content of the writing and not on the writing itself. Nor is casual-sounding prose particularly easy to produce. It takes a finely honed ear for the language and a conciseness that we do not normally apply to writing.

Another characteristic of writing for broadcast is the emphasis on the immediate. While past-tense verbs are preferred in the print media, broadcasters use the present tense as much as possible. A newspaper or web text story might begin something like this:

> A scholar in Middle Eastern studies has written a book that concludes peace between Israelis and Palestinians is closer than many people believe.

A broadcast news story might begin with this:

> A Middle Eastern scholar says peace in that region may be at hand.

Another way of emphasizing the immediate is to omit the time element in the news story and assume that everything has happened close to the time of the broadcast. In the example above, the broadcast version has no time element, since it will probably be heard on the day the scholar made that statement. Elimination of the time element is not possible in every story. Sometimes the time element is important and must be mentioned.

The tight phrasing that characterizes broadcast writing is one of its chief assets and one of the most difficult qualities for a beginning writer to achieve. Because time is so short, the broadcaster cannot waste words. The broadcaster must work constantly to simplify and condense. There are a number of techniques for achieving this conciseness. One technique is to eliminate all but the most necessary adjectives and adverbs.

■ ■ ■ ■ ■

SIDEBAR

BROADCAST WRITING STYLE

The style and customs of broadcast writing differ from those of print. Although the Associated Press Stylebook is still consulted for many usage questions, broadcast writing has some conventions of its own. Following are some of those conventions.

■ Titles usually come before names. Just as in print stories, most people mentioned in broadcast stories need to be identified. In broadcast news writing, however, titles almost always precede a name. Consequently, while a print story might say, "James Baker, former secretary of state," the broadcast journalist would say, "former Secretary of State James Baker."

■ Avoid abbreviations, even on second reference. Only the most commonly known abbreviations, such as FBI and UN, should be used in broadcast writing.

■ Avoid direct quotations if possible. Broadcast writers prefer paraphrasing to direct quotations. Direct quotations are hard to handle in broadcast copy because signaling the listener that the statement is a direct quotation is difficult.

■ Sometimes a direct quotation is essential and should be used. When that is the case, the writer needs to tip the listener to the fact that a direct quotation is being used. The use of the phrase "quote . . . unquote" is awkward and should be avoided. Instead, use phrases such as "in the words of the speaker," "in his own words," "used these words," and "as she put it."

■ Attribution should come before a quotation, not after it.

■ Use as little punctuation as possible, but enough to help the newscaster read the copy.

■ Numbers and statistics should be rounded. A text journalist wants to use an exact figure, but a broadcast journalist is usually satisfied with a more general figure. Consequently, $4,101,696 in print becomes "more than four million dollars" in broadcast copy.

■ Avoid extended description. "President and Chief Executive Officer of International Widgets John Smith said today . . . " should become "International Widgets President John Smith says . . . "

■ Avoid using symbols when you write. The dollar sign should never be used. Nor should the percent sign be used. Spell these words out so there will be no mistake on the part of the news reader.

■ Use phonetic spelling for unfamiliar and hard-to-pronounce names and words. Again, you are trying to be helpful to the newscaster. Writing "California Governor George Duekmejian (Dook-MAY-gen) said today he will propose . . . " helps the newscaster get over a difficult name. Notice that the syllable which is emphasized in pronunciation is written in capital letters. Difficult place names also need phonetic spellings. "A car bomb exploded in downtown Caracas (ka-RAH-kus) today. . . ."

■ Avoid pronouns, and when you have to use them, make sure the referents are clear to the listener. Putting too many pronouns in a story can be an obstacle to the kind of clarity a broadcaster must achieve.

■ Avoid apposition. An appositive is a word or phrase that renames a noun. In "Tom Smith, mayor of Midville, said today . . . ," the phrase "mayor of Midville" is an appositional phrase. These phrases are deadly in broadcast writing. They slow the newscaster down and confuse the listener.

■ Use the present tense when it is appropriate. Using the present tense ("the President says" rather than "the President said") is one way broadcast writers have of bringing immediacy to their writing. Care should be taken, however, that using the present tense does not make the broadcaster sound foolish. For instance, if the President made a statement yesterday, a broadcast news story probably should not have the attribution in the present tense. The past tense is more appropriate. The present tense should be used for action that is very recent or that is continuing.

Broadcasters know that their stories are built on nouns and verbs, the strongest words in the language. They avoid using the passive voice. Instead they rely on strong, active verbs that allow the listener to form a picture of the story.

Another technique of broadcast writing is to use short, simple sentences. Broadcasters do not need the variety of length and types of sentences that print journalists need to make their copy interesting. Broadcasters can more readily fire information at their readers like bullets in short, simple sentences.

STORY STRUCTURE

The most common structure for broadcast news is called dramatic unity. This structure has three parts: climax, cause, and effect. The climax of the story gives the listener the point of the story in about the same way the lead of a print news story does: it tells the listener what happened. The cause portion of the story tells why it happened: the circumstances surrounding the event. The effect portion of the story gives the listener the context of the story and possibly some insight into what the story means. The following examples show how dramatic unity works (note, too, some difference in style rules from print).

CLIMAX
Taxpayers in the state will be paying an average of $15 more in income taxes next year.

CAUSE
The state senate defeated several delaying amendments this afternoon and passed the governor's controversial revenue-raising bill by a 15-to-14 vote. The bill had been the subject of intense debate for more than a week.

EFFECT
The bill now goes to the governor for his signature. Estimates are that the measure will raise about $40 million in new revenue for the state next year. Elementary and secondary

education will get most of that money. Passage of the bill is a major victory for the governor and his education program.

CLIMAX
Many children in the city school system will begin their classes at least a half-hour later next year.

CAUSE
The City School Board last night voted to rearrange the school bus schedule for next year as a cost-cutting measure.

EFFECT
The new schedule will require most elementary school children to begin school one half-hour later than they do now. Most high school students will begin one half-hour earlier.

Traditionally, broadcast journalists think of their stories as completed circles rather than linear inverted pyramids. Whereas the pyramid may be cut without losing the essential facts, the broadcast story, if written in this unified fashion, cannot be cut from the bottom or anywhere else. It stands as a unit. Broadcast journalists and their editors are not concerned with cutting stories after they have been written to make them fit into a news broadcast. Rather, stories are written to fit into an amount of time designated by the editor or news director. For instance, an editor may allot twenty-five seconds for a story. The writer will know this and will write a story that can be read in twenty-five seconds. If the story is longer than it should be, the editor will ask that it be rewritten.

BROADCASTING FORMATS

Broadcast reporters have a variety of formats from which to choose in putting together their stories. These formats work well on the Web because each, except the minidocumentary, runs for less than a minute. This brevity is currently important for webcasts, because video and audio files tend to be large and take some time to download to individual computers. Following is a brief description of each of the major broadcasting formats.

■ *Written copy/voicers.* This format is a story without actualities or sound bites.

■ *Sound bite or actuality.* When possible and appropriate, a broadcast reporter will include some sort of sound effects from the event that is covered. This actuality may be someone speaking or it may be some other identifiable sound, such as gunshots or crowd noise, that will give the listeners an added dimension to the story. News anchors introduce the sound bite with the copy they read.

■ *Wraparound.* A news anchor briefly introduces a story and the reporter. The reporter then tells the story and includes a sound bite. The sound bite is followed by the reporter giving a conclusion or "tag line."

■ *Minidocumentary.* The minidocumentary format allows a story to run for more than a minute, and some may run for as long as fifteen minutes. The minidocumentary may include several sound bites with a variety of sources or sounds, such as interviews, noise from events, or even music. A reporter will weave in and out of the minidocumentary, guiding it along for the listener. A news anchor usually introduces a minidocumentary with a short lead-in that sets up what the listener is about to hear. This format is most commonly used on public radio news broadcasts.

Broadcast stories that include video can use any of the following formats.

■ *Reader copy.* This format is a story read by an anchor or reporter without visual or audio aid. It may have a slide or graphic in the background.

■ *Voice-overs.* A videotape of an event is shown with the sound of the event turned down. An anchor or reporter speaks over the tape to talk about what the viewer is seeing.

■ *Voice-over to sound bite.* An anchor or reporter speaks over a videotape that includes someone talking. The news copy is timed so that when the reporter stops, the sound on the tape is turned up and the person on the tape is heard speaking.

■ *Package stories.* An anchor, using what is called a "lead-in," introduces a story and the reporter. The prerecorded piece then includes a mix of video, sound bites, voice-overs, and a "stand-up" from the reporter, who explains some element of the story or summarizes the entire story. These packages may run for as long as two-and-a-half minutes.

The flexibility of the Web allows it to handle all of these formats, and the web journalist who chooses to use audio and video elements in reporting has a variety of ways in which to present a story. In earlier parts of this book, we have discussed ways in which audio and video can add to the presentation techniques of journalists who think of text as the basic element of a story—that is, print journalists.

Here, we look for a moment at the other side of that combination: broadcast journalists who report for the web. These journalists have a variety of tools not heretofore available to them.

The main tool, of course, is text. The first and most obvious use of text is that the broadcast journalist can make the script of a story available to the visitors to a web site so that they can read as well as see and hear. The journalist can go much farther than that, of course, by providing on the site the many parts of a story that can only be presented in text forms—documents, background, previous stories, and information from many other sources.

On the Web, the broadcast journalist has many additional tools for presenting a story besides text. They include graphics, pictures, and links, all of which have been discussed at length in other parts of this book.

In addition to these tools, the Web allows the broadcast journalist to think in different ways about how stories are presented. The journalist is no longer confined to the strictures of thirty-second stories and the dramatic-unity structure. A five-minute video interview with an interesting and articulate source, for example, does not have to be edited to a ten-second sound bite. Web site readers might want more than ten seconds, but do readers want the whole five minutes?

In this instance, the Web allows the journalist to divide the interview into segments so that visitors can choose the parts they want to see. Each segment may have a heading and short description to make these choices easy for the web site reader, and this introduces an element of interactivity that broadcast journalism has never known.

This example is just one of many in which the Web can have a profound effect on the broadcast journalist. The flexibility and nonlinearity of the Web gives the broadcast journalist many options in telling a story. These qualities allow an expansion of information and forms of presentation for a story, and they are ways that journalists can use to give greater context to a story. But they also demand skills that broadcast journalists have never had to use before—skills not only in working with the equipment or means of presentation, but in the conceptualizing of the story itself.

BROADCAST NEWS WEB SITES

Ideally, broadcasts will use the Web in tandem with their broadcasting facilities to relate more complete stories. Many broadcasts have begun the practice of putting an abbreviated story on the air and then encouraging viewers and listeners to visit their web site to find more detailed information. National Public Radio (NPR) has been particularly adept at this, often telling listeners at the end of their broadcast stories exactly what they will find on the web site. For instance, news reporters refer to documents that listeners can read or pictures they can view. In addition, the NPR site has an audio of the original broadcast report that allows listeners to listen again or to catch portions of the broadcast they may have missed.

In June 2002, two television stations in Maine, WPXT-TV and WPME-TV, went several steps beyond even this, by shutting down their broadcast news operations but maintaining the web site (www.OurMaine.com). This was an extreme step that is not likely to portend a trend in the industry, but it was an interesting decision on the part of Pegasus Broadcasting. "Our goal is to provide streaming audio/video reports around the clock, of local and select national and international news stories as quickly as technologically possible," the web site says. "The resources of the WPXT-TV/WPME-TV news operation will be used to gather, edit, and present local news." In addition to giving the news, the web site promotes the other programming of the station.

Just what should a broadcasting news organization put on its web site? Obvious choices are the audio and video the station has gathered and edited and the text of news stories that reporters have written. But broadcasters have found that getting their reporting onto their sites is not as simple as that. Newspapers and magazines have a relatively easy time of this, since they are already dealing with text and pictures. Many broadcasters are still using videotape cameras, and the tape must be digitized and sometimes re-edited before it can be placed on the site.

Broadcasters are also finding that their scripts are not as easily translatable as they had imagined. First, some (and sometimes a lot) of what viewers hear on the air is never written down. Reporters live at a scene usually read from notes or speak extemporaneously rather than use a word-for-word script. Consequently, the web site producers have little or no text to work with.

SIDEBAR

ON-THE-AIR TO ONLINE

The immediacy of the Web presents an aggressive television news team with a problem: How do you cover breaking news? How does the Web fit in with cameras, producers, video editing, and reporters?

Rob Kauder faced that problem directly when he joined KREM-TV in Spokane, Washington, as Internet news producer in 1999. Would the station's web site be just an add-on, or would it be a vital part of the ongoing coverage of events? Kauder reports that the station's news director provided the first answer by placing his desk in the middle of the newsroom.

"She made that decision early on in my tenure as content producer so that I would be aware of developing stories—and the management team's on-air coverage plans," he says.

Next he wrote a plan for covering breaking events, which included the following steps:

- As information comes in on a story, work with the assignments editor to confirm the story.
- Once the information has been confirmed, write a short story based on the information, making sure it's what the on-air people will be using if they cut into the regular programming.
- At the end of the story, alert readers that more information will be coming—both on the Web and on-air;
- Have a "breaking news" graphic ready to use with the story.
- Continue to update as information is available.
- When pictures from the scene are available—either stills or video—place those on the site as quickly as possible.
- If streaming is available, make sure the video encoder is live and that there is a link on the home page of the site so viewers can watch what is happening.
- Cross-promote—that is, have on-air reporters advise viewers to visit the station's web site for more information, and on the site, give the times for scheduled newscasts and other information that will get viewers to tune in to the station.

Source: Rob Kauder, "Web Workout." *RTNDA Communicator,* April 2002; the web address for KREM-TV is www.krem.com.

And when broadcasting copy is written, it is deliberately written for the ear, not for the eye. What sounds right when it is spoken may not seem as right when the words are read silently. Some broadcasting entities, such as CNN when that operation decided to invest heavily in its web site, realized that their transcripts would need considerable rewriting to be acceptable as web copy. The reporters and editors at CNN—as well as those at many other broadcast outlets—adopted a structure closer to the inverted pyramid of newspapers than the dramatic-unity form of broadcast-style writing. Some broadcasters even adjusted their on-air broadcasting style so that what they said on the air could more easily become part of the web site.

Yet another factor that prevents broadcasters from simply rolling their broadcast material onto a web site is the nature of immediacy that accompanies many broadcast reports. Much of what is heard and seen on the air, even in scheduled news broadcasts, is produced and edited for the moment of the broadcast itself. Many reports are not meant to have a shelf life. That is, they are quickly out of date, often because they are about events that are in progress. When those events are concluded, a story that says they are still occurring is not what the news organization will want on its site. Consequently, conscientious broadcasters have found that they have to update their stories— rewriting and sometimes re-reporting them so that they retain their currency on the site.

In addition, those who are serious about their sites soon realize that they may need to reformat the sound and video so that visitors can see more and have more choices about what they see. For instance, a five-minute interview can be broken into shorter segments, and an introduction can be written for each of these segments. Or, a chronology, or timeline, for the interview can be written, showing when the interviewee talks about certain subjects. Again, the viewer can go directly to the part of the interview that he or she is interested in.

Adding to these difficulties, the Web creates yet another dilemma for broadcast news operations. Most are not seeking to use their web sites to report the news; rather, they are seeking to extend their brands and expand their audiences for their over-the-air newscasts. Consequently, they do not feel that it is to their advantage to break their stories on their web sites before they can get them on the air. Let's say that a broadcast journalist puts together an important story by 2 p.m. No one else in the market has the story. If the station puts that story on its web site before the evening newscast, a competing station could work on the same story and get something on the air by the same time as the first station.

Yet many broadcast news operations feel the need to maintain active news web sites. Some do this half-heartedly, by using what is known in the professional as "wire dumps." That is, they simply run the Associated Press news wire on the site and load local stories when it is convenient. Others simply load stories and video as they can, after they have appeared on a news broadcast. A few, however, have fully committed themselves to developing a web site that enhances their news output and extends their brands to audiences beyond their broadcast ranges. These sites are working through the conflicts about the immediacy of their news. They realize that although people watch, they also read, and a broadcast and web site can be an excellent combination for a news organization.

WEBCASTING AND VIDEO ON DEMAND

Just as the Web has allowed broadcasting stations to become newspapers with their use of text, still pictures, and graphics, the Web is also letting newspapers become broadcasting stations. Webcasting is one of the many revolutionary aspects of the Web. With a relatively small investment in equipment and training, a newspaper can show live events on its web site: a city council meeting, a Labor Day parade, a high school football game, or a police–hostage standoff. The site can surround the live video with

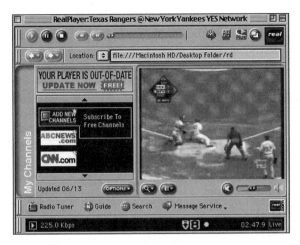

FIGURE 9.1 Baseball Webcast. Major League Baseball, like a number of other sports, is webcasting some of its games that are not available to viewers on television. These webcasts, available on a pay-per-view basis, provide the site with additional revenue.

all of the other informational elements that it has available—text, still photos, graphics, and links—to make the webcast a more comprehensive experience for the web site visitor. (See Figure 9.1.)

CONCLUSION

Audio and video have yet to become essential to a news web operation. They carry technical baggage that make their use on a web site more difficult than words and pictures. They also require training that few print journalists yet have. Still, they are valuable reporting tools that are likely to proliferate on the Web as technology improves, journalists become more versatile, and audiences become more demanding.

COOL IDEAS

Blogging with Sound

Elsewhere in this book we have discussed weblogs—the means by which a single person can set up a web site, express thoughts, and share information with an interested group of readers and possibly participants.

Weblogs are made up of text, but what if sound were added? What if the person "writing" the weblog could speak and the audience could hear? Then you would have an audioblog.

A few audioblogs have come on line as this is being written, and the numbers will undoubtedly grow. (See Radio Blogging News, http://radio.weblogs.com/0100368, and Radcliffe Blog, www.ratcliffe.com/blog.html, as examples.)

So, is an audiolog just a weblog with sound? Proponents say no. Sound has a special quality that can add immediacy and emotion to words that text can never achieve. The experience of sound is different from the experience of text, or of video for that matter.

Anyone who prefers to listen to a sports event on radio, rather than watch it on television, knows this. Sound fires the imagination and creates pictures in the brain that are far wider and richer than a television camera can provide.

DISCUSSION AND ACTIVITIES

1. Is the Web superfluous to broadcasting? That is, does the Web have nothing to add to what broadcasters do?

2. How can the Web and broadcasting work together to complement rather than just repeat each other?

3. Explore the technical reasons why there is not more live video streaming on web sites, particularly those sites that have broadcasting units.

SELECTED BIBLIOGRAPHY

Author unknown. "The Basics: Webcasting and Streaming." Apple.com (no date, downloaded September 12, 2002). www.apple.com/creative/stories/webcasting/index2.html.
De Sonne, Marcia. "Web Portals, Web Streaming, Convergence." National Association of Broadcasters (no date). www.nab.org.
Kauder, Rob. "Web Workout." *RTNDA Communicator,* April 2002; the address from KREM-TV is www.krem.com.
Papper, Bob. "New Staffs Pitch in, Do Double Duty on Web Site." *RTNDA Communicator,* June 2002.
Papper, Robert A. *Broadcast News Writing Stylebook.* Boston: Allyn & Bacon, 1994.
Stone, Martha. "Breaking Stories and Breaking Even." *Online Journalism Review,* February 1, 2002. www.ojr.org/ojr/workplace/p1015015509.php.
Stovall, James Glen. *Writing for the Mass Media* (5th ed.). Boston: Allyn & Bacon, 2002.

WEB SITES

National Association of Broadcasters (www.nab.org)
  The National Association of Broadcasters is a "full-service trade association which represents the interests of free, over-the-air radio and television broadcasters," according to its web site.

Radio and Television News Directors Association (www.rtnda.org)
  The Radio-Television News Directors Association is "the world's largest professional organization devoted exclusively to electronic journalism," according to its web site. "RTNDA represents local and network news executives in broadcasting, cable and other electronic media in more than 30 countries." The web site itself is lively, informative, and highly interactive.

National Public Radio (www.npr.org)
  The site is built to supplement the news broadcasts of National Public Radio. The site contains audio of many of the stories in its newscasts, plus additional information, pictures, and links. This site is one of the best examples of the Web and traditional media working to complement each other.

CHAPTER 10

DESIGN ON THE WEB

MAJOR THEMES

- Web site design is an important and often contentious issue in the development of the Web.
- The general principles of design for publication have been transformed to the Web and are undergoing some adjustment for that medium.
- The organization and design of a web site are inextricably tied to one another.
- Web design, like print design, must follow and support the content of the site, and the design of a site must accommodate a variety of forms of information.

Web site design provokes strong feelings on the part of many webites. Thousands of hours of argument have occurred about loading time, horizontal versus vertical scrolling, top versus left navigation, the appearance and location of links, and many other techniques and issues. This chapter will settle none of those arguments. Rather, this chapter will bring into focus some of the many design decisions that people who work with news web sites must consider. It will examine some of the commonly accepted design practices of news web sites in the early part of this century—with acknowledgment that much of what we see is likely to change as our understanding of the Web as a medium grows more sophisticated.

Many design principles have migrated from print to the Web, and they seem to be serving their purposes well. These principles are being refined to accommodate the needs of web site developers and the technical possibilities of the Web. However, the Web is fundamentally different from print as a medium, particularly with regard to its nonlinearity. The Web produces color and handles images far more easily than does print. It allows images and text to move. It gives users some choices about what they see. These and other characteristics of the Web present creative designers with many options to exercise, and many of those people are hard at work every day trying to figure out what can and should be done on the Web.

The options are so vast, in fact, that design can become *the* issue in web site development, rather than just *an* issue. As with print, the content of a web site is more important than its design. But content cannot exist without design, so editors of web sites must find the proper means for handling both.

At the end of all of these discussions, of course, is the purpose of the web site and its relationship to its audience. A news web site must deliver information to its audience. It does not exist to show how clever (or stupid) its designers are. A good design should present the content of a site to the audience in an efficient, pleasing, and sometimes entertaining way, and in a way that reflects the principles and values of the site itself.

SEPTEMBER 11 AND BEYOND

The attacks on the World Trade Center and other targets on September 11, 2001, drove a record amount of traffic onto news web sites. People were hungry for information, and in the first hours after the attacks, many sites could not accept all of the hits that were being attempted. On some of the major news sites, visitors had only a 5 percent chance of loading the site onto their screens.

To ease this burden, a number of sites took down all of their pictures, graphics, and advertising. Other sites, such as Yahoo.com, revamped their home pages to show nothing but news of the attacks and their aftermath. All of these sites had spent thousands of hours and dollars creating a look suitable to their purposes, but in that moment of crisis, they became text-only or text-dominant because that was the easiest and fastest way to deliver information to their audience. As pictures, video, and sound became available, these items began to appear on the sites, but the design remained barebones for many hours.

Web editors learned a number of important lessons from those hours of crisis. One of the most important lessons was how flexible the Web can be in responding to extraordinary situations. Another was how dynamic design should be in accommodating content and audiences. Yet another was how hungry people are in their needs for both information and for communication. (Emailing and instant messaging volume soared on that day.) Those and many other lessons will be studied for a long time to come.

DESIGN AND LAYOUT

Design is a visual process in which content is the chief factor. Design is a way of presenting a reader with information and a way of communicating to the reader something about that information. The visual is a highly important way of communicating—in fact, it is the oldest. Images predate text by many centuries.

All of us understand to some extent how important appearance is. Most people spend time grooming themselves and selecting what they wear because they know that their appearance sends a message to others about who they are. Web sites and publications are the same. They communicate to their readers what they are and what they are about by their appearance.

Unlike our basic appearance, however, web sites are not made by nature. They are the result of conscious decisions that designers and editors make. Everything on a web site or a newspaper page or a magazine layout is the product of a decision that someone has made. In publication design, nothing happens by itself.

Students learning design must understand this fact. They control everything that goes on their page. They may be following certain rules, edicts, or traditions when they put together a site or publication, but physically, there is nothing about design that they cannot change. They must then understand why design for certain types of publications is done in certain ways.

Students must also become observant about design. Our educational systems do a woeful job teaching us about design and visual logic. We spend many hours learning to write and learning to do math, but we spend practically no time at all leaning why things look the way they do. Consequently, most of us grow up completely unaware of design principles. We tend to believe that "things are the way they are" or that "they look the way they look," without any understanding of why this is so.

The following sections are meant to give students some tools to be a good observer of design as well as to teach some of the principles of information presentation. A student should look at a web site or a publication from now on and ask why the editor chose to make it look that way; why did he or she put articles in certain places, use a specific style of type, or connect elements in particular ways.

Asking these questions will help students sharpen their visual sense and will make them more aware of what can be done with a publication. People who develop their skills to the point that they can control the look of a publication often come to enjoy knowing they can create something that readers pay attention to and that has an impact on their publication. So all students interested in news, whether or not they are headed into the design field, should be aware of design and layout and should give it their critical and analytical attention.

Design refers to the overall appearance of a web site or publication. Layout is the day-to-day use of design rules and principles. Design includes not only the way the elements are laid out on any one page but also how different sections of a publication relate to each other with body type, headline, the way pictures are cropped, the positioning of advertisements, and the types of designs and shapes used in standing heads and logos.

Editors must make many decisions in developing a design for their web sites. These decisions provide the general rules of guidelines for the layout and ultimate look and feel of the site.

VISUAL LOGIC

Why do we look at things the way we do? The answer to that question is a combination of nature and training that results in what we call visual logic. When presented with a variety of visual stimuli, the eye, directed by the brain, tends to look at certain things before focusing on others. Those directions are simple to observe (see Figure 10.1).

■ *Big to small.* We see big things first, smaller things next. In content design, as in many other parts of life, size matters. We ascribe certain characteristics to "big" and other characteristics to "small."

FIGURE 10.1 Visual Logic. Designers in all media must understand the principles of visual logic. These principles describe how the eye moves from object to object. They are vital to establishing visual organization.

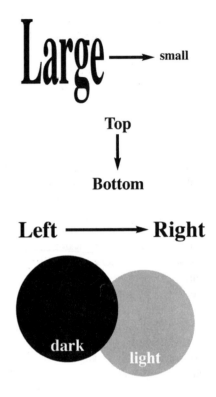

■ *Top to bottom.* For reasons that come from nature and from training, we tend to start at the top and go to the bottom. Reading material is certainly arranged in that fashion, but so are other things in life. Again, we think of the "top" as having certain characteristics, while "lower" or "bottom" has other characteristics.

■ *Left to right.* With a few exceptions, people have learned to read from left to right. This training carries over into other aspects of our lives as we encounter the world. Left-to-right is not so much a natural tendency as it is one of training, but it is so much a part of our actions that we tend to think of it as a natural reaction to the visual world.

■ *Dark to light.* We tend to look at darker (or more intensely colorful) items first and lighter (less colorful) items next. It is easier to "see" a darker item than a lighter one; our eyes have to work a bit harder on the lighter items.

These principles of visual logic are not immutable. There are exceptions certainly. But a designer adheres to these principles—wittingly or unwittingly—to send messages to the reader. Sometimes the designer can interrupt these principles to make a point.

These principles of visual logic enable designers to form hierarchies. Hierarchies are important because a reader cannot see everything on a page or a web site at once with any degree of specificity or depth of understanding. We are trained to focus on one item at a time, however briefly. Hierarchies give readers visual cues as to what items on a screen they should focus on. Hierarchies allow designers a degree of control over the sequence in which readers view the elements of a publication. Hierarchies also allow designers to attach degrees of importance to those elements.

Here's a simple demonstration. Look at the following line:

word   word   word   word   word   word   word

Chances are, you looked at the entire line and then shifted to the left. You did so because you are trained to read from left to right. Now, look at the following line:

WORD   word   word   word   word   word   word

With this line, there is no doubt that you should look to the left after viewing the entire line. Not only is there a trained tendency to do so, the reader is confirmed in that tendency when he or she sees that the leftmost word is bigger and darker than the rest. But what if the line looked like this:

word   word   word   word   **WORD**   word   word

Your tendency with this line is to forget your training to look to the left and to focus on the middle of the line, where the word is larger and darker. It would be even more so if the line looked like this:

word   word   word   word   word   word   **WORD**

Designers must always be aware of the principles of visual logic in creating hierarchies, because in doing so, they are sending important messages to the reader. If they do not have this awareness, they can easily confuse the reader. Consider, for instance, the following lists. Imagine that these are the sections on the navigation bar for a news web site.

Arts	Arts	**News**
Communities	Communities	Lifestyle
Lifestyle	Lifestyle	Sports
News	**News**	Arts
Sports	Sports	Communities

The list on the left is alphabetical, and visually, if anything, it communicates the message that the Arts section is the most important part of the site. But this is a news web site, so shouldn't the news section be the most important? The middle list makes an attempt to say that by putting News in bold type. The message is obscured, however, by the fact that it is stuck in the middle of the list. The list on the right is the visually logical list. It puts News first and in bold type. It then lists the items in a nonalphabetical order, one that conveys some message about how the editors of the site view the sections and their importance.

These demonstrations show how much can be communicated with arrangement, size, and depth (darkness) of elements. A designer must be sensitive to these principles of visual logic.

DESIGN CONCEPTS

With these principles in mind, a designer must understand some basic concepts about putting together elements on a page or on a web site. Like the principles of visual logic, these concepts are simple, and they are easy to observe—if you are looking for them.

■ *Balance.* This concept refers to putting the elements of design together so that all have the chance to be seen by the viewer. No element should be obscured. Big elements should not overwhelm small ones; dark elements should not obscure light ones. (Many web site designers like to use black or dark backgrounds, demonstrating that they are not sensitive to the concept of balance. The dark background overwhelms the type and can make it unreadable.)

■ *Contrast and focus.* Contrast is the relationship of design elements; contrast refers specifically to the difference between these elements on the screen. An element cannot be seen unless it is different from those things that surround it. That is why the concept of white space, which will be discussed below, is so important. Focus is the way a designer uses contrast to direct the eye of the reader.

■ *Economy/simplicity.* A designer can do many things with the elements on a web site. These elements can be arranged and combined in creative ways—ways that will impress other designers. The purpose of design, however, is not design itself. Design should present content. Every element used in a design should help the reader focus on the content of the publication. No element should be there to call attention to itself.

■ *Repetition/variety.* Any musician can tell you how important repetition is; any web designer should be able to tell you the same thing. Repeating elements gives strength and stability to a design. That is why designers generally choose one body type and size for their publication. Repeating that element allows the reader to focus on the content that is being presented. Good sites have specific design rules that are followed for stories, headlines, pictures, cutlines, graphics, and all of the other elements that are used.

However, the reader needs variety as well as repetition. The reader should be shown what to look at first and should be directed to certain items on the page. In musical terms, repetition is the beat of the song; variety is the melody.

Despite all of these principles and concepts, a designer has only three basic design elements with which to work: type, illustration, and white space.

THREE ELEMENTS OF DESIGN

A designer has three tools with which to work: type, illustration, and white space. Type is what is used to communicate the denotative content—that is, the words that carry the information of the site. But type also has graphic elements that can be used to send connotative messages to the reader.

Web designers should be familiar with the customs and conventions of using type, as well as various kinds of typefaces and display methods. Type is an all-important design element, and a designer must have a good sense of how type is commonly used.

The second tool of design is illustration. Illustration can be considered anything on a page other than type that uses ink; on a web site, it is anything that is not type and not negative space or background.

What we are talking about, of course, is a variety of elements: pictures, illustrations, drawings, charts, graphs, maps, symbols, icons, logos, lines, dingbats, and so on. The major purpose of these elements is to aid in delivering the content of the publication. Sometimes they are heavily content-laden themselves (such as pictures), and other times they simply play a supporting role (such as lines that separate other elements.)

Illustration can help draw the attention of the reader. It can separate elements, or it can unify them. It can give the page visual variety, or it can give the publication the repetition and consistency that we discussed earlier.

In working with illustration elements, designers should always remember that form follows function. That is, delivering the content, which is the first goal of a journalistic publication, is the primary function. The form that is created by the designer should help in achieving that goal.

White space (or negative space on web sites that use color backgrounds) is an extremely important but often ignored design tool. If it weren't for white space, we would not be able to see any of the other tools of design. Yet many people who are learning design do not recognize the importance of white space and give little or no consideration to it. They put elements too close to one another, not understanding that the eye needs "breathing room" to help it separate visuals and identify elements.

Other beginning designers sometimes do not understand that too much white space is as bad as too little. They leave gaping holes of white space on their pages, revealing that they have no idea about how elements fit together. These pages tend to look tattered and unfinished, and yet the creators cannot recognize what is wrong with them because they haven't been trained to use white space as a design element.

The key concept in using white space is proportion. There should be enough white space around an element that it can be seen. There shouldn't be so much that the white space itself becomes distracting. Larger items need more white space, smaller items less.

The idea of proportion is almost as elusive as the idea of good taste, yet a sense of proportion can be developed by careful observation and analysis. Students should look at well-designed pages and attempt to analyze what about them is good, particularly the way these pages use white space.

WEB SITE DESIGN

News web sites display a wide variety of design philosophies and approaches. These philosophies reflect views on what the news organization hopes to accomplish with its web site and how it views the audience it is attempting to cultivate. No matter the approach, however, all web sites must deal with a fundamental set of design considerations.

Readability

Viewers must be able to see and read what is on the web site. Type must be clear and precise. Pictures and images must be recognizable. Elements must be clearly differentiated from one another.

Most professionally produced web sites have few problems with any of these standards, and yet some do not view readability as of primary importance. One of the chief problems is using type that is too small to read easily. The size of type is to some extent in the hands of viewers, in that they can set their browsers to view type at smaller or larger sizes than normal. Even so, some web sites set their initial sizes so small that viewers are forced to increase the size on their browsers.

Another problem for readability on web sites—one related to type size—is that pages are too crowded. Some news web site editors believe that visitors should be given as many choices as possible as quickly as possible. Consequently, they crowd their home pages (sometimes referred to as "splash" pages) with as many words and links as possible.

Yet another problem that is found in less professionally produced sites is a background color that overwhelms the type. Black backgrounds, for some reason, are attractive to some people, but they force type into an environment that makes the type difficult to read. Professional designers understand that black type on a white background produces the greatest contrast and is thus the easiest type to read. The reverse (white type on a black background) does not produce the same contrast. Some designers try to get away from a white background by using colors with extremely soft tones or values. Even then, care should be taken that the strokes of the type are distinctive and that reading is not hindered.

Simplicity

The concept of simplicity is often undervalued in web site design. Some designers feel that animated graphics and flashy colors are necessary for a web site to gain and hold the attention of the reader. They are also seduced by the fact that it is so easy to do so many things on the Web. Sometimes the hardest thing to do in designing a web site is not to do very much at all.

The idea of simplicity keeps the designer close to the content. The designer should ask: What does it take to present the content to the reader? What does it take for the reader to see and understand the content? What hierarchies (discussed earlier in this chapter) are necessary for the design to carry its messages to the reader?

The concept of simplicity, as exemplified by the questions above, should be balanced with the natural and necessary tendency of the designer to develop a graphic personality for the site. A news web site that is simply type and pictures will probably not be very appealing to readers (although some extreme usability advocates argue that it is) and will not offer reporters and editors an interesting environment in which to display their work.

Simplicity, then, should be a controlling but not a dominant concept in web site design. Designers should have specific reasons for doing everything they do, and those reasons should have both short-term and long-term goals. In the short term, they should help enhance the readability and usability of the site. In the long term, they should assist in developing a graphic personality that will make the look of the site distinctive and project the image that the news organization wants to build.

Consistency

Hand in hand with simplicity is the concept of consistency. Some elements of design should be the same throughout the site. In most print publications, body copy has a consistent font and size throughout the publication. This standard has carried over to many news web sites. Most professional web sites maintain consistent elements such as top logos, navigation bars, and links with a consistent look throughout the site.

Consistency implies stability, which is an important concept to be associated with a news web site at several levels. A consistent design shows that the site is professional and confident in the design decisions that it has made. It also establishes a look and feel for the site that readers can count on. Once readers learn that a design will be maintained, they do not have to figure it out each time they visit the site, and they can concentrate on the content itself.

Credibility is associated with consistency, which is another reason for developing a design that readers can count on. Any news organization wants a readership that believes it will present accurate information. A consistent look helps to foster that feeling.

Consistency is not an easy thing to accomplish in a web design, however. It works at several levels. Not only should article pages look the same and have the same elements, but content—particularly links—should also be handled in the same way throughout the site. For instance, if text links are blue and underlined in one part of the site and red and bold in another, the result will be a mixed message to the reader and will be yet another vagary of the site that the reader has to deal with.

Web designers must also find ways of maintaining a consistent look while dealing with a variety of forms of information. Headlines, summaries, and stories can have a consistent graphic style, but what about video, audio, graphics, picture galleries, and the like? Each of these forms requires a different look, yet they must also maintain a visual relationship to other parts of the site. Some content itself will require variations on the consistent look of the site.

A graphics stylebook that lays out some of the basic design rules for the web site is a must for maintaining a consistent look. Not only will such a stylebook help editors understand what the style rules of the site are, it can be of great assistance when a new design challenge arises—that is, when the site wants to do something that it has not done before. A graphics stylebook can lay the groundwork for expanding the site and including new content forms.

Variety

Ralph Waldo Emerson, a nineteenth-century philosopher, wrote the much-quoted (and sometimes misquoted) line: "A foolish consistency is the hobgoblin of little minds adored by little statesmen and philosophers and divines." If all that designers had to worry about was consistency, their jobs would be relatively easy. Finding the proper balance between consistency and variety is possibly a designer's most difficult task, but the effort can save the site from becoming the hobgoblin of which Emerson wrote.

Designers should abide by a general principle: design should offer the readers consistency; content should offer variety. That is, it should be the content—packaged in a consistent design—that gives the site its flavor and uniqueness. Variety can be achieved by adding and subtracting elements such as pictures, pull quotes, graphics, and links.

Still, with the unpredictability of news, no design will be able to anticipate all of the content and situations that a news web site will encounter. Sometimes the design will have to change to fit the content, as it did on September 11, 2001 (see the beginning of this chapter).

Purpose

Why does the web site exist? What do the editors want visitors to do? These two questions should always be present in the minds of web site designers. The designs they form should advance the purposes of the site. The design should also make it easy for the visitors to do whatever the editors intend.

ORGANIZING A WEB SITE

The design of a news web site is inextricably tied to the site's organization. Newspapers have news, sports, and feature sections; television news broadcasts have news, weather, and sports sections. So, too, must news web sites have a way of organizing the content. Web site editors do this because they assume readers are unwilling to comb through everything on the web site and because they need a way of organizing their staffs efficiently so that every necessary task is performed.

Any organizational scheme must reflect the purpose of the web site, the actions that editors want visitors to take (see the previous section), and the expectations of the visitors themselves.

A good organizational scheme is one in which the divisions are clearly defined and clearly named. In the minds of most journalists and media-savvy people, the difference between "news" and "sports" is obvious and well understood. Less obvious is the difference between "leisure" and "books." No set of rubrics for the content of the sections of a news site will be completely clear and discrete; there will always be the possibility of overlap (as there is even between "news" and "sports"). News sites must assume that they can educate readers to certain expectations by having a consistent presentation of content within a section. Over time, "leisure" or "home life" will come to mean something to the reader.

All of the rubrics used in an organizational scheme should have some initial meaning that is generally common to all visitors. Terms such as "community," for instance, may indicate that the section contains news coverage of the site's surrounding communities, or it may mean "communities of interest." Editors should be extremely careful in selecting the words they use, especially if these words are developed from current technology and web practice.

Another characteristic of good organization is comparability. Sections that are alike and are of equal value should be grouped together. What's wrong with the following list?

News
Sports
Business
Classified ads
Lifestyle
Hobbies
Help wanted
Editorials

Several things. The difference between "Lifestyle" and "Hobbies" is certainly unclear. More serious is the inclusion of "Classified ads" with what are obviously news sections of the site. More confusing still is the existence of "Help wanted," which is usually a subsection of classified ads.

Figuring out an organization scheme for a news web site is neither easy nor obvious. Naming the sections can require a great deal of brainpower.

So far, what we have been discussing are the primary links of a web site. These are the links that are likely to appear on every page on the site so that readers can always go to another section or back to the main page no matter how deeply he or she gets into the site. These links usually connect to "section front" pages that contain more news stories, pictures, video, graphics, and other content having to do with just that section.

These section fronts may also contain their own set of links that show how the section itself is divided. For instance, a news section might be divided into local, regional, national, and international news. A sports section could contain secondary links to baseball, football, basketball, golf, auto racing, and the like. These are called secondary links, and they add another layer of content to the site. They lead to section fronts that have content especially related to the subject, and they may even have their own subset of links. For instance, baseball might be divided into Major League, Minor League, College, Local, and so on.

At some point, the hierarchy of the organization must end, however. Readers should not be forced to click too many times into the depths of the site before they discover the content they want. Consequently, some web sites have developed ways of showing third-level organization at the second level. Sometimes they do this with rollover buttons (rolling the mouse over a word makes a new list appear) or simply with an indented list.

All of the factors of organization have design implications for the site. First, the organizational scheme of the web site must be clearly visible to the viewer. The designer must create the visual hierarchies that correspond to the schematic hierarchies of the site. To do this, the designer must understand the organization scheme of the site thoroughly. The designer must also know the definitions that the editors have in mind when they use certain names for the sections. Often, the designer participates in the selection of those names.

The design of the links themselves should be clear and unmistakable. In fact, the links should be set apart in some kind of navigation bar or column (which we will discuss in the next section), so that they do not look like anything else on the page. Front pages, section fronts, and article pages should reflect a visual hierarchy. For instance, each of these might contain a version of the web site's flag—but the front page will have the largest version, the section fronts a smaller version, and the article page the smallest version.

Variations in the design that are made to accommodate special content should not violate the organization scheme's hierarchy. Let's pick up on the example from the previous paragraph—the size of the flag. If a special design is developed for presenting video, for example, the flag presented in this design should not be larger than the one on the front page or the section fronts.

All in all, designers must be extremely sensitive to the organization of the site and to the visual hierarchies that the site has established. They cannot venture out on their own to develop "cool" designs that have nothing to do with how the site is divided up. Such designs are likely to confuse the reader and damage the look and feel that the site is attempting to develop for the reader. Designers must make sure that readers will always know where they are and how to get to other parts of the web site.

WEB PAGES

Much of this book so far has dealt with the idea that the Web is an "unlimited" medium; that is, although there are certainly physical limits to the amount of content that can be stored on a web server, those limits are not yet in sight for most web sites.

However, the Web is limited in a very real and immediate sense by the size of computer screens and the limitations of the technology that the reader is using. These limitations mean that a reader can see only a certain amount of content at any time. This in turn confines what a designer can do. Content and design elements must be chosen with great care.

In considering these limitations, web designers have to deal with three practical factors at the very beginning of their design work.

Horizontal Scrolling

Although the standard width of a computer screen has grown during the late 1990s and early twenty-first century, it is still limited to about 10 inches. A web page can be far wider than that, but one of the almost immutable laws of web design is that readers should not be made to scroll horizontally. It is simply too hard to read copy when one has to use the scroll bar at every line. Consequently, no professionally produced web site at the time this book is written extends beyond 10 inches in width.

Vertical Scrolling

Readers find vertical scrolling to be far less trouble, and most pages on news web sites extend beyond the length of the screen itself. There is a belief among many web producers, however, that there is a fairly short length beyond which readers will not go. Web journalists have borrowed a couple of terms from newspapers to use in discussing this issue—"above the fold" and "below the fold." A full-size newspaper comes off the press folded in half. A story, picture, or other item can appear above the fold or below the fold. In journalistic webese, what can be seen without vertical scrolling is "above the fold"; anything else is below the fold. Some web editors believe that the length of a front or section page should be severely limited because readers will not scroll far below the fold. In fact, some sites are designed so that readers should not have to scroll at all.

Load Time

Load time refers to the amount of time it takes for a web page to show up on a user's computer. A number of factors contribute to load time, including the size and speed of the user's computer and the type of Internet connection the user has. Another factor is the size of the items on the page itself—particularly the size of the images.

During the first years of the Web, a feeling built up among web denizens that users were an impatient lot and would not wait for more than a few seconds for a page to appear on their computers. Consequently, one of the rules of web design was that pages should carry only a small number of images at the smallest sizes possible, so the pages would load quickly.

As the Web has matured and as people have acquired larger and faster computers, load time is no longer the ominous monster that overshadows web design. Still, it is a consideration that restrains designers from piling on large and heavy graphics and images onto a site.

THE FRONT PAGE

Front pages of news web sites have many different looks, but not as many now as there were in the late 1990s. In those days designers were trying a variety of approaches to introduce their sites to readers. One approach was to give readers as many choices as possible as soon as the page loaded. These pages would be filled with links and small type, rarely displaying any graphic features at all. Another approach was to emphasize a single story, usually with a substantial picture or graphic. Links to a couple of other stories might be included, but sometimes these pages would not even include a navigational bar for the site. Instead, there would simply be a link to the inside of the site. For a time, the *Chicago Tribune*'s front page was a headline, summary, and image related to a single story, with a couple of links to other stories; all of this was contained within a small, television-like window. The *New York Times,* seeking to simulate its print front page, made GIF images of its headlines on its front page using the same typeface that is standard in its print headlines. (Both of these approaches have since been abandoned by these web sites.)

Although no standard look has emerged, most news web sites have developed a visual design that falls in between the maximum-links and the moderate-links approaches described above. Most use a basic set of elements that are the building blocks of the design (see Figure 10.2).

FIGURE 10.2   The Front Page. This front page has most of the basic elements that you will find on most front pages of news web sites: a flag or top logo, a navigation bar, labels, headlines, summaries, pictures and cutlines, and a bottom navigation bar. This site has chosen a clean look with a limited number of links.

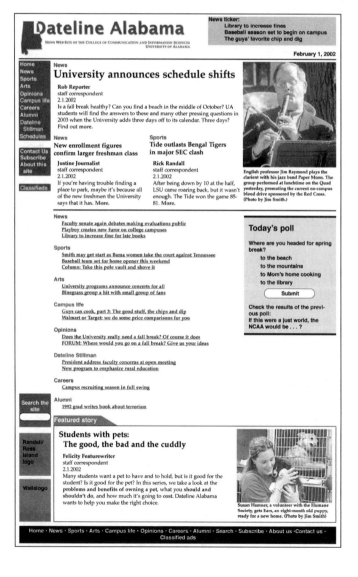

Flag

The name of the web site, contained in the flag (nameplate, top logo), is the site's most important graphic element. It is the image that is most likely to be repeated throughout the site. The flag tells people where they are and establishes the site's brand. The flag should not be so large that it overwhelms other elements on the page and takes a long time to load onto a user's computer. It does not need to contain much denotative information (web site address, phone numbers, etc.). Rather, it should be simple, direct, and clearly visible. Its size and weight should be proportional to its importance in relation to the other elements on the page.

Navigation Bar

The navigation bar, or navbar, is the second most important graphic element on the page. The bar contains the links to all of the major sections of the site. In addition, a navigation bar may also contain links to other parts of the site that are not considered major sections. For instance, most sites have a "Contact us" page that tells readers how to get in touch with the people who operate the site; many contain an "About us" page that gives the history of the site and tells something about its operation. Other common features of navbars are subscribe sections and search functions.

Placement of the navbar is a major design decision for the editors of the site. The two most common placements are what is called "top navigation" and "left navigation." Top navigation, as the name implies, puts the navigation links horizontally across the page, usually just above or below the flag. Left navigation places the navigational links in a column that runs down the left side of the page. Occasionally, a site will use a right navigational column. Some sites use both top and left navigation, with some obvious difference between the types of links that each bar contains.

Another navigational device that many sites use—no matter what they have at the top of the page—is a bottom navigation bar. This is a standard element at the bottom of every page, and it has a specialized function and structure. Most navbars at the top of a page are image-based; that is, they are a set of images that designers have created because they like the look that they produce for the entire page. Some site visitors set their browsers to prevent the downloading of images onto their computers. They are satisfied to have only the text, and such settings often reduce load time dramatically. What these viewers do not get is the image navbar. Consequently, the bottom navigation bar usually includes text only, not images, so that it will download for these users, and they will have a means of getting around the site.

Another reason for having a bottom navigation bar is for the convenience of all users. It alleviates the need to scroll back to the top of the site to find a navigation bar that will allow the user to go to a different part of the site.

Promotions

Many news web sites have a habit of promoting stories, pictures, or other items found on the inside of the site on their front pages. Sometimes, these promotional items are simply text links. Sometimes they are far more elaborate, resembling an advertisement with words and graphics. They are designed to get the reader into the site by offering something of interest. These promotions are often found under the left navigation column, but they can appear anywhere on the page.

Headlines, Summaries, and Links

All of the items described above are usually static. That is, they may not change from day to day, and they are what gives the site its "look and feel." The heart of the front page, however, is what does change: headlines, summaries, and links. Web designers have found many ways to handle these items. Some sites select the top three or four stories, put large headlines (14-, 16-, or even 18-point type) on them, and write summaries for them (see Chapter 5 on writing). A link is provided that takes the reader directly to the article page. Many sites then list in smaller type the top headlines of all of the major sections of the site. This list is updated periodically, from once a day to once every few minutes. These items are why the reader returns to the site.

Pictures, Cutlines, and Graphics

Most front pages contain at least one picture or graphic near the top of the page. These images emphasize the news content of the page and are usually accompanied by a cutline and a link. They may also be there to promote some special part of the site. As noted in the previous section, pictures slow the loading time of the page. For this reason, they are usually small, and their number is limited to one or two. See Figure 10.3, however, for a dynamic use of a large picture.

Other Items

Some news web sites contain other items that editors believe their readership will expect or appreciate. One of the most common is a weather box that gives the current temperature, conditions, and forecast. Another feature found on many sites is a web poll that gives readers the opportunity to respond to a daily question. Sometimes a site will try to provide other services, such as a list of the latest help-wanted classified ads to aid readers in finding new jobs.

SECTION FRONTS

Section front pages often mirror the look of the front page of a news web site with regard to placement of the flag (usually smaller than on the front), the navbar, and the headlines and summaries. A secondary navigational bar for the section itself (as we discussed earlier) may appear somewhere on the page, usually above or below the primary navbar. Headlines, summaries, and links are often presented in the same format in which they appear on the front page. More headlines may have summaries under them than showed on the front page, and there are likely to be more headlines. A section front will usually give readers some means of getting to the previous day's headlines.

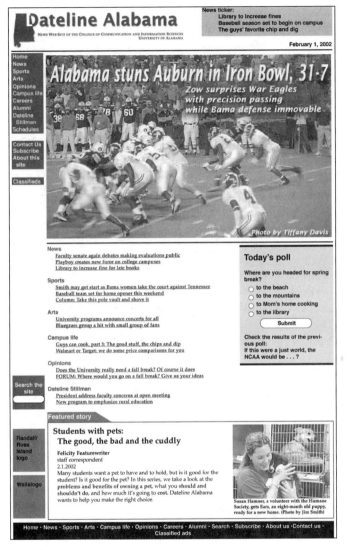

FIGURE 10.3
Alternative
Approach to the
Front Page.
A major story and
an excellent photo-
graph came together
to allow the editors
of this site to have a
picture or graphic
dominate the page.
Here the reader has
little choice but to
look at this picture
and consider click-
ing on a link to a
story, even if he or
she is not interested
in the subject.

Pictures are likely to be somewhat more plentiful than on the front page, but editors are still restrained by the specter of long loading times. Consequently, pictures
may still be relatively few in number.

A section front is a second layer of information for the reader, not only about
the site but also about particular stories on the site. Sometimes, section fronts offer
more detailed summaries about stories or other information about a particular story.
The dual purpose of this is to give the reader more information and to help the reader
decide to go more deeply into the site for even more information (see Figure 10.4).

Whereas a front page is designed for scanning and little reading, a section front
is built for both scanning and somewhat more reading. Visitors will still scan through

FIGURE 10.4   Section Front.
This section has many of the
standard features of a section front
page. The name of the section is
prominent, and while the latest
stories are emphasized with larger
headlines, a series of headline
links gives readers many choices
within the section.

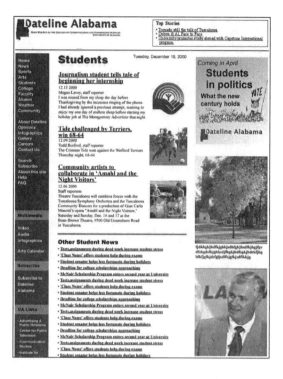

the information, but the feeling among many web professionals is that if a visitor gets
to a section front, he or she is willing to spend more time considering what information is there.

ARTICLE PAGES

The design assumption of article pages is that the reader is there to stay, at least for a
little while. Readers may, in fact, scan articles, and articles should be written and designed with this in mind. Article pages should be set up to make the scanning process
productive (see Chapter 5). Still, easing the act of scanning is not the major purpose
of the designer; these pages are meant to be read.

Article pages should mirror the general look of the site that has been established
by the front and section front pages. They are likely to contain a flag, though smaller
than the section front flag. They should also include some navigational device that will
take the reader back to a previous page, back to the section front, or forward to another
part of the site. A standard part of navigation has become a link on every part of the site
that will take the reader back to the front page (often called the "home" page).

Headlines on an article page will probably be larger than anywhere else on the
site. They are large because they need to establish a visual dominance over the body
copy, which will be the most extensive graphic element on the page. Some news web

sites include a summary under the headline. Links to related stories, pictures, graphics, or other information are grouped together close to the top of the page or at the end of the body copy. (See Figure 10.5.)

Body copy for a story is smaller than the headline, and the main criteria for selecting a font is its readability. (Editors, of course, should keep in mind that the browser a reader uses can default to a size and typeface they have not chosen, so the editors do not have complete control of this visual aspect of their site.) The type should be set on a background (preferably white) that enhances its readability, and the maximum length of a line should be from 3 to 4 inches, depending on what else is on the page.

Pictures, pull quotes, graphics, and sets of links can be inset into the body copy to give it some visual variety. Placing these items at the optimum locations in the story—that is, where they are referred to in the body copy itself—is an ideal that some

FIGURE 10.5.   Article Page. This article page has a prominent headline, summary, and picture. The look of the page is in keeping with the general visual openness of the site. The navigation bar on the left allows the reader to go back to the section front or directly to the front page.

sites strive to achieve. This placement is not always possible given the structure of HTML (HyperText Markup Language), other web construction codes, and some content management systems.

Some web sites divide longer articles into two or three pages, believing that users will appreciate the decrease in loading time for the page (see Figure 10.6). The trade-off is that at some point, the user will have to click to the next page in order to continue reading. Many people have opinions about whether this is a good practice, but no consensus about it has yet formed.

SPECIAL SECTIONS

Not everything on a news web site becomes an article, of course. Sometimes web editors must create special designs for special kinds of content. These designs should be visually different from the more standard parts of the site, but they should also contain elements that tie them back to the site itself. The most obvious and necessary of these elements is the site's flag, which (as we have noted previously) should be a part of everything on the site.

One of the most common types of special content is the picture gallery. This is a special set of pages created to display pictures that are related to one another in some way. (The pictures do not have to be about the same subject. The *Washington Post* has a standard feature called the Day in Pictures that exhibits the best pictures of the day

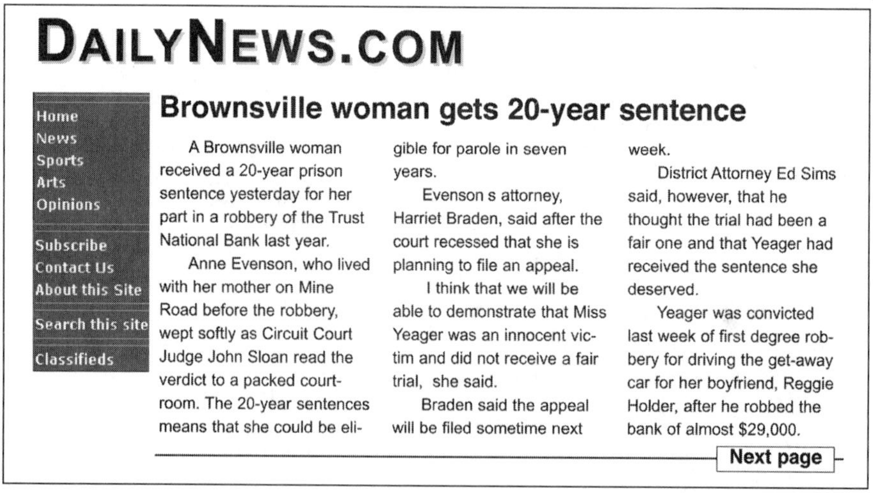

DAILYNEWS.COM

Brownsville woman gets 20-year sentence

Home
News
Sports
Arts
Opinions

Subscribe
Contact Us
About this Site

Search this site

Classifieds

A Brownsville woman received a 20-year prison sentence yesterday for her part in a robbery of the Trust National Bank last year.

Anne Evenson, who lived with her mother on Mine Road before the robbery, wept softly as Circuit Court Judge John Sloan read the verdict to a packed courtroom. The 20-year sentences means that she could be eli-

gible for parole in seven years.

Evenson s attorney, Harriet Braden, said after the court recessed that she is planning to file an appeal.

I think that we will be able to demonstrate that Miss Yeager was an innocent victim and did not receive a fair trial, she said.

Braden said the appeal will be filed sometime next

week.

District Attorney Ed Sims said, however, that he thought the trial had been a fair one and that Yeager had received the sentence she deserved.

Yeager was convicted last week of first degree robbery for driving the get-away car for her boyfriend, Reggie Holder, after he robbed the bank of almost $29,000.

Next page

FIGURE 10.6   No Scrolling. This alternative page design, pioneered by sites such as the *International Herald Tribune* (www.iht.com) does not force readers to use the vertical scroll bar. Instead, when the story is longer than a page full of type, the reader can click at the lower right corner and continue with the story.

from both their own photographers and the Associated Press and other news services to which the newspaper subscribes.)

Picture galleries usually appear in pop-up windows that can handle both horizontal and vertical pictures. These windows—and the pictures themselves—should not exceed the side of the screen; readers should not have to scroll to see the whole picture. The chief concern of the designer, however, is navigation within the gallery. This is usually accomplished by simple NEXT and PREVIOUS buttons, but sometimes more elaborate devices are built. One of the most popular is to set up thumbnails of all of the pictures in the gallery and make them links to the pages that contain those pictures.

Editors may want to group a series of stories or a special section of information into a single package that readers can use as a starting point. These special sections can be as simple or elaborate as the time the news organization decides to invest in creating them. Often, a special section page will differ little from a standard section front page, but occasionally it will be radically different, with large images and a different navigation scheme than is found in other parts of the site.

CONCLUSION

The age of web design has passed infancy but is probably still in the toddling stages. As indicated in this chapter, we have borrowed much from many generations of publication design, and many of those principles seem to work well on web sites. News web sites are developing a more standardized look as reader expectations have been developed.

Nothing is settled yet, however. Many creative people are being drawn to web journalism, and they have little training in or reverence for the customs and conventions of print or broadcast design. Their creativity, combined with advances in technology for web development and delivery, make it easy to predict that one day soon web sites, and particularly news web sites, will have a very different look and feel to them.

DISCUSSION AND ACTIVITIES

1. In the section of this chapter on "Visual Logic," a set of three lists of navigation bar categories is shown, and the third list is said to be the most visually logical. What is being communicated to the reader by this list?

2. This chapter describes and shows several approaches to front page design. Which do you prefer? Why?

3. Find a news web site that has many links (Alabama Live, www.al.com, is a good example) and one that has much more limited links (such as MSNBC.com). Which do you like better? Which is more effective in engaging readers? What is the logic behind the decisions the editors have made about their front pages?

SELECTED BIBLIOGRAPHY

Moses, Monica. "Why Usability Matters." Poynter.org, August 12, 2002. www.poynter.org/centerpiece/
081202_matters.htm.

Small, Jay. "What We Think We Know about Interactive Design." Originally published in 1997 by *Editor
and Publisher,* updated at the following address: http://smallinitiatives.com/modules.php?op=
modload&name=Sections&file=index&req=viewarticle&artid=11.

Small, Jay. "Ink-Stained Designers: Don't Write Off New Media." *Sensible Internet Design,* August 7,
2002. http://smallinitiatives.com/mail/archive.php?id=2&issueID=2.

Stovall, James Glen, and Edward Mullins. *The Complete Editor.* Dubuque, Iowa: Kendall/Hunt, 2000.

Williams, Margot. "A Primer for a Good Web Page." *Seattle Times,* March 29, 1998. http://archives.
seattletimes.nwsource.com.

WEB SITES

Sensible Internet Design (http://smallinitiatives.com)
   This is an excellent web site produced by a commercial web design company. The site contains a
   great deal of up-to-date information about web design and about current trends and controversies.

Adrian Holovaty weblog (www.holovaty.com)
   Holovaty is a web designer for the Atlanta (Georgia) *Journal Constitution.* Many people interested in web site design check into his log and offer their opinions. It's a good place to keep up
   with some of the latest thinking in web design.

■ ■ ■ ■ ■

CHAPTER 11

ENGAGING THE AUDIENCE

MAJOR THEMES

■ More people are spending more time online; faster computers, broadband connections at work and in the home, more information and services on the Web, and the growth of a web culture have encouraged more people to use the Web for more things.

■ What audiences expect from the Web is unclear, particularly to people involved in traditional media.

■ Journalists who seek to provide news to an audience via the Web will have to build a nontraditional relationship with the audience; the nature of that relationship is not yet well defined.

The *Seattle Post-Intelligencer,* a morning newspaper in Washington's largest city, puts out an edition called the 4 O'Clock News every day. The edition is put together usually by one editor sometime between 2 and 4 p.m. each day. It contains traffic information (Seattle has become one of the most congested cities in the United States), entertainment events scheduled for that evening, the latest sports news (Seattle is a sports-crazy place, according to the editors), an item or two about eating out, the latest news headlines, and often something just a little bizarre.

The 4 O'Clock News doesn't hit the streets, of course. It hits the web site. There's a special top logo and a design that deviates somewhat from what visitors see at other times of the day. (See Figure 11.1.)

The only reason the 4 O'Clock News exists is that there is an audience for it. The *Post-Intelligencer* web site editors looked at the daily traffic and found that there was a slight spike in page views between 4 and 5 p.m. "People were calling up our site sometime just before they left work," an editor say.

The editors then tried to figure out what these people were looking for. They decided on a mixture of "news you can use," such as traffic conditions, the ever-popular sports, a few breaking headlines, and some suggestions about what to do that evening.

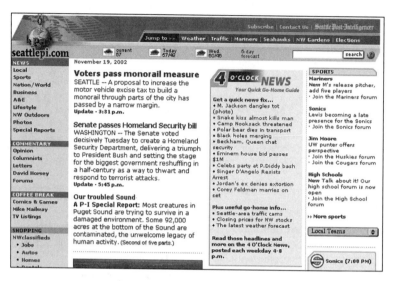

FIGURE 11.1   The 4 O'Clock News. The *Seattle Post-Intelligencer*'s 4 p.m. web edition is a response to an audience that calls the site up sometime just before they leave work. The newspaper's web site editors gather content they feel the audience would want at this time of day, such as breaking local news and traffic reports.

And the bizarre. The site features a story or picture that might not make it to the top of a regular news cycle, but as one editor said, "People really love that stuff."

The editors tried several formulas, tinkered with the design, and watched to see what happened to the page hits. Slowly, the number of hits began to increase. More tinkering led to more page hits.

The audience for the 4 O'Clock News is not huge—just a few thousand hits above the other hours of the afternoon. Yet it does exist, and it is distinct, and the newspaper devotes part of the working day of at least one staff member to serve it.

THE DEATH OF ALL MEDIA

Some commentators have speculated that the Web will mean the death of all media as we know it. Their speculations have a doomsday flavor but should not be dismissed out of hand, because they are based on questions that journalists find difficult to confront.

Why should a newspaper be delivered to someone's front door when that person can get more news and more up-to-date information by turning on a computer? Why should a person turn on a television or radio and wait for news, when that person can find out exactly what he or she wants immediately by turning on a computer?

If these things *can* occur, they *will* occur, futurists say. Furthermore, it is likely that people will become engaged with their computers rather than with the organizations that are actually delivering the information. Speed and specificity will replace quality, depth, and a community of shared information as the guiding values of the media.

In this brave new media world, information exchange—through email and personal messaging—will replace the one-to-many structure of communication of the traditional media. Audiences will be built through weblog types of web sites. Just as our current age seems to have lost its sense of propriety and civility, the Web will hasten the loss of discretion and the value of information.

This pessimistic outline ignores many of the factors that make up the media–audience relationship today, and it is easy to dismiss these speculations by saying that they can never happen. Doing so, however, should not be a license to ignore one of the most important changes that will occur with the growth of the Web: a shift in the journalist–audience relationship. That shift is occuring now. How the audience for news engages with news organizations, to what uses it puts the information it receives, and what gratifications it gains from the information are questions of immediate concern as we enter the age of the Web.

A GROWING AUDIENCE

Web audiences and Web use are growing. More people are doing more things and spending more time on the Web. By the summer of 2002, depending on how you define and calculate usage, between two-thirds and three-fourths of the population of the United States had access to the Web and used it regularly.

Just what are people doing on the Web? Many people say that the Web is helping them do their jobs. Students are finding more educational resources on the Web (although often not as much as they think is there). People are using the Web to communicate, to pursue hobbies, and to establish a voice for themselves through participation in weblogs (see Chapter 2). Some people are playing games. Others are finding relatives and ancestors.

The events and aftermath of September 11, 2001, brought many of these activities into sharp relief. According to a study by the Pew Internet and American Life Project, about half of all Web users got some news about those events from the Web, but more significantly, about three-quarters used the Web to communicate personal messages to other individuals. Thousands upon thousands of email chains—a message sent to you as part of another's email list is sent on to everyone on your email list, and so on—rattled through the Internet. These messages—concern, grief, comfort, information (sometimes even false reports), and the like—multiplied into a phenomenon of communication that the world had never seen.

The Pew report quotes e-newsletter writer David Weinberger as saying, "Now, for the first time, the nation and the world could talk with itself doing what humans do when the innocent suffer: cry, comfort, inform, and, most of all, tell the story together" (Pew Research Center, 2001).

Fortunately, of course, not every day is like September 11 and not all news events have the impact of that day's tragic occurrences. Eventually, life more or less returned to normal, and we found that the events of that September 11 did not necessarily constitute a breakthrough for the Web in terms of gaining a permanent audience for news. Nor did it mean the abandonment of the traditional media. People still use newspapers, magazines, radio, and television in much the same way they always have.

Still, the growing audience for the Web inevitably means a larger audience for news web sites. Indeed, most news organizations have reported that the number of visitors to their sites has risen. Newspapers are reaching not only out-of-circulation audiences but increasing numbers of people within their circulation area. In some cases, though not all, this increasing audience has had a positive effect on both subscriptions and single-copy sales of the paper. Some research is also beginning to show that as people spend more time on the Web, they are spending less time watching television.

Why should people look for news on a web site rather than in a newspaper or on television? In some cases, though not all, it is more convenient—and possibly the only medium that is available. This is certainly the case in many work environments, where people have a computer and Internet connection as part of their tools.

Another reason is the immediacy of the Web, particularly where television is not available. (Again, think about a work environment.) People may want to find out the latest news, not the information that was available when the newspaper was printed but what has happened in the last hour or minutes. And even where television is available, people may not be able to access specifically what they want to know on television (baseball scores, stock market prices, etc.).

Still another reason for using a news web site is the amount of information that a site can carry, although this reason has yet to prove particularly potent for the audience. A web site can certainly carry more information than a newspaper can print or a television news show can broadcast. However, this information may be difficult for an individual to access because it is poorly organized by the news organization or because it is simply inconvenient for the individual to use the Web.

THE INTERACTIVE AUDIENCE

Throughout this book, we have repeatedly referred to the interactivity quality of the Web as one of its main characteristics. The lines of communication between a journalist and the individuals in the audience are very short, and if the news organization chooses to do so, it can make the lines between the individuals in an audience much shorter than they have ever been. This characteristic has the possibility of changing much about the way journalism is traditionally practiced.

As never before, web journalists will need to concern themselves with the audience, both as individuals and as a group. For traditional media, the audience is an amorphous mass that can occasionally be individualized by a phone call, letter, or even face-to-face contact with the journalist. That contact can be limited by the journalist or the news organization in a variety of ways, and these limitations have reinforced the top-down distribution of information. Journalists, including editors and publishers, control what, when, and how information is reported. The audience has little influence on news decisions, and the expectation has been that it has little to say about these matters. The audience simply has to accept what the news organization does. There is no way to hold it or the journalists accountable.

One other characteristic about this journalist–audience relationship should be noted. It is generally limited by geography. Newspapers have circulation areas, and television stations can be picked up only within certain distances from their towers. Even national news publications and broadcast outlets are limited by geography. Newsmagazines have broken the geographic barriers to some extent, but with great trouble and at great cost.

The Web makes a new journalist–audience relationship possible and even likely. Although interactivity is nowhere near reaching its full flowering, it does not take much of a seer to understand that the audience will come to web journalism on a far more equal basis than it has ever had with traditional media. An individual has always had the power to select which stories to read or view. For traditional media, finding out what selections an individual does or does not make is a difficult and expensive thing to do. Consequently, traditional media has viewed the audience in two general categories, readers (or viewers) and nonreaders (or nonviewers). Any reading or viewing puts an individual into the reading or viewing category, even if the reader or viewer did not read or watch everything.

The Web gives a news organization much more precise information about the choices an individual reader makes. By recording page hits (not just site hits), the Web can give a publisher or editor data on how many people have looked at a story. This makes it possible to know not only how many people have landed on a particular page of the web site, but also how many people have *not* made that selection. The act of not selecting a story, previously lost in the mists of the unknowable, is now part of the data set that an editor receives, and the implications of how an editor might use such information are profound. (Will an editor assign stories about topics that he or she knows will draw large numbers of hits? Will the editor look at these data to see how large an audience a reporter is drawing for his or her stories?)

Let's say that a reader does choose to look at or read a story on a news web site. How will the journalist–audience relationship change then? If the reader chooses to do no more than read the story, there seems to be little that will be different from the relationship in traditional media. The Web provides the opportunity for a more active relationship, however. Many news web sites are providing email addresses and telephone numbers for the reporters at the end of their stories. (One collegiate web site, Dateline Alabama, with which the author is associated, lists the email address of the reporter *and* the copy editor.) Sometimes these addresses come with an active link to make it easy for readers to respond to a story. Readers may also choose to get in touch with editors as well as reporters, provided the news site lists editors' email addresses somewhere on the site.

What will reporters do when they get an email from a reader? The content of the reader's response will determine that to a great extent, of course. In general, reporters and editors should take serious responses seriously and respond in kind. The web site, by listing email address, has indicated to the reader that this audience participation— at least on this basic level—is important. Should the individuals on the site fail to follow through properly in this area, they will be doing serious damage to their ability to engage an audience.

Another simple means of inviting audience participation is the web poll. Web polls are questions with a closed-end set of answers and a means of allowing readers to select an answer that fits most closely with how they feel. Once an individual has responded, a graph shows how many people have selected each answer. (Web polls should not be mistaken for scientific surveys; they do not produce results that can be generalized to a larger audience.) Writing meaningful questions and responses is not an easy task. Questions should be posed in a way that allows for true differences of opinion, and responses should include all of the relevant responses that might be given to a question.

A news site can take the additional step of setting up a discussion forum that not only allows readers to respond to an article or topic but also allows them to see the responses of others. Readers can then take the additional step of getting in touch with other individuals who have read the article and share an interest. Should reporters and editors participate in these forums? That is a question of policy that the news organization itself must address, but there are certainly advantages to having journalists part of the active discussion on a story that the site initiated.

A reporter can answer questions or clarify impressions that readers have gained by reading a story. The reporter can also provide additional information that he or she may not have been able to include in the original article. More important, participation in public forums by journalists demonstrates a willingness to engage with the audience in a way that few reporters in traditional media get to do. However, participation in a news forum does have its downside. Participation takes time that reporters and editors may need to devote to other tasks. And reporters may reveal attitudes or biases that the news organization prefers to keep hidden.

Answering emails and participating in forums are not the only ways a journalist can engage with an audience. A particular story may offer a special opportunity for a web site to engage the audience. When President George W. Bush was preparing to deliver the State of the Union message to Congress and the nation in January 2002 and there was much speculation about what he would say, the *Christian Science Monitor* set up a gamelike section of its site titled "My Fellow Americans." In it, the editors provided information about political speeches and invited readers to write their own State of the Union messages, giving them options about various topics that the President might cover. It was an interesting exercise that told readers something about how speeches are written and about the major issues of the day.

Some journalists have realized that some stories they cover had special meaning to a significant number of people within a larger audience, and they have taken some steps to cater to that audience. For instance, in March 2002, Ken Sands, a reporter covering a local high school basketball tournament in the Spokane, Washington, area, decided to make his reporting more participatory. He first notified an email list of local basketball fans (to which the newspaper had access) that he would be covering the tournament and invited them to be sources. As he was covering the tournament with his laptop computer, he filed a series of short items throughout the day to a weblog that he had set up; these items included email messages that he had received from fans throughout the day. The response to the quirky items he posted, and the stories that he wrote, were beyond anything he had seen before in his reporting days. He received more than two hundred emails and many more personal contacts. "The blog (weblog) got so popular, and I was so recognizable by the end of the tournament, that fans and even players were approaching me to tell me stories," he said later. "I've never seen anything like it in my 21 years here."

Other reporters have made similar discoveries. People are very interested in what is happening to them and in what reporters are saying about it. Many of these people have information and ideas that do not receive proper attention or expression through normal journalistic methods. In the near future, web journalists will be looking for ways to build their audiences into communities of interested participants.

The idea of an Internet community is something of a radical departure for traditional journalistic thinking. These "communities" may be short-term and topic-oriented. They may not be confined to the geographic areas that have traditionally defined audiences for journalists. They are likely to dissipate once the issue that brought the individuals together fades. On the other hand, they may survive and thrive beyond the control or the participation of the journalist who began them. In short, we do not yet have a good idea about how Internet communities will work.

Some have taken the idea of Internet communities and extended it beyond the boundaries that even web journalism might want to venture. In an article for the *Online Journalism Review,* Dale Peskin predicts that news will evolve into a "collaborative, participatory activity," one in which anyone can be a journalist. Communication, he says, will be more important than content. As this happens,

> A new group of consumers—the Millenials—emerges. They have no loyalty to news organizations. They don't read newspapers. Their habits and behaviors have no context in traditional news products. By sheer numbers, they have the power to transform consumer markets. (Peskin, 2002)

Peskin's vision of the future of news may be giving too much credit for the ability of "participants" to become journalists and too little credit for journalists themselves to be innovative in meeting the challenges of the Web. Still, it is clear that the rules of engagement for journalists and their audiences will be different from those we have known before, and participation and interactivity are terms and concepts that will be important to the future of the profession.

AUDIENCE-ORIENTED FORMS

News web sites, as they are constituted in the early part of this century, reflect both the content and the forms of the traditional medium from which they sprang. Much of the news is text written in inverted-pyramid style. Feature stories, editorials, sports columns, photographs, book reviews, and the like appear much as they would in print. What little video is on the Web has the same look and feel as video produced for nightly television shows.

The audience, most of whom were trained in the traditional media, seems perfectly content with these forms. They may complain that text is difficult to read on a screen, but they are not demanding new forms of presentation. Yet new forms of presentation are coming (as we have discussed in other parts of this book). These forms will not develop because of audience demand; they will come through the innovations of journalists who develop an understanding of storytelling and information presentation on the Web. Journalists, by interacting with the audience, will begin to understand what audiences want and need and how the Web can help them fulfill these needs.

The Web's abilities to link and to present information in a variety of forms are the major tools that will be used in the early stages of this development. In turn, audiences will form expectations about what they will see on news web sites and how information is presented to them.

Despite the lightning speed with which the Web has developed and people have taken to it, none of the news audience-oriented forms is likely to gain dominance overnight. Journalists are trained to think linearly in their presentation styles, and they are comfortable with the inverted pyramid and other structures. It will take some time for them to reformulate their thinking, just as it will take time for audiences to get used to something new.

PERSONALIZATION: THE DAILY ME

The question is probably as old as journalism itself: Should a news organization give the audience what it wants or what it needs? Attempts to answer this question force journalism into a logical dead-end. They provoke additional questions, such as: If a news organization doesn't give an audience what it wants, how can it survive? If the organization doesn't give the audience what it needs, how can it be journalism? Are audience wants and needs necessarily contradictory? And doesn't the very question (between wants and needs) demonstrate the arrogance of journalism?

The question of the audience's wants and needs does point out the distance between journalism and its audience—a distance that is both lamented and celebrated. That distance creates a tension that will always be part of journalism, no matter what the medium.

What does this have to do with the Web? The Web brings a new dimension to the question of audience wants and needs by allowing the possibility of audience choice. The technological structure of the Web lets individual users select what news they see, not the items that editors select for them. It can also tell editors what articles a user has selected previously, so they can formulate a "front page" based on those choices. In other words, the Daily Me.

Personalization of news web sites was recognized in the mid-1990s as one of the great possibilities of the Web. The first grand visions of personalization pictured an actively involved user giving a web site a set of preferences, and the web site that showed up on the user's screen would reflect those preferences. For instance, a user might tell a site that he is interested in all news from Tennessee, that he is a St. Louis Cardinals fan, and that he wants any information the site has to offer about high blood pressure. The user is also interested in U.S. art, bluegrass music, the Great Smoky Mountains National Park, and U.S. history. Along with this information, the user has given the site his zip code (he lives in a state other than Tennessee), his age (54), and his occupation (he's a college professor).

Based on this information, the front page of the web site that shows up on his screen the next morning contains headlines and summaries of the following stories:

- Congress considers the President's proposals on Social Security.
- A proposed highway near the user's house will likely cause environmental damage.
- The St. Louis Cardinals have traded a star player for two Chicago Cubs minor leaguers.
- The Tennessee legislature is struggling with a budget crisis.
- Local weather and headlines.
- A new ACE-inhibiting pill for high blood pressure, which can be taken weekly rather than daily, has been approved for use in Europe.
- Papers signed by James Madison have been found in a Virginia barn.
- Several Ivy League universities are raising tuition again this year.
- A bluegrass festival will be held 50 miles from the user's home this weekend.

A different user would get a different set of stories that was based on a different set of preferences. All users would have access to other stories on the site, but they would not be displayed prominently.

Traditional journalists and others who are accustomed to a standard news presentation found this vision of the news troubling. They continue to do so. On one level, it negates the "expertise" that professional journalists have acquired in sorting news for its audience. It also obscures news that may be very important to the user (such as a stock market plunge) even though the user has not designated it as personally interesting. The worst thing about the Daily Me, as described in the example above, is that it destroys the common pool of information that a newspaper or television news program creates for a local constituency. Because commonly shared information is one of the necessary factors in creating a community, this reliance on the Daily Me could damage the community itself.

The picture is even scarier for traditional journalists when one considers that none of this news delivery has to take place through a news organization itself. An independent program, possibly from the Internet service provider, can troll through the Web looking for items that match the preferences of the user and bring them together on a single page. No human judgments would be involved in the immediate selections.

This vision of the Daily Me is still around, still viable, and in some instances has been put into practice. Despite its charms and possibilities, however, it has yet to become the dominant mode of web news distribution. News consumers, it turns out, are a conservative lot and have not particularly embraced this change. They seem, at present, to be satisfied with the familiarity that news web sites have to their traditional print and broadcast partners. Consumers also seem not particularly motivated to make the choices that editors have always made for them. Despite personal preferences that are often ignored, they do not appear to be willing to take on the responsibility of choosing news for themselves. Many consumers are unwilling to give the Web the kind of personal information it would take to draw up an appropriate list of preferences, fearing that this information could be used in ways they would find detrimental.

The Daily Me has failed to blossom for other reasons as well. The main one is economic. News organizations that would have to devote resources to setting up a personalized web site are not certain that profits would result from their efforts. Advertising departments would have to adapt a new way of selling ads, and circulation offices would need to be revamped to deal with subscription revenues. It would require rethinking throughout the organization, on both the editorial and the business sides, and few established news entities are prepared or willing to undergo that.

Finally, the idea of commonly shared information has salience with both news professionals and consumers. The fact that we all read the same newspaper or watch the same news broadcasts is a bond that many people find useful and valuable. We may not all be personally or financially interested in vagaries of the stock market, but when it soars or crashes, we recognize that as information that needs to be shared. News events such as a market crash transcend our personal preferences.

Still, although the personalization of news has not yet come to dominate web journalism, it has made inroads. News organizations are now offering email alerts to individuals who express an interest in certain types of items. On many web sites, if you type in your zip code the site will produce weather information for your area each time you visit. Baseball scores, stock prices, and traffic reports appear regularly in personalized form on news web sites. News organizations are finding ways to serve their audiences without turning their web sites into ones that deliver only personal preferences. They are likely to continue in this direction, and consumers are likely to develop greater expectations in this regard.

PAYING FOR IT

The Web is free, right? Well, not exactly. First of all, someone has to pay for the computer and the software. And someone has to pay for the Internet connection, both the hookup and the monthly fees.

But the information you can access on the Web—now that's free, isn't it? To date, for the most part, that answer has been yes. You can get information from the *New York Times,* the *Washington Post,* CNN, MSNBC, and many other news web sites, large and small, and never pay an extra dime. Many non-news web sites are deep wells of information from which users can draw at any time, at no additional cost. In the first decade of the Web, so much information has been offered to consumers without any direct charges that many people have the idea that this is how it should be. Survey after survey shows (not surprisingly) that vast majorities of Web users say they would not pay subscription fees to web sites. In fact, many people have come to believe that it is their right to receive information free from a web site, and they resent the suggestion of a subscription fee.

But news is not a natural product. It is man-made, and a news organization spends an enormous amount of money producing it. Economic logic says that a news organization cannot give away its product any more than Nike can give away its shoes. However, in order for web sites to begin charging for their information, a number of things need to occur (and undoubtedly will occur in some form).

First, news organizations and consumers alike need to get past the idea that consumers will not pay for content or services from a web site. Consumers may not want to pay, as aptly demonstrated by the results of surveys cited above, but there are plenty of instances where consumers are indeed paying. Music web sites, such as Emusic.com, charge monthly subscription fees and in turn allow subscribers to download music without restrictions. Sports web sites, such as Major League Baseball, charge a fee for premium services such as the ability to listen to radio broadcasts of games and insider information about teams and issues. On the news side, the *Wall Street Journal* has two levels of fees, one if you subscribe to the print edition and one a Web-only fee. Other news sites, such as those of the *Washington Post* and CNN, charge fees either for archived articles or for premium information and service. The fact is that consumers will pay for information.

Some advocates of free Web information argue that the Web should adopt a broadcasting model, by which advertising pays for most of the cost of production and distribution. Although web advertising is a growing industry, most news organizations have not been able to generate a real profit from advertising revenue alone. Advertising will continue to be an important part of the revenue stream of a news web site, but it is doubtful that advertising alone can sustain a site.

In addition, news organizations will have to change if they are to charge consumers. The organizations themselves will have to place a higher value on the articles, photos, video, and other information they produce. They will need to understand what various segments of their audiences want and what they would be willing to pay for, and they will need to devote staff and time toward producing that information.

As monopolies for more than a generation, most newspapers have never had to think much about their audiences or the quality of information they generate. That sense of value needs to exist within the news organization before it can be translated to the consumer. Once that happens, consumers will be willing (though not necessarily happy) to pay for information. In turn, the consumers themselves will value the information they receive—much more so than they do now. Charging subscription fees, then, will be the ultimate way in which a news web site can engage its audience.

THE AUDIENCE SUPREME

As an audience-oriented and often audience-controlled medium, the Web redefines the relationship that journalism has with its consumers. The arrogance with which journalists as individuals and news organizations as corporations have operated within traditional media is not likely to continue or thrive. Dialogue in many forms with individuals in the audience will become a standard part of web journalism.

DISCUSSION AND ACTIVITIES

1. How do you feel about paying to see a web site? What would you pay for? What do you think should be free?

2. Have you ever tried to interact with a news web site? How? What were the results?

3. One of the trends that many studies show is that we are using the Web to do more and more tasks in our lives. Are you using the Web for anything now that you weren't just a few years ago?

4. Take a look at the section in this chapter on personalization. If a news web site were personalized just for you, what kinds of things would it have on its front page? You should not think necessarily in terms of traditional news. What are you interested in?

5. If you were to start a weblog about a particular topic (other than yourself), what would it be about? What are you most interested in? Who shares that interest? Do you think those people would participate?

SELECTED BIBLIOGRAPHY

Associated Press. "Survey Says Internet Cuts into TV Time." *The New York Times,* November 29, 2001.
Dube, Jonathan. "What Readers Want." Poynter.org, March 15, 2002. www.poynter.org/web/031502jon.htm.
Lasica, J. D. "The Promise of the Daily Me." *Online Journalism Review,* April, 2, 2001. www.ojr.org/ojr/lasica/1017779142.php.
Lasica, J. D. "The Second Coming of Personalized News." *Online Journalism Review,* April 2, 2001. www.ojr.org/ojr/lasica/1017779244.php.
Olsen, Stephanie. "The Battle over Getting to Know You." News.com, February 20, 2002. http://news.com.com/2102-1023-841419.html.
Outing, Steve. "Interactive News Is Newspaper-Wide Effort in Spokane." *Editor and Publisher,* March 13, 2002. www.editorandpublisher.com/editorandpublisher/features_columns/article_display.jsp?vnu_content_id=1400396.
Outing, Steve, and Rusty Coats. "To Charge or Not to Charge: Searching for the Holy Grail of Revenue Models for News Sites." Poynter.org, April 10, 2002. www.poynter.org/centerpiece/revenue.htm.
Peskin, Dale. "Preparing for the Coming Era of Participatory News." *Online Journalism Review,* March 26, 2002. www.ojr.org/ojr/future/1017170352.php.
Pew Research Center. "The Commons of the Tragedy: How the Internet Was Used by Millions After the Terror Attacks to Grieve, Console, Share News, and Debate the Country's Response." Research report, October 10, 2001. www. pewinternet.org.
Scasny, Randall. "Online News Users Have to Pay." *Online Journalism Review,* November 23, 2001. www.ojr.org/ojr/business/1017776541.php.
Stone, Martha. "A Time to Compare the Numbers." *Online Journalism Review,* August 15, 2002. www.ojr.org/ojr/business/1029471539.php.
Wendland, Mike. "Developing the Internet Community." Poynter.org, January 5, 2002. www.poynter.org/web/010502mike.htm.

WEB SITES

Pew Internet and American Life Project (www.pewinternet.org)

This project conducts and funds research on how the Internet is affecting all phases of U.S. life. "The Project aims to be an authoritative source for timely information on the Internet's growth and societal impact, through research that is scrupulously impartial," according to its web site. It is an initiative of the Pew Research Center on People and the Press.

Nielsen//NetRatings (www.nielsen-netratings.com)

This commercial company is a partnership of several firms that have come together to do Internet audience research. The company posts some of its findings on its web site, and its comparisons of audiences among web sites are becoming a standard for the industry.

CHAPTER 12

MEDIA LAW ONLINE

BY AMELIA PARKER

MAJOR THEMES

■ Many of the major legal issues concerning the Internet and the Web are far from settled.

■ Decency, privacy, free speech, and intellectual property (copyrights, trademarks, etc.) all provide major legal battlegrounds for Web litigation.

■ In addition to these traditional issues, the Web is spawning new legal problems with regard to how people use the medium.

When a group of college researchers created the Internet in the 1960s, it was intended to link information between universities, the military, and government agencies in case of a wartime communication melt-down. Instead, by the 1990s, the Internet had become the World Wide Web, linking together people all over the planet with news, merchandise, and a general riot of knowledge, all at a click of a mouse.

In our increasingly litigious society, it was inevitable that the Internet would become a breeding ground for legal disputes. Some of these cases were similar to those seen when television and radio hit society; others were offspring of a medium no one could ever have imagined.

This chapter will explore some of the major areas of media law, libel, privacy, copyright, and obscenity, and how they have come to apply to the Internet. First, however, it will be beneficial to take a look at another era, the heyday of radio and television. By looking at the history of these media, we can better understand how the government has tackled the regulation of new technology in the past.

BROADCAST REGULATION

In their day, radio and television created a buzz similar to the flurry of legal battles the World Wide Web is creating now, because there were no preceding cases to follow.

Regulation of the two media continues today, almost a hundred years from the time of the first radio broadcast.

Most people consider Reginald Fessenden's 1906 broadcast from Brant Rock, Massachusetts, to be the first radio transmission. Music entered the airwaves in 1909 in California, and by 1916, Lee De Forest was reporting the results of the Wilson–Hughes presidential election on the radio.

Radio was first regulated in 1912 after the *Titanic*'s maiden—and final—voyage. Broadcasting licenses were first distributed in 1921. The initial owners of these licenses were newspapers, as many paper owners hoped to continue to control local news reporting.

Unlike a daily newspaper, however, radio had no physical boundaries. A broadcast could reach into the next town and over state lines. This resulted in a confusion of the airways, with too many stations trying to broadcast in the same area.

The government's solution to the problem was the Radio Act of 1927. The act established the Federal Radio Commission (FRC) and a list of regulations that set standards for every corner of the industry. The FRC quickly assigned frequencies to different stations, eliminating most of the crowding problems.

There was still a fight for radio to produce programming benefiting public welfare, similar to the United Kingdom's British Broadcasting System (BBC). People believed the airwaves were public property and should not be used to promote only the interests of large advertisers or station owners. It was eventually decided that the public's airways could be used by radio stations, so long as they kept the public's interest close to heart.

By the 1950s disk jockeys were keeping their bank accounts close to heart. When news of "payola" scandals hit newsstands, the nation learned that popular disk jockeys had been given cash bribes, free vacations, and other favors by record companies to get new artists air time. The government investigated, and payola became unheard of until the late 1970s and once more in the mid-1980s. Though some insist that payola is still a factor in the music industry, broadcast staffs must sign a statement swearing they will not accept any form of payoff for song play.

Commercial radio got its in-home entertainment competitor in 1927, the same year it was first regulated. Philo Fansworth sent the first TV picture using a cathode-ray tube that year, but because of patent disputes and financial concerns, commercial television was delayed for another decade.

The Federal Communications Commission (FCC) was established in 1934 to succeed the FRC. It ruled over all things wire and radio, including radio, television, and telegraph. The commission decided in 1937 that television was not ready for national service and would not grant rights to commercial sponsorship.

This didn't stop manufacturers. In the late 1930s the first television sets hit department stores, ranging in cost from $125 to $600.

Fourteen different companies created their own television broadcast systems, and in 1941 the FCC decided on an industry standard so that commercial television could be made available to all, no matter which brand of television they purchased. By May 1942, ten stations were up and running.

In the years during and immediately following World War II, television grew faster than the FCC could control it, and the FCC stopped granting licenses to new stations in 1948 until a more systematic approach to channel assignments and technical equipment could be developed.

During the four years between 1948 and 1952, television advanced by leaps and bounds. More sets were sold, increasing the medium's saturation level, and classic shows, such as the *Ed Sullivan Show* and *I Love Lucy* debuted, ushering in the Golden Age of television.

By the 1990s the Golden Age of television was long over, and violence on TV had become a national concern. The Television Violence Act of 1990 gave broadcasters three years to staunch the on-air blood flow. Children's programming was a special concern of activists. Networks agreed to place "violent content" and "parental discretion" disclaimers at the beginning of programs that warranted them. Despite efforts to contain the problem, children's programming continues to be a hotly debated topic among many today.

Later in that decade, the FCC initiated the Telecommunications Act of 1996. This act expanded the number of television stations a single company or person could own, creating a mad rush of buying and selling to capitalize on the lighter restrictions. It also introduced the television viewing audience to a consistent ratings system and the V-Chip, a device that reads a television program's rating. This allows parents to block shows they do not want their children to see.

DECENCY ONLINE

Broadcast, which includes television and radio, has always been highly susceptible to government regulation in the United States. Even as late as 1996, television was facing new measures, such as ratings and the V-Chip, to ensure that it produced what the government deemed proper for viewers to watch.

Though TV was under fire in 1996 for its portrayal of violence, the Internet had yet to face any sort of major regulation on its content.

By the mid-1990s, the continuously growing online community had become more than just a place to exchange information; it had become a market for all sorts of entertainment, including pornographic photographs and other adult ventures. The federal government decided it was time to step in.

Later that year, Congress passed what was known as the Communication Decency Act (CDA). The CDA prohibited obscenity and indecency of any kind on any part of the Internet that was accessible to children. Anyone who violated the CDA could be convicted of a federal crime.

At the time, lawmakers viewed the online media as they viewed broadcast media. Broadcast is highly regulated because it is easily accessible to children. Broadcast is also regulated because it is considered intrusive, pervasive, and because it confronts people in their homes, sometimes without warning. These same assumptions were being applied to the Internet, a medium unlike any the world had seen before. The CDA was written to try and make the Internet adhere to these standards.

The early pioneers of the Internet had created a somewhat anarchic community, one that didn't take to what they viewed as unfair restrictions. The whole act was based on regulating "decency," a term that has a murky legal meaning, which outraged much of the Internet community.

The American Civil Liberties Union (ACLU) decided to take the case to court, naming U.S. Attorney General Janet Reno as the defendant. *ACLU v. Reno,* which reached the U.S. Supreme Court in 1997, proved to be a key Internet law case.

During the trial, ACLU lawyers hailed the Internet as a widening of the "marketplace of ideas," a theory first set forth by J. S. Mill, a nineteenth-century British philosopher. The theory states that people, and not the government, should be allowed to choose their own ideas. Mill believed that everyone should be presented with all the information available and then they would make rational, informed decisions for themselves. The theory is often used to interpret the vague First Amendment to the U.S. Constitution.

Another key point in the case was the fact that the Internet contains both commercial and noncommercial speech. Under the First Amendment, noncommercial speech is more protected than commercial speech. In *ACLU v. Reno,* the Supreme Court found the government to have no compelling interest to regulate noncommercial speech on the Internet. The Court also decided that no revisions to the CDA could make it meet these qualifications.

After hearing arguments from both sides, the Supreme Court decided that the Internet deserves as much protection by law as does print, the most protected medium. Much of the CDA was deemed unconstitutional. It had failed to do what it set out to: check "indecent" and "patently offensive" speech on the Web.

DEFAMATION

A person's reputation, or how others perceive someone, is highly protected under the law. Reputation is regarded as something a person owns, much like a car or a piece of jewelry. If those possessions are wrecked or lost, it is possible to attain monetary damages for them. The same is true of a reputation: if someone damages yours with false information, an action called defamation, it may be possible to bring legal action against them.

Defamation Basics

There are two kinds of defamation, libel and slander. Slander is oral defamation, and libel is written. "Libel" is the term applied to cases of publication, such as print, broadcast, and other media.

The most important thing to remember about any sort of defamation is that the information must always be false. If there is truth to a statement, then a claim of defamation will not stick.

When it comes to what can constitute libel, the list is long and flaming. There are, however, several "danger areas" of which one should be wary. These include accusing someone of extremist political beliefs, such as calling a person a Nazi; claiming someone has a mental illness that might cause social stigma; remarking negatively on someone's professional ethics or competence (this can also apply to a corporation, an entity considered one person under the law); claiming someone has a "loathsome disease," such as AIDS; expressing views on someone's sexual orientation or promiscuity; and accusing someone of a crime.

During a libel case the plaintiff, the one whose reputation has supposedly been damaged, must prove several things to the judge. The first is publication. The plaintiff must show evidence that the libelous information was communicated to at least one person. Second, the plaintiff must prove that he or she was identified by the information, which can sometimes be difficult if the information applied to a group of people and not just an individual. Next, the plaintiff must provide proof that damage was done to his or her reputation in some way or another, be it through loss of business revenue or more deliberate actions such as hate crimes.

Lastly, a plaintiff must prove fault, the action most difficult of all to pinpoint. A famous 1964 case, *The New York Times v. Sullivan,* has proven to be the pivotal piece of modern case law in defamation claims.

The New York Times v. Sullivan

In 1960 a group of civil rights activists took out a full-page advertisement in the *New York Times* with the intention of raising money to support Rev. Martin Luther King, Jr. The ad contained accounts of demonstrations, including one that had taken place in Montgomery, Alabama. A great deal of the information in the ad was false. For example, the ad said that students had been expelled from the Alabama State College for singing on the steps of the state capitol building. Students had been expelled for asking for equal service at a courthouse eatery, but not for singing.

L. B. Sullivan, commissioner over the Montgomery police, urged the *Times* to print a retraction. The *Times* refused, so Sullivan, along with several other Alabama politicians, sued the paper. Sullivan said he had been defamed by the ad because it mentioned Montgomery police in a negative light, and he oversaw the department.

An Alabama jury and the Alabama Supreme Court both found in favor of Sullivan. The case made its way to the U.S. Supreme Court by 1964, where the decisions of the previous courts were unanimously overturned.

The Supreme Court found that limiting criticism of public officials like the Montgomery police "dampens the vigor and limits the variety of public debate."

Instead of defendants like the *Times* having to prove the truth of their statements, public figure plaintiffs like Sullivan would now have to prove that the statements were false. Also, defendants had the added responsibility of proving "actual malice." Actual malice means the statements were published with both knowing falsehood and reckless disregard for the truth.

The Court found that the *Times* did not publish with actual malice because employees responsible for the ad did not know that any of the information was false.

Since *Sullivan,* private citizens must only prove negligence by a publisher to win, but the burden of proving actual malice makes it more difficult for public figures. Defendants, on the other hand, must prove only that their published statements were true.

Libel Online

In defamation cases, publishers, such as newspapers or television stations, are usually sued along with the reporter who wrote the offending statement. Publishers are legally responsible in a libel suit because they have control over the content before it is printed or broadcast. All copy goes through an editor or even several editors before it is shown to a public audience.

This is not true when it comes to common carriers, such as the phone company. Common carriers carry the messages of others, unedited and for a fee.

A 1991 New York state district court ruled that Internet Service Provider (ISP) Compuserve was not responsible for libelous information that was posted on its electronic bulletin board service. Compuserve had no or a very minuscule amount of editorial control over the actions of its subscribers, so it could not be held responsible for what they wrote about other people online.

In the mid-1990s, a citizen sued Prodigy, an ISP, for libel. Prodigy edited some of what users posted to its bulletin boards, making sure the boards were "family oriented." Prodigy lost the case, and a New York court said that ISPs that edited must assume responsibility in a libel case.

The Telecommunications Act of 1996 overturned the Prodigy ruling. In Section 230, Congress said that even if ISPs exercise some editorial control, such as limiting "objectionable" messages, they were still not considered publishers.

Several cases tested Section 230 in the late 1990s. A 1997 ruling found that America Online (AOL) was not at fault when a user sold t-shirts baring slogans such as "McVeigh for President 1996" shortly after the bombing of the Alfred P. Murray building in Oklahoma City (Timothy McVeigh was convicted of carrying out the bombing). The user sold the t-shirts under the name Ken Zeran, a Seattle man who had no connections with the bombing or the attempted business venture. Section 230 was used again in an AOL case concerning Matt Drudge's "Drudge Report." Drudge, an AOL user, accused a White House employee of marital abuse online. The court ruled that AOL was not responsible for Drudge's actions. The statement was later withdrawn.

A simple lesson for ISPs: edit a tiny bit, or don't edit at all. Many news web sites publish message boards, which can give rise to accusations similar to those against ISPs. Chatters should be made aware of a site's policies on libelous statements and agree to them before they can post.

PRIVACY

Compared to the centuries of precedence in libel law, the right to privacy is a relatively new concept in media law. Normally, privacy is traced to an 1890 *Harvard Law Review* article that argued for legal protections of privacy because of technological advances such as photographs. Samuel Warren and Louis Brandeis, the attorneys who authored the article, probably could not have imagined a technological advance like the Internet, but what they set forth in their article is still applied to online media today.

Privacy Basics

The Constitution makes no specific mention of the right to privacy. The Fourth Amendment forbids government searches of homes and businesses that are deemed unreasonable. Courts have extended the meaning of this statement to apply to media, saying a person's privacy rights can be violated if a journalist accompanies officials on any kind of search.

However, most privacy laws have come out of common law and are not set forth in an official document such as the Constitution. There are four areas that generally apply to the media: the publication of private facts, intrusion, "false light," and appropriation.

What exactly is a private fact? It is a concept that is loosely defined by the law. A private fact is something that if published (1) "would be highly offensive to a reasonable person" and (2) "is not of legitimate concern to the public." In the past, things such as sexual matters, physical or mental health, eccentric behavior, criminal activity, and poverty have all been considered "private" facts. There is not much case law in this area, and some wonder if publication of private facts will cease to become a legal matter. Publications can defend themselves against a privacy suit by asserting that the facts in question were newsworthy or that the person agreed to the publication of the information.

An ethical area of privacy pertaining only to the media falls under the publication of private facts: publishing names of victims of sexual crimes, such as rape or abuse. Legally, publishers have the right to do so. Most reputable publications and journalists choose not to publish this information, feeling that it violates their personal code of ethics.

Intrusion is another area of privacy law and refers mostly to the use of secret recording and video equipment to gather information. Common law defines intrusion as a "highly intrusive physical, electronic, or mechanical invasion of another's solitude or seclusion." Secretly using tape recorders, employing telephoto lenses, and aggressively pursuing a subject can all be violations of someone's privacy under intrusion law. Offenders are often charged with both trespass and intrusion.

Presenting someone in a "false light," or in a manner other than they actually are, is also an area of privacy law. For the false light tort to apply, a person must have been portrayed in a way that is (1) highly offensive to a reasonable person and (2) publication must be done with actual malice, or knowing, reckless disregard for the truth. Because their subject matter can be so similar, libel cases and false light claims are often filed at the same time.

Appropriation is the last area of privacy law that applies to the media. Appropriation is unauthorized, commercial use of a person's "persona," and most often applies to celebrities. For example, it is permissible to print Britney Spears' likeness on the cover of *People* magazine, but you cannot use her picture in an ad for hair care products unless she agreed to it. Bette Midler won an appropriation case when a car company ran a commercial featuring a singer with a Midler-esque voice. Johnny Carson sued a portable toilet company when they marketed their product as "Here's Johnny," a phrase used for years to introduce Carson as host of the *Tonight Show.*

Outrage, or the infliction of emotional distress, is not an area of privacy law but is worth mentioning when it comes to publication of potentially offensive material. This tort can be applied if conduct is "outrageous and exceeds the bounds of decency so far as to be intolerable in a civilized community." Infliction of emotional distress is often thrown in when privacy cases are tried. Television evangelist Jerry Falwell sued *Hustler* magazine under this when it ran an ad featuring Falwell in a compromising position with his mother. The case made it to the U.S. Supreme Court, and the ad was found to be an exaggerated political cartoon and therefore protected by the First Amendment.

Privacy Online

Though much attention has been paid to online privacy issues, there are actually few laws that deal with the area. The very nature of the Web allows incredible amounts of information to be stored, and some of this information may be something a person would rather keep under wraps. Unfortunately, the "Big Brother" aspects of the Internet may not allow this. It is fairly simple to locate a wealth of information about any person. Addresses, phone numbers, employers, and even emails that one sent in 1999 can all show up when a person's name is typed into a search engine.

Though this practice can be useful for journalists, it can put the average person on edge. Potential employers can do background checks on interviewees, finding out information about political beliefs or health histories.

Internet surfing patterns can also be detected if a site has the right technology. "Cookies," small text files or programs placed on a user's hard drive by a website, can send information about viewing habits back to web sites. For example, a brief visit to this author's cookie bin shows that she frequents news web sites, Amazon.com, and entirely too many sites that sell clothing. Cookie use came under fire in 1999, when RealNetworks used them to conduct market research about people who used Real's streaming audio and video players. Real stopped its cookie munching when users complained about invasion of their privacy online.

When people send out email, they are also placing their privacy at risk. The Electronic Communications Privacy Act, passed in 1986, does place restrictions on unauthorized accessing of emails. There are several exceptions to this law. Email service providers are allowed to access emails; after all, they have to access it in order to send it. Employers are also allowed to access employees' professional email accounts, but only if the employee has consented to being monitored. There are restrictions on the monitoring so that personal information gathered from emails, such as knowledge about personal health issues or social lives, cannot be used against someone.

A child's privacy is also at risk when the child surfs online. Information about children is easily obtained by web sites, as kids must often register to play games or search certain areas of sites. The Children's Privacy Protection Act, signed into law in 1998, limits the actions of sites aimed at children under age 13. These sites must provide parents with notice on their information gathering, and they must obtain parental consent before collecting or using a child's personal information.

Parents can protect their children online by carefully monitoring their kids' Internet use. Programs such as NetNanny and CYBERSitter block potentially offensive sites when installed on a computer. There are also search engines aimed at young people, such as Yahooligans and Ask Jeeves for Kids.

Kids are not the only web surfers who face invasion-of-privacy concerns. The Internet has turned into one of the venues of choice for political debates, and those involved run the risk of having their personal information, not just their political opinions, splashed around the Web.

In the late 1990s, the Nuremburg Files site was established, denouncing those who supported abortion. The site contained personal information about families of doctors who performed abortions and a "hit list" of doctors' names, with those who had been murdered crossed out. The site proclaimed one doctor's killer as a "hero." Planned Parenthood filed a case against the American Coalition of Life Activists, publishers of the Files. The Federal Access to Clinics Law, which prohibits intimidation of those seeking abortions, was used to decide the case. The Nuremburg Files was shut down, and the publisher was fined.

Internet users should constantly remain aware that their online activities are being monitored, and usually without their consent. Personal information, such as credit card numbers and home addresses, should not be given out without careful consideration of a collector's reliability.

COPYRIGHT

When an artist, author, or songwriter creates a new work, he or she can regulate the copying and uses of the work by obtaining a copyright. Copyright protects any kind of creative work, such as songs, movies, advertising campaigns, and books. The Internet has greatly affected copyright regulation, providing the public with an easy venue in which to pirate copyrighted works. Music, movies, software, and text, when digitalized, can be traded between users quickly, causing the creators of these works to lose profits they might have made otherwise.

Copyright Basics

Article I, Section 8, of the U.S. Constitution gives Congress the power to create copyright law. The writers of the Constitution wanted to give people an incentive to create, and so provided a way for creators to have a monopoly over what they produced.

Copyright applies only to tangible works—that is, works that are fixed in a "tangible medium." Examples of tangible media include books, articles in newspapers or magazines, films, paintings, sculptures, and recorded music. Ideas cannot be copyrighted, but the way an idea is expressed can be copyrighted. For example, a news story contains ideas—the facts and events the story described. These are not copyrightable. The way the story is expressed—the method the writer chose to string together words to convey the facts and events—is copyrightable.

Individual works, such as a particular song or photograph, can be copyrighted. Compilations, such as those countless *Now That's What I Call Music* CDs, can be copyrighted as well. Derivative works, works that transform or adapt an existing work, may be copyrighted. An example of a derivative work is a book that was originally written in English but was translated into French to be sold in France. Performances of a work, such as your college's production of *King Lear,* may also be copyrighted.

A copyright protects a work for the length of its creator's life and seventy more years. Works created by a corporation, such as a movie, keep their copyright protection for 120 years from the time of their creation or 95 years from the time of their first publication.

When someone creates a work for a corporate entity, such as a freelance writer working for a magazine, the corporation owns the work unless someone else is specified in a contract. However, in June 2001 the U.S. Supreme Court found in favor of several freelancers whose older work for the *New York Times* had been published in a digital database without specific permission from the freelancers. The case, *Tasini v. New York Times Co., Inc.,* began when the *Times* authorized a CD-ROM that included old articles from both the *Times* and the *New York Times Sunday Book Review* and *Magazine.* The freelancers felt the CD-ROM infringed on their copyright to the work they had completed for the *Times.* The Supreme Court focused on the individual articles in their decision. Because one could view a single article, outside the context in which it appeared in the *Times,* the Court found that the freelancers' rights had been infringed.

Copyright Online

Freelancers are not the only people facing copyright infringement because of new technologies such as digital databases and the Internet. The music industry and the world of e-commerce have brought their fair share of cases to courts in the last few years. The number of new copyright cases may cause lawmakers to look at revising copyright law even further. The current basis for copyright law is the Copyright Act of 1976, which made the law more uniform by preempting state copyright laws. The Copyright Act has already been revised several times, making changes for cable television, VCRs, movie rentals, and the Internet.

One of the most interesting copyright battles in recent times has been the battle over online MP3 trading. MP3 is a file format that allows audio files to be compressed into a fairly small size. This allows traders to send the files over the Internet at a fairly rapid pace without losing any of the music quality. Even better, trading MP3s allowed music fans to get their tunes without paying $15 to $18 for a CD at the music store.

In 1999, losing millions to a music "black market," the Recording Industry Association of America (RIAA) sued Napster, a company started by a college kid. Napster was the originator of point to point, or p2p, technology, which allowed users to download software to help users search for and download MP3s and other media files. By the close of 2000, even under legal fire, Napster had about 30 million members.

The RIAA said that Napster and other similar companies violated the Digital Millennium Copyright Act (DMCA), passed in 1998. The DMCA, along with the Digital Performance Rights in Sound Recording Act (1995), gave record companies royalty rights to all digital audio transmissions of music to which they hold copyright, including when that music is streamed over the Internet.

Napster was shut down in July 2001, but continued to attempt to strike deals with various record companies. The company filed for bankruptcy in spring 2002, but plans to reorganize and relaunch its services in the future.

Meanwhile, former Napster users have turned to other, less convenient file-sharing providers, such as Morpheus and KaZaA. The RIAA has also attempted to launch its own trading service online, allowing users to pay to download files "legitimately." And because the popularity of DVDs, the digital version of VHS videotape, continues to grow, more and more movie files have also begun to be pirated online.

In August 2002 Congress began to pressure the Justice Department to enforce the little-known No Electronic Theft (NET) Act, signed into law in 1997 by then President Bill Clinton. The NET Act prohibits a person from sharing copyrighted works, such as music or movies, if the value of the work exceeds $1,000. Violation of the NET Act is a federal crime, and it is punishable by one to five years in prison.

Researchers have recently released evidence indicating that online media trading will begin to decline after 2005. The Yankee Group predicts that illegal audio file swapping will reach nearly the 7.5 billion mark in 2005. In the next year Yankee predicts that only 6.33 billion illegal files will make their way over the Web. The findings measure swapping among those aged fourteen and older. Another research group, Forrester, says that unlicensed file swapping will decline after 2005 because record companies plan to release their own, subscription-oriented services that year. According to Forrester, online sales will make up 17 percent of record company profits by 2007.

Media file sharing is not the only copyright issue created by the Internet. "Deep linking," a practice employed by many web programmers, has often come under fire in the courts. A deep link is a hyperlink that sends a user to any page other than a site's home page. For example, a front-page link to CNN online would be www.cnn.com. A deep link to CNN online would be www.cnn.com/LAW/, which would take a user straight to CNN's section on legal news.

Linking first entered the legal realm in 1997 when the *Washington Post* sued Total News, Inc., for copyright infringement. On its web site, Total News deep-linked to *Post* stories. When a user clicked for a *Post* story, the *Post*'s web site would come up, "framed" by Total News advertisements and navigation bars. While linking to another site is generally considered good practice, framing another site with your own is not. The *Post* argued that readers could not distinguish between material from the *Post* and material generated by Total News. The case was settled out of court, and Total News was allowed to link only with permission and if it did not use frames.

Similar cases have followed, most notably in 1997, when Ticketmaster sued Microsoft. Microsoft had created Sidewalk sites that attempted to be online guides to various cities around the United States. The Sidewalk sites listed events occurring in the cities and posted deep links to Ticketmaster's site, where Sidewalk users could go to purchase event tickets. Because the links were deep links, Ticketmaster argued, users missed Ticketmaster's front page, where most of its major advertising was located. The case was not settled until 1999, when Microsoft agreed to link only to the front page of Ticketmaster.

Generally, most webmasters do not mind if you link to their site. It is a good rule always to look into a site's linking policy before you do so, as some sites, such as

Ticketmaster, do not permit deep linking without prior permission. Framing, in addition to being visually unappealing, is not good web protocol and should be avoided.

Something else that should be avoided is violating a company or person's trademark. A trademark is any word, symbol, or device used to distinguish one product from another. A good trademark example is Nike's famous "swoosh," which appears on its athletic shoes. Having a trademark gives someone rights similar to those of a copyright, except that trademarks are viable as long as a company pays to renew it.

The Internet has created trademark problems for many companies and celebrities. A 1996 case, *Panavision International v. Toeppen,* gave domain-name rights to trademark holders. Still, "cybersquatters," those who buy domain names in hopes of selling them for a profit, continued to be a problem. For example, a cybersquatter would buy a domain such as bradpitt.com, and then attempt to sell the name to actor Brad Pitt. In 1999 the Anti-Cybersquatting Consumer Protection Act was passed, allowing plaintiffs to sue cybersquatters for up to $100,000.

Famous-name cases were brought after the act was passed. Julia Roberts and Madonna won rights to juliaroberts.com and madonna.com, while Warner Brothers, Inc., won the rights to harrypotter.com, the main character of the popular book series to which Warner Brothers purchased movie rights in 1998.

Domain-name struggles have continued, as there are only so many names under the current top-level domains (.com, .org, etc.). The Internet Corporation for Assigned Names and Numbers (ICANN), the group responsible for assigning domains, is continuing to create new top-levels, which may alleviate some of the pressure to snap up names quickly.

Meta-tags are another trademark issue on the Internet. Meta-tags are the online version of false advertising. When a search engine crawls around the Web, looking for things to add to its database, it searches for what is included in sites' meta-tags. For example, a site about college football might include "NCAA" and "SEC" as keywords in its meta-tags.

Playboy magazine won a case involving meta-tags. The word "playboy," a trademark of Playboy Enterprises, was being used as a meta-tag keyword by sites that offered photographs of a sexual nature. Because the sites were not affiliated with Playboy, but were attempting to profit from Playboy's trademark, the sites were forced to remove the keyword.

Similarly, cosmetics company Estee Lauder won a case relating to online perfume sales. When browsers typed "Estee Lauder" into Excite's search engine, they were directed to the web site for The Fragrance Counter, Inc. The Fragrance Counter did not sell Estee Lauder's brand, but had included the trademark in its keywords to attract attention from Web surfers.

OBSCENITY AND INDECENCY

Because sex is a subject of such interest to the human race, courts have always had to struggle with obscenity and the regulation of indecency. The Internet did not help matters, bringing the public an easier way to exchange obscene and indecent materials.

To understand the laws concerning these two issues, one must first take their definitions into consideration. Obscenity is defined as pornography that is so morbid and shameful, it is said to appeal to the "prurient interest." Obscenity has no protection under the First Amendment. Indecency is defined as sexual material that is less erotic or less explicit than obscenity. The First Amendment fully protects indecency in the print media and on the Internet.

Obscenity and Indecency Basics

One of the hardest facets of obscenity law was defining the term. In 1973, *Miller v. California* resulted in a three-part test to determine if something is obscene. To be considered obscene, a work must meet all three parts of the test.

The first part of the Miller test is whether an average person, applying their community's standards, would find the work appeals to the prurient interest. The "average person" is defined as a normal adult, someone who is neither a prude nor a person with strange tastes. The "community's standard" aspect was included in the test because of differences in people's views across the country. People from urban areas generally are considered to be more tolerant of indecent material than are people from rural Alabama. It is not fair to make urbanites conform to the standards of others who may be more conservative than they are.

The second part of the test is whether the work depicts, in a "patently offensive" way, conduct defined by state law. This will, of course, differ from state to state. The more excessive the sexual detail, the more "patently offensive" the work is considered. Nudity and four-letter words are not considered to be patently offensive.

The last part of the Miller test concerns the "serious literary, artistic, political, or scientific" value. If the work, taken as a whole, can be found to have any social value, then it is not considered offensive. For example, a detailed photograph of female genitalia would probably be offensive in a newspaper, but it would have scientific value if it was included in an anatomy textbook.

When it comes to obscenity, the U.S. Supreme Court has decided that adults may possess it and receive it, so long as they are in their own homes. There are, however, very strict regulations on the sale and distribution of obscenity, making it illegal to send it through the mail.

Indecency is not as strictly regulated and has full protection under the First Amendment, so long as it is in print media or on the Internet. Cable television has a fairly loose leash when it comes to indecency, though there are some restrictions on what time of the day certain things may be shown.

Obscenity and Indecency Online

As part of the Telecommunications Act of 1996, Congress passed the Communications Decency Act (CDA), which attempted to ban indecency online. The CDA prohibited obscenity or indecency of any kind on any part of the Internet that was available to children (people under eighteen years old). Allowing dissemination of obscene or indecent materials to minors online was considered a federal crime, placing both companies and individuals under fire. ISPs were excluded from the CDA, so long as they could prove they acted " 'in good faith' to take 'reasonable, effective, and appropriate actions' to prevent minors from receiving indecent material through the Internet."

The CDA was eventually struck down by the Supreme Court in the 1997 case *ACLU v. Reno,* as discussed previously in this chapter.

Since that decision, several cases about blocking or filtering indecent material online have come into the courts. In 1998 there was a case in Virginia concerning public libraries' use of filtering of software. The library, a government-supported institution, was using software to block child pornography, obscene material, and content it deemed harmful to minors. Library patrons filed suit, claiming the software blocked nonobscene sites as well. A federal District Court ruled that libraries must prove compelling interest before limiting their users' access to sites. The court also said that the restrictions must be narrow enough so that nonobscene sites, protected under the First Amendment, are not blocked. The library was allowed to continue blocking child pornography and obscene material, because these are not protected by the Constitution.

Congress is currently considering legislation that may help parents control what their kids can see on the Internet. The "Dot Kids Domain Name Act" is currently in subcommittee. Under this bill, ICANN would have to create a top-level domain name, ".kids" (or "dot kids"), which would only house material approved for children under the age of twelve. Other examples of top-level domain names at this time include ".com," ".gov," and ".edu." The two senators who introduced the bill have said they want to create an "Internet playground" for children.

ICANN has considered dot kids before, but rejected it because the organization felt it would be too hard to police. One country's government could not decide who got to be under dot kids because the domain would apply to the whole world. For example, a site might be considered unsuitable for U.S. children, but it might be thought okay for kids in Italy.

If the dot kids bill is passed, ICANN would have to create the ".kids" domain within 30 days, before it created ".biz" and ".info," domains that were approved at an ICANN convention in November 2001.

CONCLUSION

The Internet, which began as a series of networked computers on university campuses in the 1960s, has grown into a major facet of everyday life for many people in the world. People use the online world to trade stock, buy clothes, get the news, and, in larger cities, buy groceries. It has become a major player in the world of commerce, as more and more people use the Internet to complete everyday commercial transactions.

Congress, the courts, and other restrictive agencies have long recognized the Internet's importance to the future of the world. How to regulate it is still a question that needs to be answered. Some of the first attempts to impose restrictions failed. For example, the Supreme Court shot down the Communications Decency Act of

1996, and many lower-court rulings against the Internet have been overturned by higher courts.

One of the most influential decisions concerning the World Wide Web was to declare its level of First Amendment protection. In its decision about the CDA, the Supreme Court found the Internet to deserve the highest amount of constitutional protection, similar to print media. Writing for the majority, Justice John Paul Stevens said that the Web is a "unique" medium, dissimilar to any other sort of media known today. Unlike broadcast, there is no physical restriction on the Internet to stop its users from sending information at any time. At any given time, "tens of thousands of people are discussing a 'huge range of subjects,' " with content "as diverse as human thought," the Court said. The Court also recognized the Internet's value as a "marketplace of ideas," and that it could not be regulated as harshly as other media, such as broadcast (*ACLU v. Reno,* 1997).

Still, one of the main problems in policing the Internet is its worldwide nature. As was noted earlier in the chapter, at least one worldwide organization, ICANN, has been set up to deal with domain-name problems, on top and other levels. Other groups, such as the World Intellectual Property Organization, have used their international influence to help settle Internet disputes between countries. Many nations impose rigid regulations on their citizens' Internet access, as well as what content is allowed for viewing. Some of the strictest regulations have come from more undeveloped countries. Yahoo, a Western-based Internet company, recently signed an agreement to limit its online offerings in China, a nation that has been called the "Great Cyber Wall" because of its restrictions on online content. North Korea has forbidden its citizens to use the Internet at all, instead running its government web sites on Japanese servers. In Western nations, Internet regulation has been less stern, with attempts at lawmaking regularly struck down by more liberal courts.

As the "digital divide," the number of people with Internet access versus those without it, continues to shrink, more and more people will inhabit the digital world. A recent survey by Scripps Howard News Service and Ohio University found that all U.S. generations under the age of sixty-five can be considered "cyber savvy" and report logging onto the Internet at least weekly.

Now more than ever, lawmakers and those based in the technological world face controversy from the Internet. While most U.S. legislation to regulate the Web has failed, eventually Congress and the courts will agree on some method to restrict the dissemination of such things as indecent material online. For now, though, most prefer to let the Web regulate itself through technological means.

DISCUSSION AND ACTIVITIES

1. In your opinion, what is the biggest legal issue facing web journalism?

2. Legally, is the Web more like print or more like broadcasting?

3. Can the Web be controlled legally, or do too many people have access with too much freedom already?

SELECTED BIBLIOGRAPHY

Black, Jay, Jennings Bryant, and Susan Thompson. *Introduction to Mass Communication* (5th ed.). Boston: McGraw-Hill, 1998.

Delaney, John F., and William A. Tanenbaum. *Representing the New Media Company: Guiding Your Clients through a Changing Economy.* New York: Practicing Law Institute, 2002.

Grossman, Mark, and Bradley Gross. "A Review of Online Privacy: Few Laws Offer Protection." Gigalaw.com, August 2000. (www.gigalaw.com/articles/2000/grossman-2000-08.html.) See also Gigalaw.com's other articles on this topic: www.gigalaw.com/articles/privacy.html.

Landreau, Michael. "Questions and Answers about the Napster Case." Gigalaw.com, May 2001. (www.gigalaw.com/articles/2001/landau-2001-05.html.) For further reading on the Napster and Mp3 cases: www.gigalaw.com/articles/copyright-napster.html.

Middleton, Kent R., Robert Trager, and Bill F. Chamberlin. *The Law of Public Communication* (5th ed.). New York: Addison Wesley Longman, 2000.

Morris, Stan. "The Limits of Free Speech on the Internet." Gigalaw.com, January 2000. (www. gigalaw.com/articles/2000/morris-2000-01.html.) See also Gigalaw.com's other articles on this topic: www.gigalaw.com/articles/freespeech-defamation.html.

Schrees, Julia. "House Refines Virtual Porn Ban Rules." Wired.com, June 27, 2002. www.wired.com/news/business/0,1367,53510,00.html.

WEB SITES

Gigalaw (www.gigalaw.com)

Gigalaw is a comprehensive site devoted to Web and Internet legal issues. Most articles are written by law professors. In addition to the references cited above, see the sections on trademarks, www.gigalaw.com/articles/domainnames-trademarks.html, and international law, www.gigalaw.com/articles/2001-all/yu-2001-04-all.html.

Wired (www.wired.com)

This web site keeps up with the latest news about the Web, particularly on the technology side. Its legal reporting is first rate.

CHAPTER 13

JOURNALISM ACCELERATED
INSIDE MSNBC

MAJOR THEMES

■ MSNBC.com and CNN.com are two of the top news web sites in terms of size of audience.

■ The marriage of Microsoft and NBC News gives MSNBC.com technical and resource advantages that allow it to be a leading light in the development of news on the Web.

■ The journalism that is practiced at MSNBC.com in many ways mirrors the journalism that occurs in traditional media.

The Web, as we have seen throughout this book, handles and enhances journalism in any form—text, pictures, graphics, audio, and video. It can present these forms in ways that are similar to those of traditional media. That is, text can run in columns very much like what a newspaper would print. Pictures can be accompanied by text cut-lines. Headlines can appear in type sizes that are larger than body copy. Audio can be heard just as it is on the radio, with no text or pictures. Video stories can be shown with voice-overs and text crawling at the bottom of the screen.

However, the qualities of the Web that distinguish it from traditional media—capacity, immediacy, flexibility, permanence, and interactivity—combine to let journalists explore different ways of information presentation and storytelling. These combinations allow journalists of the twenty-first century to find, along with their audiences, a journalism that could not be imagined less than a generation ago.

Yet only a relatively few news organizations are conducting this exploration. Most are bound by the weight of workloads, economics, and traditional practices. News is a difficult, labor-intensive product to produce. To be acceptable to both the audience and the professionals who produce it, information must go through an extensive and exhaustive process—a process that occurs in a relatively short amount of time, often only a few hours. These institutional imperatives and processes have precluded consideration of the Web as a medium and the development of its journalistic possibilities. The Web has been a low priority for news organizations for these reasons and because the journalism industry has never been particularly interesting in investing in research and development.

A few exceptions to this general description stand out. The *New York Times* and the *Washington Post* have developed web sites that show the industry some of the possibilities of the new medium. The innovations of these two newspapers have demonstrated much in the way of information presentation and customer personalization. The web site of the Cable News Network (CNN.com) follows the tradition of its parent in emphasizing the immediacy of news and blanket coverage of breaking news events. Its partnership with Time Inc. publications and other journalistic entities (such as Business 2.0) adds to its depth and reach.

The remaining giant in the field of web journalism is MSNBC, an odd hybrid of Microsoft and the NBC television network (owned by General Electric) that was established in the mid-1990s to explore the commercial and journalistic possibilities of the Web.* This joint ownership and unusual set of corporate parents has imposed an organizational structure and set of institutional imperatives that other news web sites do not face. The purpose of MSNBC.com, in its own words, is to "inform, engage and innovate with the highest quality of news and information, anytime, anywhere." With such well-heeled parents as Microsoft and NBC News, the staff commands an impressive array of resources. At this writing, the site ranks among the top three most visited news web sites in the world, with about 17 million unique visitors each month.†

MSNBC.com is the news web site for the MSNBC cable channel and for NBC News itself (see Figure 13.1). That gives it access to NBC's staff of editors, producers, and reporters who cover news around the world. It also provides a strong promotional tool to drive people to the web site. *Dateline NBC,* for instance, often mentions that "more information can be found" or that "people can vote" on an issue at MSNBC.com. Audiences for the site also come from MSN, the Microsoft network that provides email, shopping, and other services to its visitors. Finally, MSNBC.com has partnership agreements with *Newsweek,* the *Washington Post,* and the *Wall Street Journal* to use some material from each of these publications. In fact, on occasion *Newsweek* columnists produce a piece especially for the Newsweek web site (Newsweek.com), which MSNBC.com can also use.

---

*Much of this chapter is based on a two-day visit the author made to the MSNBC newsroom on the Microsoft campus near Seattle, Washington, on October 24–25, 2002. During this time, the author conducted extensive interviews with many of the editors, producers, and journalists on the staff there. In addition, significant breaking news events occurred during the visit (the capture of the D.C. sniper on the first day and the plane crash that killed U.S. Senator Paul Wellstone and members of his family and staff on the second day). These events allowed the author to watch the operation handle news that was breaking on a minute-by-minute basis. Many people whom the author interviewed are listed in the acknowledgments section of the Preface.

†As of September 2002, MSNBC had 17,169,000 unique visitors, behind only CNN's 18,058,000. The other top news web sites were Yahoo! News, 14,958,000; ABC News, 9,162,000; USA Today, 8,739,000; and the New York Times, 8,684,000, according to Neilson/Netratings (www.netratings.com).

FIGURE 13.1 *Dateline NBC.* MSNBC.com and its partners, particularly the NBC news programs, use each other to cross-promote themselves. The web site is mentioned on television programs, and the web site carries items about the television shows. MSNBC.com is the web site for NBC News and its programming.

Physically, MSNBC.com is located in two places. One staff operates in Secaucus, New Jersey, at the NBC television news operation. The main staff, however, is in Redmond, Washington, on the campus of the Microsoft Corporation. The Redmond staff maintains general control of the site, posting new material on an hourly basis—and much more frequently when the news demands it. The MSNBC.com staff itself is a relatively small number of reporters, producers, editors, and photographers who process content from the site's partners and also create original content for the site. Many of these people have had significant experience in newspaper, magazine, and broadcast journalism, and much of what happens at the site on a day-to-day basis resembles the operation of a medium-size newspaper.

The major difference, of course, is that instead of one deadline and one press run every day, this is web journalism, and every minute is a potential deadline. When news breaks, millions of people bring the MSNBC.com web site up on their computer screens. They expect to find the latest information about the latest event, even if that event occurred only a few minutes before.

It is journalism accelerated.

IMMEDIACY: INSTANT INFORMATION, JUST ADD WORDS

Call up MSNBC.com on your computer screen at various times during the day, and the first thing you will note is that it changes regularly. New stories appear, and older ones disappear. Stories are updated as new information comes in. The front-page image changes to reflect this new information, and sometimes it changes to highlight a new top story. The site promotes programs on MSNBC television, and these promotions also change throughout the day.

Like most other news organization, the day officially begins at 9 a.m. Pacific time, with a morning news meeting of many of the major editors for the site (see Figure 13.2). These people gather in a room where they can project the web site on one wall to discuss what they have in hand and what will be happening that day. The meeting also includes representatives of MSNBC.com in New Jersey (just outside New York City), NBC News, *Newsweek,* and MSNBC-TV. Each editor and representative describes what his or her organization is producing for the site, and they discuss ways to collaborate on subjects or stories. This meeting is a short one, usually less than a half-hour.

A front-page producer or editor is on duty at MCNBC.com twenty-four hours every day, charged with keeping the site updated and fresh. The editor understands that regular users will call up the site several times a day, and one of the basic principles of the site is that it should be consistently different. Consequently, even on a "slow

FIGURE 13.2   MSNBC.com News Meeting. Twice each day, news meetings take place in the Seattle office to determine what will be on the web site that day. Conference calls are used to communicate with editors on the East Coast.

news day"—a day when there is little or no breaking news—the site changes throughout the day. An updating cycle occurs every hour, and the front-page producer oversees the efforts of the staff to post new information.

At night and on weekends, a front-page producer may work virtually alone, but during normal hours he or she is surrounded by editors and writers. All of these people are seated in front of a large wall of television screens, where they can see MSNBC-TV, CNN, CNN.com, and other news channels. They also have access to the Associated Press and other wire services, so they can stay on top of the news no matter what the source. All of these people stay in visual, verbal, and electronic contact with each other, and their communication constitutes an important part of the process by which items get onto the site. (These few people constitute the heart of the news operation, but they are not the only ones working to produce content for the site. Various editors, writers, and producers work on other parts of the same floor.)

An afternoon news meeting occurs at 2 p.m. Pacific time, and again editors and representatives from the site's partners gather to assess the day's news and update each other on what has been happening in their organizations. As with the morning meeting, important decisions are made about what will appear on the site that evening and into the next morning.

At the morning and afternoon news meeting, editors discuss what they know will happen—a presidential speech, a vote in Congress, a sports event, or even a major weather system. They plan their coverage, trying to coordinate who will be doing what, where information will be coming from, and when it will be coming in. However, the nature of news is that the unexpected will also always occur, and when that happens, the site has to be ready to respond instantly.

Many of the people who work at MSNBC.com have newspaper or broadcasting news experience, and they have carried the culture and practices of the newsroom with them into this new medium. When breaking news occurs, journalists are driven by a number of factors, such as speed, competitiveness, and the need to present information accurately. All come into sharp focus at a news web site such as MSNBC.com when a significant and unexpected event occurs.

Information about the event is posted as quickly as possible, and the top image on the front page of the site is changed to reflect the news. The major concern of the staff from the beginning of an event is the words they will use to describe what they know. A writer is designated to put together a coherent version of what is known about an event when it begins to break. That writer has to absorb information from a number of sources, recognize what is important, interesting, and significant, and resolve conflicts in various reports that he or she is receiving. Then the writer has to formulate the language to produce a coherent and sustainable version of the information.

Conversations fly around the room about what information means and how it should be stated. Words and phrases are considered; story structures are debated; sources of information are compared. Into this mix come the reports of competing web sites (CNN.com, the *New York Times,* ABC and CBS News, etc.) The writer has to listen, think, and write. A news story needs to be produced, and the deadline is now.

A writer may produce only a paragraph or two before it is taken over by an editor to be edited, proofed, and sometimes even rewritten. Depending on the speed with which the information is to be posted, the editor may send what he or she has done into the production queue, so that it can be posted onto the site. Or, if there is time, the editor and writer may discuss the entire story before sending it forward. Even when a breaking news story is "complete," the writer continues to work because information keeps coming in, and the site will need to be updated again in a few minutes. The event itself dictates the pace of the work. When there is a lull in the event—a hostage crisis, for instance, will have an initial flurry of activity and then settle into a siege before more activity occurs—writers and editors can sit back for a moment to catch their breaths. They may even be able to do some additional tinkering with their copy, but they are also thinking ahead to what might be the next event, what information they will need, and how they will restructure their story.

Despite the technology that surrounds the journalists of the news media, the journalism itself remains old-fashioned. Words are carefully considered; phrases are tried and rejected; information is weighed again and again until it is found to be substantive. Whereas newspapers and broadcasters might deal with one or two deadlines each day, the Web forces minute-by-minute deadlines onto the process, but the process itself stays the same. The journalism of the Web is a word business, and the words are labor-intensive. No amount of technology makes this easy.

CAPACITY: GETTING TO THE "SECOND CLICK"

Got text? Fifty words, 5,000 words? No problem, except that the text has to be written and edited.

Pictures? One photo or a dozen, no problem, but the pictures do have to be taken, selected, edited, cropped, and made Web-ready.

Video? Some is okay, but not too much. Visitors may not have broadband connections, so it may be difficult to download. Besides, many site visitors do not show much inclination to play video on their screens—at least, not yet.

Audio? That's easier to post and download. Still, visitors may not be all that interested.

Graphics, maps, and charts? Hard to produce but easy to load and include with articles.

Interactive presentations? No problem there, except that some visitors may not have the memory or the plug-in software on the computers that allow them to be played. Still, they can be offered to the visitor without making the site too heavy.

Links? Easy to do. Linking is what the Web is all about, and the ability to link to other parts of the site or to information off-site is limited only by the time and inclination of the journalists.

Journalists at MSNBC.com have enormous resources to call upon when gathering information. And as we see from the list above, they have many ways in which to present this information. Finally, they are working in a medium in which sheer capacity to hold the information in whatever form it takes is not often an issue.

However, there are limitations that these and other web journalists encounter each day. They come in three forms—limited human resources to produce information, limited screen size, and user inclination. Each is a powerful check on the idea that the Web is a medium with unlimited capacity.

MSNBC.com employs about 150 people, and about half of these are writers, editors, producers, and other media specialists. In addition, as we mentioned earlier, the site has the people and resources of NBC News to call upon, as well as limited partnerships with the *Washington Post, Newsweek,* the *Wall Street Journal,* and *Slate* magazine. With the wire services and picture and video services that the site subscribes to, the site could become a classic portal site—that is, one that simply presents information from these various sources without much selection or editing. (The news portion of Yahoo.com, http://news.yahoo.com, is a good example of a portal.) Instead, MSNBC.com takes the many resources at its command and molds them into a site that has a unique blend and flavor. To do that takes the full efforts of all of the employees and contributors. Consequently, editors and managers are constantly making decisions about what not to cover and what information not to post on the site because of the limited human resources they have.

The second limiting factor is screen size, and hand-in-hand with that is the issue of design. Like the proverbial tip of the iceberg, a web site may be huge, but a visitor will see only a very small portion of it at a time. As with the tip of the iceberg, you know there is much more to it, but you just can't see it. Consequently, the tip—in the case of a web site, the front page—is enormously important, and web sites devote many hours of thought, discussion, and work to the right design for the front page.

So it is at MSNBC.com. The basic design philosophy of the site is that it should be unique visually and easy to read. These considerations have to be combined with the fact that a user's screen may be only about 100 square inches (as opposed to about 260 square inches for a full-size newspaper). This pursuit of visual distinction has led the site producers to a design that emphasizes a single story over all others at any given moment. This emphasis is an image with a limited number of words laid on top of it, and the image is meant to draw the eye of the reader immediately. This image, or "slide," may take up about 15 to 20 percent of the viewing area that the visitor sees initially (without having to scroll vertically), and after the site's logo, navigation bars, and banner ads are accounted for, there is relatively little room left for headline links to other stories. (See Figure 13.3.)

Scrolling, of course, increases the space available for other items, but MSNBC.com limits itself to a relatively "short scroll." That is, viewers do not have to scroll far before they reach the end of the page. (By contrast, the web sites for the *New York Times* and the *Washington Post* are "long scrolls.") An MSNBC.com user can extend the front page by asking for local weather, but even then the site has a fairly short scroll. And the number of links to items inside the site remains limited.

All of which brings us to user inclinations. Most news web sites realize that users are not going to "go inside" a site unless they have some reason to. Some visitors do use the standard navigation bar to take them to section fronts such as "News," "Sports," "Business," and so on, but many will only click on some specific link they find on the front page. Consequently, the front-page links to specific items on the site take on enormous importance. They give readers an idea of what the site has to offer, and they direct readers to those specific items.

FIGURE 13.3   MSNBC.com Front Page. The front page of the web site has a design that gives it a different look from any of its competitors. This design does not allow as many links on the front page as some other sites have, so getting an item linked from the front assures that it will have a fairly large audience.

These links are, in the parlance of the web industry, the "first clicks," and they are important because relatively few readers will make a "second click." Increasing the number of "second clicks" is one of the goals of any web site, and MSNBC.com makes every effort by providing many internal links and a great deal of content that editors feel will attract and hold readers. Knowing that, at present, many readers are not inclined to make the "second click" in effect limits what the site can do and how it should spend its resources.

FLEXIBILITY AND INTERACTIVITY: BUT IS IT JOURNALISM?

The flexibility of the Web extends beyond the fact that it can handle information in various forms as the traditional media do. The power of the Web is that it can put all of these forms at the reader's fingertips to create something that is new and different. These combinations of traditional media forms can create a new environment in which information is presented and understood by the reader or viewer. Journalists working on the Web have developed three levels at which these combinations generally occur, and all three are on display daily on the web pages of MSNBC.com.

Linking is the first and most common level at which the flexibility of the Web becomes apparent. Links to other information—and other types of information presentation—are inserted in most stories that are posted on the site. Some web sites group their links on one part of an article page, either at the top of the article or at the bottom, but MSNBC.com's current style is to sprinkle links throughout the story, often in the parts of the text where they are the most appropriate (see Figure 13.4). Writers can learn the tags that need to be placed in their copy to make these links appear, and they work closely with audio, video, and picture editors to make sure that such links are available.

Presentation is the next level at which the power of the Web can be tapped. Presentation means taking traditional media forms and using them in ways that go beyond the media from which they come. Again, we can look at the most common form of this presentation level: the picture gallery. A picture gallery presents a sequence of still pictures, usually accompanied by a text cutline. Considered as single pictures, there is little difference here from print. The fact that the Web allows photography editors to sequence the pictures creates an experience for the reader that is quite different from print.

Some web sites go beyond simple sequencing and add audio to the pictures to create yet another storytelling environment for the reader. As noted earlier in this book, on some web sites the photographers discuss their experiences while covering a story as the pictures are being shown. In its Pictures of the Week and Sports Pictures of the Week galleries, MSNBC.com editors try to interview photographers about what it was like to take the picture itself, so that the reader can get a sense of being with the photographer.

The presentation level can include even more sophisticated forms of information that include text, sound, motion, and graphics. The forms, usually created with Macromedia's Flash software, may require that readers begin the presentation with a click of a mouse (as do most picture galleries), but once they begin, the reader can simply sit back and watch or listen. Not much interactivity is required from the reader.

The final level is the interactive presentation, in which the information environment is completely different from what is available in any other medium and that engages users in the presentation. At MSNBC.com, these presentations are created by a small Interactive team, which conceives the presentation and then executes it using whatever tools are necessary, from simple HTML to Javascript to Flash.

The team can create and save templates that allow writers easily to incorporate polls or interactive divisions of text that the users can choose, depending on what kinds of information they want.

Sometimes, however, these presentations are far more elaborate. One such presentation was part of a package that won an award, "Creative Use of the Medium," from the Online Journalism Association in 2002. The package investigated the state of airport security in the wake of the post-September 11 changes instituted by the federal government (www.msnbc.com/modules/airport_security/airsecurity_front.asp). The presentation showed users what it was like to be an airport baggage screener, and it challenged users to spot dangerous materials in bags and briefcases as they slid under a scanner (see Figure 13.5). The users who participated in this interactive presentation were given some information about how to spot certain items and were then put through a two-minute drill. When they stopped the bags from traveling through

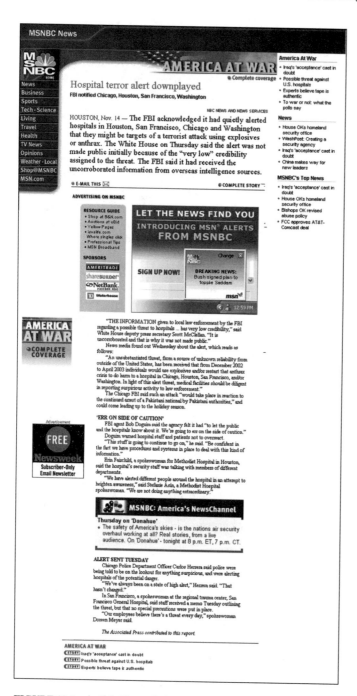

FIGURE 13.4   Article Page. Article pages carry some of the elements of the front page, to promote consistency of design throughout the site. Links are inserted onto the article pages in several ways.

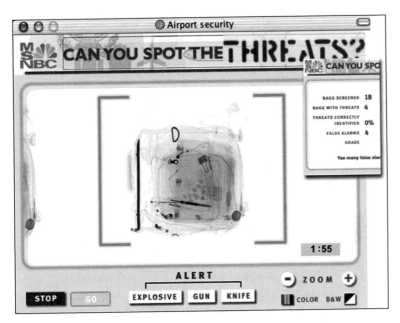

FIGURE 13.5   Airport Security Simulation. Editors and producers put together a Flash presentation that allowed users to get a feel for what it is like to be a baggage checker at an airport. This simulation used authentic images from the scanning machines at an airport. Those who went through the simulation were timed and given a score showing how well they were able to detect dangerous items.

the simulated screener, voices could be heard complaining about how long it took to get through the line. At the end of the two minutes, participants were rated on their performance. The point of the presentation was to let users stand in the shoes of the baggage screeners for a couple of minutes and experience what they go through to do their jobs.

Another presentation that was rolled out during the end of the 2002 baseball season was a strikeout game that lets users make decisions about where to pitch to certain batters. Participants were given certain game situations and told something about the hitter or about how they were feeling at that point in the game. They had to decide how to pitch to the next batter by choosing a pitch (fastball, curve, or slider) and clicking on the part of the strike zone where they wanted the ball to go. (They were also told that not all balls go where the pitcher wants them to.) The game ended with the user being either the winning pitcher or the loser. (See www.msnbc.com/modules/sports/pitchinggame.)

Interesting, and sometimes fun, but is it journalism? The journalists who produce these interactive items (and many have substantial news media experience) debate this point constantly. They are presenting information, as all journalists do, but they are also creating experiences that no journalist has previously had the opportunity to create. They ask four questions when considering ideas for interactive presentations: Is the subject important? Is it newsworthy? Will users participate? Will the presentation have lasting value (that is, will it still be useful beyond the immediate story to which it is tied)? A confident yes to all four questions is required before they develop the presentation.

Many people believe that this new form of storytelling—giving the reader information but also creating an experience—is where the Web is taking journalism. Attempting to put the user inside the head of a baggage screener or on a pitching mound to face Major League hitters are things that a good reporter and writer may be able to do. Asking readers to participate in the experience can only be done on the Web.

THINGS TO COME

MSNBC.com is certainly not the only site on the Web that is practicing all-out web journalism or exploring the possibilities of the medium. But like few other sites, the MSNBC.com team often has the time and resources to go where other sites cannot yet go. As new ideas for web journalism are formulated, tested, and developed in the next few years, sites such as MSNBC.com will be the ones to watch.

DISCUSSION AND ACTIVITIES

1. Find a news web site that is doing comparable work to that of MSNBC and compare them. Look at the content generally to see what is produced. Then keep tabs on the site as a breaking news story occurs. Keep an hourly log comparing what each site posts and how it handles the information on a breaking news story.

2. What are the dangers of "journalism accelerated," to use the author's phrase?

3. How do the presentations, such as the ones referred to in this chapter on airport security and being a Major League pitcher, differ from traditional journalism? Do you consider these presentations to be journalism?

4. MSNBC regularly wins awards from the Online News Association. Check out the association's web site to see other award-winning entries from other sites (www.journalists.org).

CHAPTER 14

PRACTICE AND PROMISE

MAJOR THEMES

- Despite its progress in technology and its success in gaining an audience, the Web is still in its infancy as an information medium.
- The best people and the best ideas for web journalism are yet to come.
- To date, the chief effect that the Web has had on journalism is to accelerate the process, but overemphasis on that aspect will obscure the new ideas and the changes that the Web will eventually bring to the profession.

The Web acts like no other news medium. It is not a newspaper, magazine, radio, or television. The fact that journalists are currently treating it as if it were an extension of these traditional media is understandable at this stage of the Web's development, but that will not always be the case. Web journalism eventually will be something quite different from the forms of journalism we know in the early twenty-first century. Without being too futuristic, this book has attempted to examine some of the possibilities the Web might hold for the journalistic process.

This book is built on an exploration of the five major characteristics that the Web brings to journalism: immediacy, capacity, flexibility, permanence, and interactivity. This final chapter reviews those characteristics in light of what the information about web journalism and its practice is telling us.

IMMEDIACY: THE ACCELERATION OF PRINT

Print news organizations that have web sites are beginning to discover the power of immediate news, and they are taking advantage of this power in ever increasing numbers. Many newspapers now advise their readers in the morning edition that important local events will be occurring during the day, and they should call up the newspaper's web site for "the latest information." Newspapers have always had this sense of immediacy as their press deadlines approach and news is breaking. The Web turns the tables on this practice to some extent by creating a deadline situation every time there is breaking news, no matter what time of day it occurs.

In doing this, the Web puts newspapers in direct competition with local television, and this situation is far different from anything that either organization has ever known. Newspaper and local television news staff have competed for information, but they have rarely competed directly for audience. At this stage of the game, neither organization is quite sure how to conduct this competition.

The immediacy of the Web has had more important effects, however. Journalism is an exciting profession, and every daily journalist will tell tales about the breaking stories that he or she was involved with and about the adrenaline-producing effects these events can have. The Web heightens this effect, particularly for print journalists.

However, it also increases the dangers that accompany the practices of journalism-on-deadline. One example of those dangers is the posting of incomplete or unconfirmed information in order to be the first news organization with that information (a journalistic point of pride). While no good journalist will publish clearly inaccurate, incomplete, or unconfirmed information, the shades of gray in these situations are many, and decisions about whether to post or not rely on the best judgment of the editors.

When a print editor faces such a situation, he or she has to consider that the information will be in the form of ink on paper. The print copy will exist, no matter what else is learned after the fact. That thought is a powerful check on the tendency to publish.

The Web provides no such check. In fact, the ease with which the web can be changed not only removes that check but also provides an incentive to treat information with less care. The editor may think, consciously or subconsciously, "If we're wrong—or if the information needs to be adjusted—we can always take it down." The Web allows mistakes to be corrected; that's a good thing. But that fact should not lighten the responsibilities that editors feel to make every effort to ensure their information is correct before it is posted the first time.

That's just one example of the effect of the Web on journalism. The accelerated pace that the Web brings to journalistic practice will likely produce many other examples. Timeliness is a basic value of journalism. The immediacy of the Web enhances that value. In doing so, the Web calls on journalists to cast a strong light on what they do and how they do it.

CAPACITY: UNLIMITED BUT LIMITED

The Web has virtually unlimited space to hold information in a variety of forms. Filling that space—or even a portion of it—with quality news and information and getting an audience to that information have become the two major considerations in this area of the development of web journalism.

News that meets traditional journalistic standards, as we have discussed elsewhere, is difficult and expensive to produce. It is rich food for the Web, and the Web is a beast that demands more and more. The Web dramatically decreases the expenses of journalism associated with the distribution of information, but it has done relatively little to decrease production costs. Despite many technological advances that help humans produce news, news as a product remains an expensive commodity.

Daily newspapers have dealt with these production demands for years. Many newspapers have become so efficient at producing news—whether they use their locals staffs to gather it or buy it from a wire service—that they usually have more news than they can fit into their medium. The issue with these organizations is what must be left out, not what must be included.

The Web solves that problem by providing enough space to hold any information the organization has,* but there is a catch.

Web news organizations are discovering that no matter how deep and rich their sites are, getting an audience inside the site remains difficult. Most web sites realize that the front page of their site is what almost everyone who visits the site will see. Getting people into a site and having them spend time looking at what the site has to offer is the real measure of the site's success.

Web sites have not yet discovered the appropriate degrees of transparency and density for the front pages of their sites. That is, they do not know how many choices they should provide to their initial audience and how to inform the audience at first glance about how much depth there is to the site.

Time and practice may help solve both of these dilemmas. Just as readers understand that there is more to a newspaper than its front page, Web users will also develop an understanding that they can expect certain information and experiences as they progress into a site. They will train themselves to understand the site's organizational and navigational schemes. However, the news organization must constantly remind itself that information will not be viewed just because it is somewhere on the site. The organization will have to find ways to make that information easier and easier to find.

FLEXIBILITY: MANY TOOLS, ONE JOB

As the most flexible of all media, the Web can handle just about any form of storytelling or information presentation. However, the practice of journalism on the Web, and the state of the technology, limit the ways in which these forms are used. For instance:

- Video does not yet work well on the Web, although the sending and receiving technology is improving. Video takes time and bandwidth to download, and often it is not the smooth flow of images that one finds on a television screen.
- Text, too, is still not completely adapted to the computer screen. The pixelization of text makes it difficult for some to read, and the nonportability of stationary

---

*Fortunately, while the Web is a demanding medium in terms of information, it does not demand to be filled every day. Consequently, web news organizations can avoid the fate of twenty-four-hour television news. In the 1980s, when twenty-four-hour television news organizations began showing up on television cable systems, they discovered that it was simply too expensive to produce news for that much time. Instead, they filled the time with inexpensive talk shows that emphasized opinion over information and noise over substance. Thus was born the "babbleratti," a class of talking heads that may entertain but add little to the public's knowledge.

computers continues to make the Web an inconvenient medium. Here, too, technological advances are being made, and they will undoubtedly improve the Web's viability as a medium, but the level of dissatisfaction with text and non-portability remains high.

■ Photographs, to be conveniently viewable, are limited to the size of the screen, and what size that is takes an educated guess by the web producer. Although they may have some control over the size of the text they see, viewers cannot easily (if at all) resize a web site to fit their screen or personal preference.

■ Audio is possibly the least developed of the storytelling forms for the Web, from both the journalist's and the user's point of view. Most journalists do not know how to produce audio reports, and most users are not in the habit of accessing such reports.

Despite these limitation, all of these tools are available and are being used to some extent by web journalists. They represent a powerful arsenal of weapons with which to present information, and together they have the potential of taking journalists far beyond the text/photo/graphic tools of the print journalist or the video/audio tools of the broadcaster.

The joys of the convergence of these tools into one reporter's backpack (see Chapter 4) sometimes overlook the problems associated with the Web's flexibility. One major problem can be stated simply: what is the best way to tell a story?

That question arises to a limited extent with the traditional media, but its consideration is limited because the tools are limited and because there are precedents. That is, journalists cover stories in the same way they have covered similar stories.

In web journalism, the question demands more consideration. With more tools and with fewer precedents, journalists are faced with continually deciding what are the best ways to inform the reader. They can rely on the traditional forms (such as inverted pyramid with photos or video with voice-over), or they may use the characteristics of the Web to form new storytelling structures, as we saw in examples in Chapters 1, 3, and 4.

A look at the near future indicates that the "Flash presentation," in which images are combined with text and audio, is becoming a new and standard storytelling form for the Web. We still do not have many standard subforms of this way of presenting information, nor are there rules or guidelines for its use. But the Flash presentation, as practiced by the *New York Times* photo gallery section, MSNBC (see Chapter 13), and other news web sites, is an emerging form that students of web journalism will do well to study.

Another major question concerning the flexibility of the Web is: can a journalist actually use all of the tools at hand to cover a story?

Print reporters who take a still camera with them on a story often find it cumbersome. It is difficult to know when to stop taking notes and start shooting pictures. Their pictures can then be disappointing because they do not understand the shooting techniques of a photojournalist. The Web asks them to consider using audio and video equipment as well, which means not only must they be able to shoot and record, they also need to know something about editing both types of media.

■ ■ ■ ■ ■

SIDEBAR

WHAT MAKES YOU SMART

"It turns out that the real secret to success in the information age is what it always was—reading, writing and arithmetic, church, synagogue and mosque, the rule of law and good governance. The Internet can make you smarter, but it can't make you smart."

Thomas L. Friedman, Pulitzer Prize-winning journalist for the *New York Times,* January 9, 2001.

Can they do it? Journalism professionals and educators are deeply divided on the question, and the implications of the single, multimedia journalist versus the one-dimensional specialist are profound. What news organizations decide they want will have a great impact on how journalists are trained and what they are asked to do. And these things, in turn, will have a great effect on what kind of journalism they produce.

The job of the journalist is to inform the reader. The Web opens new possibilities as to how that can best be done.

PERMANENCE: BUILDING THE ICEBERG

The Web, as we have seen, never has to lose any information. Whatever is created for the Web can remain as a permanent part of the site and can be retrieved at will. That's the theory.

The practice is far different. To date, web sites have not done a good job of saving and archiving their information. Instead, web journalists have treated yesterday's news much as they did when they were newspaper or television reporters. They have discarded it without much thought.

Hand-in-hand with this neglect is the general lack of development of strong search engines for the internal parts of a site. Many sites display search capabilities for their sites, but few of these operations are entirely satisfactory for the user who is unfamiliar with the site to begin with. Web sites have not standardized internal searching so that users can be reasonably confident they can find what they want to find. Instead, users are forced to remember routes to information that they may have seen before.

One of the most powerful aspects of the Web is its ability to retain everything. The Web is the most permanent of media because it does not deteriorate easily and because it can be duplicated quickly. Yet news web sites, for the most part, have not tapped this power, either for themselves or for their users.

The conceptual and technological problems of searching and retrieving information are not simple or easy to solve. They involve not just harnessing the power of the Web but also consideration of the kind of information the site is producing. The fact that this is difficult, however, should not deter editors from recognizing that permanence and access are characteristics of the medium that cannot be matched by traditional media.

Another aspect of the permanence of the Web has to do more directly with the practice of journalism. Web journalists, in putting together information for today, need to keep their eyes on the future and need to ask, "Can this information be used again?" If they do this, they can allay one of the major criticisms of modern journalism—that it is too episodic; that is, stories are reported without the context necessary to understand them. The Web, if used correctly, can provide that context.

The methods for doing this have not yet been developed, and that development represents one of the major challenges for journalists in the near future.

INTERACTIVITY: THE BIGGEST QUESTION OF ALL

What will Web users do, and when will they do it?* And how many of them will show up to do it? The audience for the Web is growing, and the safe prediction is that it will continue to grow. More people will gain access to the Web, and more uses will be found for it. Technological advances will enhance the way that people receive information and may even shift the reception device from the personal computer to something else—telephone, hand-held, television, and so on.

The relationship that the audience has to web journalism remains the biggest question of all in looking at the future of the profession. The audience will continue to be, for the foreseeable future, receivers of information, even passive receivers. But that relationship will likely evolve into something different, as more people experience the Web and as they find different ways to respond to what they experience. The relationship of the audience to traditional journalism—an almost completely passive relationship—has been based on the system of delivery, in great part. That is, people waited to have their newspapers delivered or waited until a radio or television station decided to broadcast its news. Because of geography, most people have had few choices of traditional media—one newspaper and maybe two or three broadcast stations.

With the Web, those relationships change. The audience no longer has to wait for the newspaper to show up or the television station to broadcast. A user can go onto a web site and get news anytime.

The audience is no longer confined to a few choices. There still may be only a few outlets that offer local news, but if the user looks beyond that, the choice is greatly expanded.

And if the user wants to respond to a news web site, he or she can go beyond a letter to the editor or a phone call to the station. These means of responding may be provided (and controlled) by the web site, or they may not. Conceivably, a user could create an alternative news web site if he or she felt ill-served or unsatisfied by the traditional news site.

---

*Historical note: These questions mirror those asked by Senator Howard Baker of Tennessee during the Watergate political scandal in 1973. Baker was on the investigating committee that looked into the misdeeds of the administration of President Richard Nixon. The central questions, he said during the hearings, were, "What did the President know, and when did he know it?" That question became part of the lexicon of politics for more than a generation.

In short, the Web changes the media–audience environment and relationship in ways that we can only guess at. The challenge of web journalism is to avoid complacency, remain sensitive to the wishes of the audience, and attempt to serve that audience in ways that are appropriate and profitable.

GETTING THERE

The Web offers journalism an opportunity to maintain its traditions and expand its reach. What form journalism will take in one or two decades will be decided by how the Web is perceived and used.

The best ideas for how journalism should use the Web and what structures, procedures, and practices are appropriate are yet to come. They reside with people who

■ ■ ■ ■ ■ ▬▬▬▬▬▬▬▬▬▬▬▬▬▬▬▬▬

SIDEBAR

KEEPING UP

The increasing interest in web journalism and the effects of the Web on journalistic practices and procedures has fostered a number of institutes and research centers. Each of these has a slightly different focus, but all are worth watching and provide information, training, and programs that will be valuable to the web journalist. Here are four:

■ *J-Lab: Institute for Interactive Journalism* (www.j-lab.org). This center at the University of Maryland is sponsored by the Pew Center, and its principal goal is "to empower people to be global and civic players by pioneering interactive ways to participate in news and information." The Pew Center's mission is to increase civic participation, and the J-Lab studies the media's role in this regard.

■ *Newsplex* (www.newsplex.org/home.shtml). The University of South Carolina center, sponsored with funding from the Ifra Centre for Advanced News Operations, studies the way news and information will be handled in the newsroom of the future. "Tomorrow's newsroom must be different than today's," according to its mission statement. "It must work across multiple media simultaneously and in real-time. It will be the hub of an information-based service company, more content-driven and less product-limited."

■ *Institute for New Media Studies* (www.inms.umn.edu/about.html). This institute at the University of Minnesota focuses on research about new media and journalism. "The Institute's goal is the creation of new knowledge and new understandings in the still uncharted world in which content must find its place. The Institute will work to anticipate the impacts that new technologies will have on the industries and organizations which create content."

■ *University of Southern California Annenberg School of Journalism* (www.ojr.org). USC offers a master's degree concentration in online journalism, and it publishes the *Online Journalism Review,* an indispensable source of information on the expanding world of web journalism.

may not yet have even thought about journalism as a career or yet understand the nature of news and information. But these are the people who will honor the traditions that brought us to this point and who will look forward to the future as an exciting place, full of possibilities.

DISCUSSION AND ACTIVITIES

1. Go through this chapter and find where the author has made predictions. Considering that this text was composed in 2002, have any of these predictions come true? Has journalism on the Web developed in a different way from what the author talked about?

2. One of the things the author is referring to in the subsection on flexibility is Slate.com's Enron Blame Game (slate.msn.com/id/2061470/). That item is a storytelling form—or is it? What do you think of the idea of presenting information in the form of a game? Will this become a standard storytelling form on the Web?

3. How interested are you in learning to:
   a. Write an inverted-pyramid news story
   b. Shoot and edit a two-minute video
   c. Create a pie chart showing the number of students in each class at your university
   d. Edit an audio story to include sound effects, actualities, and voice-overs

   Do you think a journalist should have to learn to do all of these things?